The River and the Land

THE RIVER AND THE LAND:

A HISTORY OF WINDSOR, ONTARIO TO 1900

PATRICK BRODE

BIBLIOASIS
WINDSOR, ONTARIO

FIRST EDITION

Library and Archives Canada Cataloguing in Publication

Brode, Patrick, 1950-, author
     The river and the land / Patrick Brode.

Includes index.
Contents: v.1. A history of Windsor, Ontario to 1900
Issued in print and electronic formats.
ISBN 978-1-927428-89-4 (v.1 : bound).--ISBN 978-1-927428-90-0 (v. 1 : epub)

    1. Windsor (Ont.)--History. I. Title.

FC3099.W56B763 2014   971.3'32   C2014-905989-2
                                                          C2014-905990-6

Edited by Dan Wells
Copy-edited by Allana Amlin
Typeset by Chris Andrechek
Cover designed by Kate Hargreaves

Biblioasis acknowledges the ongoing financial support of the Government of Canada through the Canada Council for the Arts, Canadian Heritage, the Canada Book Fund; and the Government of Ontario through the Ontario Arts Council.

PRINTED AND BOUND IN USA

Photo credits:
Windsor Community Museum, Windsor, Ontario: 13, 49, 68, 72, 78, 92, 100, 126, 147.
McCord Museum of Canadian History, Montreal, Quebec: 29.
Charles Mady Collection: 89, 128.
Patrick Brode: 22, 30, 70, 110, 138.
Windsor Star: 44, 117, 123, 132, 136, 143.

Contents

Introduction

FIRST, THERE WAS THE RIVER. What would become the city of Windsor was intrinsically formed by its location along "*La Rivière du Détroit*," the river at the strait as the French explorers called it. On August 11, 1679, a Jesuit priest, Father Louis Hennepin, stood on the deck of the exploration ship, the *Griffin*, and left a vivid picture of what he saw before him as he entered the southern approaches of the Detroit River: "The banks of the Strait are vast meadows, and the prospect is terminated with some hills covered with vineyards, trees bearing good fruit; and the groves and forests so well arranged that one would think that Nature alone could not have laid out the grounds so effectively without the help of man, so charming was the prospect." Inland there were "herds of buffaloes that trample down the flowers and grass as they rush around in their clumsy motion."[1]

Father Hennepin would not be the last to be enthralled by the location, and others would be alive to its economic possibilities. The river would dominate life for those who lived near it and its importance as a means of transport grew over the decades as it became a crucial link in the early fur-trade system of North America.

Then, there was the land. As the narrowness of the strait was an obvious military asset, a fort, an outpost of the French Empire, would be built in 1701. In order to supply the military garrison, a farming community comprised of settlers on both sides of the strait would be fostered. Similar to the land grants of Quebec, ribbons of land with a narrow frontage along the river would be granted to the arriving settlers. The future layout of the area would continue to reflect this pattern of settlement, with roads running straight back from the river. So it would continue into modern times and when the farms became thoroughfares, the names of the original farmers would be preserved in the street names. Beyond that, the early French settlers on the southern or Canadian shore would leave a cultural legacy in the area that marked it as a distinct entity from the rest of what was to become an Anglo-Protestant province.

As time went on, the border region would inevitably be buffeted by outside events. While Father Hennepin saw it as one region divided by a small strip of water, by the 1790s, distant political authorities in Washington and London decided the area should be partitioned. As a consequence, an invisible, international border divided the river and separated its people. Especially in the early 19th century, the towns at the strait would be caught between the emergence of a dynamic, democratic republic on one side, and the cautious toryism of British America on the other. This would result in the area literally becoming a battleground in which the inhabitants would have to choose which political destiny they favoured. Throughout the 19th century, the passionate issues of the day—democracy versus constitutionalism, slavery versus freedom, and even the cause of Irish liberty—would be fought out along the border. However, unlike many other cross-border conflicts, these struggles would not leave a legacy of bitterness. Perhaps the similarities of culture and interest between the two peoples at the strait were too intimate to permit enduring enmities. But this century of conflict would leave its mark, and in Windsor a prominent black community would remain as a reminder of the brutal American struggle for freedom.

Situated across from the American metropolis of Detroit, the ferry landing began to emerge as a separate community. English-speaking Loyalists, and a dynamic cohort of Scottish entrepreneurs would set up shops in an effort to control commerce. Individuals such as James Dougall and S.S. Macdonell came to dominate the area's burgeoning trade. Even while it grew, the settlement along the Canadian shore would never have one central focus during the 19th century. Rather, it would be divided between the three embryo communities of Sandwich, Windsor, and later Walkerville. Each of these towns had distinct origins, proud traditions, and would be separated from each other by slender fingers of rural land. Sandwich, the oldest of the trio, was the government town, and while it retained its legal significance, it could not keep pace in the commercial struggle to expand. Very much in contrast to Sandwich was the town at the northern end of the strait, Walkerville. As the creation of one man's ambition, Walkerville would foster a continent-wide business and generate the first industrial complex in the area. The history of Windsor in the 19th century is essentially the history of these three border towns. While each of them would struggle through this period to retain their individual identities, only Windsor would emerge as a hub for transportation and this factor would have a profound effect on its future prospects.

With the coming of the Great Western Railway in 1854, Windsor became far more than a mere ferry stop. It had the potential to become a transit point on one of the most important transnational lines on the continent. This is the story of how Windsor fought to take advantage of the opportunities that circumstances presented to it. It was certainly not a rosy story of continuous or predictable growth. Industrial moguls in the great metropolises had no particular interest in Windsor's future, and it seemed at times as if the town might be bypassed in favour of more accommodating localities. Moreover, Windsor would suffer during the depressions of the late 19th century and businesses would stagnate or move elsewhere. As it endured this rollercoaster of booms and busts, Windsor was a town much like many others in southern Ontario. Its population rose during prosperous times and in lean years families left and looked elsewhere. Windsor's growth was not particularly remarkable, and in some ways it lagged behind comparable municipalities such as London or Hamilton.

Yet, it fostered some extraordinary individuals. Dr. John Coventry would defy his superiors and a hostile press to advocate on behalf of public health. With a single-minded determination, he endured ridicule to campaign for greater measures to protect residents against tainted water that was a constant menace to life. James Dunn demonstrated that a black man could be a leading figure in business and politics. With few resources at his disposal, Dunn would lead a fight against the segregation of Windsor's schools, and he would successfully overcome the prejudice that kept black children from an adequate education. John Tringham would harness the forces of new scientific advances in previously unheard of ways. He would demonstrate the possibility of a single individual in spurring technological innovation and industrial growth. These were the outstanding exceptions.

Windsor during the Victorian period remained largely a city of conventional thoughts and actions. Its one defining mark, other than its railroad connections, was its link to its American neighbour. The trade policies of the late 19th century had encouraged Detroit capitalists to invest across the river and, far more than most Canadian municipalities, Windsor would be affected by Sir John A. Macdonald's National Policy with its inducement to American businesses to avoid tariffs by crossing the border. Detroit companies would build their Canadian subsidiaries just across the river where they could keep their eyes on their investments and supervise their plants with American staff. The result was an economic fusion in which businesses and workers crossed the international border almost as if it did not exist.

By the end of the century, the riverfront had lost the bucolic splendor described by Father Hennepin, and its vast meadows had become a grimy shore lined on each side with factories and warehouses. Yet, the significance of the Detroit River region lay in the fact that it functioned very much as one economic unit. Between them, Detroit and Windsor were beginning to create a distinctive, regional community, united culturally, linguistically, and by the reality of commerce. While the existence of a separate region was already apparent by the end of the 1800s, the full impact on the area would not come into full effect until the following century.

Throughout this book, reference was frequently made to two scholars whose work have set a standard for the history of the Detroit River area. The writer acknowledges the influence of Rev. E.J. Lajeunesse and his *The Windsor Border Region*, as well as R. Alan Douglas and his *Uppermost Canada: The Western District and the Detroit Frontier 1800–1850*. Any history of Walkerville must also acknowledge the lifetime scholarship of Ronald Hoskins and his studies of Hiram Walker and his career.

The assistance of the following institutions and persons is also gratefully acknowledged: Madelyn Della Valle, Heather Colautti and Melissa Phillips of the Windsor Community Museum, Tom Vajdik of the Local History Collection of the Windsor Public Library, and Michael Fish of the Windsor Municipal Archives.

Chapter One
Naming Rites:1836
September 6, 1836

WHAT TO CALL IT? When a community reaches the size that it needs a recognizable name, it has attained a certain sense of its own existence. The tavern and hotel owners, the local farmers and labourers who lived at "The Ferry," the hamlet where the ferry boat from Detroit, Michigan, stopped on the Canadian shore, thought it was about time they had a name. Some called the place "South Detroit," an accurate enough geographic description for a Canadian community that was south of its American counterpart. For a time the name "Richmond" (after the Duke of Richmond, a former Governor General) had been in use and had been touted by the prominent merchant Joseph McDougall. A public meeting was called for the evening of September 6, 1836, to sort this out and reach a consensus. Legend has it that the meeting was held at "Hutton's Tavern" and there, likely amid swirls of pipe tobacco, a debate ensued over what would be most suitable. Some speakers dismissed the existing titles as too prosaic or confusing (the Richmond name was already in use by another municipality) and thought that something more grand such as "Bellevue" or "Montpellier" was appropriate. One wag suggested that the place should be named after the local squires, the Baby family, and henceforth be called "Babylon." The discussion seemed to be stalemated on Richmond versus South Detroit when a young Scottish merchant, James Dougall, proposed "Windsor." He thought that this name had a fine air about it, and as well it evoked the royal town on the Thames. The deadlock was broken and the ferry landing became the hamlet of Windsor, a postal address within the Township of Sandwich. John Hutton was so pleased by the result that he renamed his establishment the "Windsor Castle." The local newspaper, the *Canadian Emigrant*, simply reported that:

11

"The meeting for the purpose of naming the village at the ferry, on the 6th instant, resulted in its being called 'Windsor.'"[2]

It is an amusing story, but like many things about Windsor's past, it also carries an element of mystery. The above account comes largely from James Dougall's 1888 obituary, which proudly proclaimed him as the "father" of Windsor. But in fact, tavern keeper John Hutton did not open a shop in Windsor until 1842. Another individual, S.T. Probett, had inaugurated the "Windsor Castle Ale & Beer House," but in May, 1838—a year and a half after the name selection.[3] All that can be said with any certainty is that in September of 1836 the name "Windsor" had been decided on—and that was that.

The James Dougall who may or may not have proposed the name would later go on to have a decisive impact on the community. He had come with his father, John Sr., and brother John from Paisley, Scotland, first to Montreal and then to York (Toronto) in the mid-1820s. The Dougalls were a cultured, literate family with sharp business acumen and willingness to work hard. They were getting by in Scotland but thought that Canada offered greater opportunities to make a significant fortune. When their dry goods store in York burned down in 1830, they considered moving farther west. They had the option of going to either of the two largest settlements: Amherstburg, the port and military fort, or Sandwich, the district capital. They chose neither. Instead, the Dougalls opened a general store, "J & J Dougall," at the site where the boats from Detroit landed on the Canadian shore. Relying on their contacts in the Montreal wholesale business, the Dougalls were able to sell not only to the hamlet, but to a wider region including Detroit. One observer noted that while the newly minted village of Windsor had fewer than a hundred residents, "two large retail and wholesale stores are established here; and much wealth has been rapidly accumulated by the proprietors, in vending their merchandise to all classes in Michigan."[4]

The Dougalls were but one family in a wider Scottish diaspora. Statistical analysis of early business elites in Canada indicates that Scots were prominent in all business and industrial circles. Yet to advance even farther, it helped to be part of the local elite. Two years after he had arrived in the area, James married Susanne Baby and thereby became the son-in-law of the local seigneur, François Baby. Marrying into French-Canadian Catholic families was not uncommon for upwardly mobile Scots. Religion was not a huge obstacle, for the father's faith prevailed and the seven children of the marriage would be raised as Presbyterians. The union of the Dougall and Baby families provided continuity in the role of the French families in the region, for the growth of the border towns would be intimately connected with the original French settlements of the 18th century.

ANCIEN RÉGIME

Antoine Laumet dit de Lamothe, Sieur de Cadillac, the first French commandant at Detroit had expressed his view that the lands at the strait of Detroit were "the earthly paradise of North America." When Cadillac arrived in 1701, it was for the purpose of turning this rich natural area into a resource to enable the French military to control the continent's hinterland. Cadillac's fort at Detroit would be on the north of what would become the American side of the straits. To the south lay a tribe of Huron Indians. The Jesuit mission to the Hurons

James Dougall.

was founded in Detroit by Father Armand de la Richardie in 1728, and after several attacks it changed locations until it settled at La Pointe de Montréal, where the Ambassador Bridge now crosses the Detroit River. Ottawa Indians already lived five kilometres farther east along the shoreline and a Potawatomi tribe occupied an area near Fort Pontchartrain. Perhaps as a result of Cadillac's machinations, the first decades of the 1700s would see a vicious series of inter-tribal conflicts known as the "Fox Wars."[5]

The J & J Dougall store.

From 1734, French settlers had been allowed to create farms outside the fort and spread along the river in narrow strip farms similar to those in the St. Lawrence valley. By the late 1740s, the lower lakes had become the scene of greater conflict both with various tribes and the English to the south. In 1749, the Governor of New France called for settlers to populate and fortify Detroit and its region and offered inducements to encourage settlement. Both sides, or *côtes,* along the straits were to be settled, and this included "Petite Côte" on the southern side of the river below the fort. These lands just north of Turkey Creek (Rivière aux Dindes) seem to have been selected for their sandy beaches; however, the lands were of poor quality and it soon became known as "Côte de Misère." Many settlers moved north towards the village of the Ottawas, and by 1751 lands had been granted as far north as modern Goyeau Street.[6] This settlement, "Côte du Sud" or "Côte de la Pointe de Montréal," was almost directly across the river from Fort Pontchartrain. These grants were narrow ribbons of land in which each settler was guaranteed access to a small waterfront. A typical grant had a frontage of three arpents (175 metres), but a depth of forty arpents or more. Over time, these holdings were divided among sons and as a result they became increasingly narrow. The families who held these grants, the Ouellettes, the Goyeaus, and Parents, would eventually have their names perpetuated in Windsor's streets.

During the Seven Years' War of the 1750s, the settlers were reduced to near famine as their harvests were seized to support the armies. Their poverty lasted into the 1760s in part because they were so far from markets and shipping was expensive. There seemed little need to produce beyond their own needs and this caused their priest, Father Potier, to complain that half of his parishoners, "have already wasted all their wheat in drink." Heavy drinking was already a prominent feature of frontier life.

The community on the south shore ceased to use the reference to La Pointe de Montréal after 1776 and was thereafter known by the Jesuit mission to the Indians name of L'Assomption. It was becoming a small outpost of French life and, as would be the case with so many of the ethnic groups that succeeded them, the Church would be the hub of their community. Ste. Anne's Church in Detroit was the parish church on both sides of the river and until 1761, all children were baptized there. By the 1780s, the Hurons had largely withdrawn from the area and moved westward or resettled near Lake Erie. The remaining settlers on the south shore, drawn from the descendants of Quebecers and in some cases their intermarriage with Indians, were determined to have a church of their own separate from Ste. Anne's. From 1781, the parish priest, Jean François Hubert, zealously devoted himself to this end, and in the summer of 1787 the timbered Church of L'Assomption was dedicated by his successor,

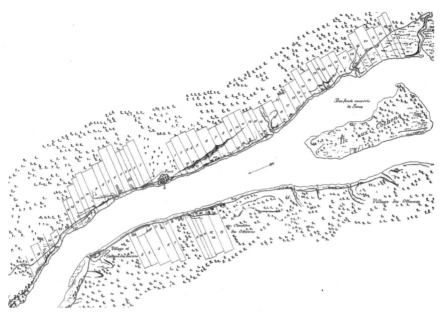

Fort Detroit and the allocation of strip farms along the Detroit River.

Father Dufaux.[7] The original structure is now gone, but the pulpit of this frontier church has been preserved in the modern day Assumption Church.

French authority at the strait came to an end in 1760 after France's defeat during the Seven Years' War. When the area came under the British Crown, the rationale for the settlement as a military outpost against Britain ceased, but its role in the continent's trade remained as important as ever. That trade was in fur, and the flow of pelts from the north-west found its way through the Detroit straits and from there to Montreal. From the beginning, transportation was the lifeblood of commerce. Trappers and voyageurs caught and then shipped the luxuriant fur pelts of the beaver, mink and fox down the lakes by the only way they could be transported: water. After 1760, Detroit "became increasingly important as a supply centre for the region beyond Lake Superior and as a point for the repacking and transshipment of furs to Montreal."[8] Scottish intermediaries such as Alexander Duff and Angus Mackintosh were the face of the North West Company. These were the men who saw that the trappers were paid off and that their harvest of furs was bundled and sent on for shipment. They would leave their mark on the strait in many ways. Duff's 1798 mansion on Russell Street in Sandwich would last through the centuries and the iron hook in the entry hall for weighing furs would remain as a tangible legacy of this past. Mackintosh's wife, the French-Indian, Marie Archange Saint-Martin, was proof that the pragmatic Scottish traders knew the importance of alliances with the peoples who fed their trade.

Even though French authority was gone, the lands at the strait remained most indelibly French, and French language and ways predominated on both shores of the Detroit River. As one American official reported from Detroit in 1796, the local "inhabitants are generally French except for the merchants who are all Scotch." French settlers had literally planted a new landscape at the strait. Instead of erecting a cross, they planted orchards of apple, pear and plum and by so doing "they created a distinct landscape and asserted ownership to land." Perhaps some of the trees came from France by way of Quebec. Although commonly called the "Jesuit pears," there was no basis for linking them to the arrival of the Jesuit missions. The presence of so many orderly lines of fruit trees was one of the most noted aspects of the area. A Scottish traveller, John Howison, observed in the 1820s that the French farms along the Detroit River were the "Eden of Upper Canada" because the fruits of their extensive orchards "exceed in size, beauty, and flavour, those raised in any other part of the Province."[9] As Father Lajeunesse noted in his study of the area, the settlers continued French ways and the *coup-de-main* or bee was the way in which the community joined together to accomplish a major task such as raising a barn or bringing in a crop. Afterwards, the landowner was expected to provide liquid refreshments to his helpers. In this remarkably flat terrain, grain threshing was still done by the windmills whose gently rotating sails were a fixture on the riverfront.

After the transfer to British rule life continued much as before, at least for those in authority. Jacques Baby, the eldest son of the leading French family, easily shifted his allegiance to the British Crown. With the conclusion of the American War for Independence and the secession of the upper Great Lakes area to Britain, many Loyalists moved into the district. They demanded their own government independent from Quebec, and as a consequence Upper Canada was created in 1791. For the first time, the land at the strait came under British law and custom. The Detroit River area became part of the Western District, a vast portion of the western part of the colony which took in much of the lands north of Lake Erie and extending up to Lake Superior. In 1790, the Superintendent of Indian Affairs, Alexander McKee, concluded a treaty whereby the Ottawa, Ojibway, Potawatomi and Huron nations surrendered most of the southwestern lands to the Crown. The Huron Church Reserve, located just south of Assumption Church, continued to be set aside for that tribe.

Detroit remained effectively a part of Upper Canada until it was occupied by American troops on June 11, 1796. When that happened, merchants such as Jacques Baby and Angus Mackintosh, who wished to retain their British connection, were compelled to relocate across the river. Mackintosh bought farm lot 93 in the first concession of Sandwich Township (roughly the lands between Gladstone and Moy in modern Windsor) and built "Moy Hall," a grand mansion "reputed to be a place of lavish entertainment," on the British side. Built of hand-sawn walnut, Moy Hall was both an imposing residence and a vital centre of the fur trade. In addition to the mansion, the complex contained a storehouse, a store, and wharf on the river. From Moy Hall, Mackintosh would supervise the trans-shipment of furs from the upper lakes at Michilimackinac to Montreal. To grease the wheels of trade, he kept a vast array of products stored at Moy Hall including "black ostrich feathers, cream-coloured gilt-edge china" as well as scalping knives, prayer books and brass candles.[10] Commerce united men such as Mackintosh to their American counterparts. While the people on both banks of the straits remained intimately connected, after 1796 the political growth of the two communities would be markedly different.

To compensate for the loss of Detroit, colonial authorities established Fort Malden in Amherstburg as a port and military facility. Next to the Huron Church Reserve, the British resolved to erect a new town, and in 1897, the provincial administrator, Peter Russell, reported to Lieutenant Governor Simcoe that:

> The British Merchants at Detroit having solicited me to give them a town on that river, where they may reside and carry on their trade with equal convenience, I purchased from the Indians the Gore (triangular land parcel) near the Huron Church for their accommodation and named it Sandwich, and I am informed that several houses have already been built there and that it promises fair to become soon the most beautiful town in the Province.[11]

Sandwich became the Western District's capital and "was a mirror image of the Detroit that its residents had just departed, right down to neighbours in Detroit turning up as neighbours in Sandwich."[12] Laid out in a triangular form, the town's base extended along the river, while one side ran along the lot of Assumption Church and met the other side of the triangle at an apex. Sixty-one acres along the river near the church was reserved for the Huron Indians. Town lots of one acre each would form the residential area near the river while larger park lots were available at the rear. Three parallel streets, Bedford, Russell and Peter were run across the frontage of the town lots. More land became available for settlement when in 1800 the greater part of the Indian reserve was granted to the Crown as the Hurons had largely abandoned the area. As the capital, Sandwich was home to the courthouse and, after 1808, the Grammar

School of the Western District. Despite this, Sandwich grew slowly, and by 1810 it was estimated to have only a dozen houses.

While Catholic residents had the "French Church" of Assumption at their disposal, Protestants had neither clergy nor church to dispense the sacraments. It was not until 1802 that a deacon, Richard Pollard, provided Anglican services in Sandwich. Pollard held a multitude of official posts, including sheriff and judge of the Surrogate Court and registrar of deeds. It was said that Pollard could arrest a criminal, hold him pending trial, probate his will, take his last rights, hang him, and then conduct his funeral. Despite his "Gilbert and Sullivan combination of roles," his religious zeal was entirely sincere. He would found the Episcopalian church in Michigan, construct churches in Amherstburg and Chatham, and in 1820, see to the completion of the "English Church" (after 1838, St. John's) in Sandwich.[13]

Land was power in the early 19th century, and instead of commerce, land speculation seemed the road to riches. Men such as John Askin and Alexander Grant accumulated huge holdings across the county and held them indefinitely in the hope that they would yield an eventual gain.[14] Nevertheless, the Great Lakes remained the lifeblood of commerce with pelts headed down the straits to Montreal while supplies for the trappers headed north. Any additional business was a mere offshoot of the fur trade. In the absence of any cheap way of transporting products, most agricultural products were consumed locally. However, the windmills of Sandwich milled some grain for export and "high wine" or distilled spirit was sent to the east.[15]

War and Aftermath

When war broke out between Great Britain and the United States in June, 1812, it might have seemed to many of the inhabitants that their incorporation into the American republic was inevitable. On July 12, 1812, General William Hull's American troops landed where the town of Walkerville would eventually be located. Meeting no opposition, they advanced down the Detroit River side to the ferry and set up a small fortification named "Fort Gouie" and a headquarters at the recently built mansion of François Baby. One American soldier described how "The inhabitants (nearly all Canadian French) welcomed us as friends. White handkerchiefs and flags waved from every house and the expression 'We like Americans' came forth from every dwelling."[16] General Hull observed that, "The Canadian militia are deserting in large numbers." Not only did they not resist, several settlers offered to organize a cavalry troop for the Americans and lead foraging parties into the countryside.[17]

Meanwhile, American scouts probed the defences of the British fort at Amherstburg, but were repulsed. That August the American offensive stalled, Hull abandoned the fortifications at the ferry and retreated to Detroit. The British commander of Upper Canada, General Isaac Brock, arrived in Amherstburg on August 13th, 1812, with regular soldiers, militia and Indian allies. Shortly after his arrival he met and joined forces with the great Shawnee warrior Tecumseh. Brock generously excused the absence of the local militia and presumed that they were anxious to attend to their harvest. Nevertheless, he impressed upon them that now was the time for action. Adopting an aggressive stance, he formed his small force into three brigades and crossed the river on August 16th. The previous day, Brock had demanded Detroit's surrender and in an aside, warned Hull that while "It is far from my intention to join in a war of extermination… you must be aware, that the numerous body of Indians who have attached themselves to my troops will be beyond control the moment the contest commences." Brock had barely formed his troops up for an assault when Hull, fearful of what the Indian warriors might do to the civilians of Detroit, suddenly surrendered his command. Before battle could even be joined, the Americans had given up an enormous cache of prisoners and arms and opened up the Northwest to further British offensive action. Moreover, the inhabitants of Sandwich and those at the ferry again found themselves united with their compatriots across the river.

The reunion was short lived. At the Battle of Lake Erie in September, 1813, the British squadron was defeated and the western part of Upper Canada was left exposed to American attack. Realizing his precarious situation, Colonel Henry Procter, the commander at Fort Malden, decided to evacuate the area. While his Indian allies, including Tecumseh, protested, there seemed to be little else he could do. Before leaving, Procter formally disbanded and disarmed the Essex militia. Taking away their weapons was an embarrassing but necessary step to keep them from falling into American hands. Procter's forces retreated through Sandwich and along the way burned Detroit's public buildings. Closely pursued by the Americans under General William Henry Harrison, Procter turned to face them at the Battle of the Thames (Moraviantown). He was decisively defeated and Tecumseh killed. For the rest of the war, the American army would occupy Amherstburg and Sandwich and make occasional destructive forays deeper into the colony.

After two and a half years of devastating but inconclusive warfare, peace was signed in January 1815. The pre-war boundaries were confirmed by the treaty and both sides returned to the same arrangement that had existed before all the bloodshed. When news of the peace reached the Detroit frontier in February, 1815, there was profound relief and residents organized "A public dinner & ball given at Detroit on account of a peace having taken place."[18]

The years of war had a disastrous effect on so many of the settlers as their log cabins and barns had been razed and their crops plundered. Two years after the war, the Scottish agronomist Robert Gourlay was going about the colony collecting information for a general report on existing conditions. At a meeting held in Sandwich Township, he was informed that the residents lamented the overall lack of progress and that "No lands have recently sold in the township; the settlement has long been at a stand. Only one road in front on the river… The back part of the township unsettled, except for a few scattered houses…"[19] Growth was also slow on the opposite side of the river. Michigan territory was considered to be inferior farmland, so land grants to veterans were usually made in Ohio and Indiana. The land at the straits remained a bucolic backwater. One American traveller sailing upriver to Detroit in 1819 pictured Amherstburg as "a small, dirty town, of a few houses and a British garrison." He described Sandwich a little more charitably as "small but handsome." What impressed him above all was the beautiful river bank bounded by "fine farms covered with orchards."[20] Indeed, the district was overwhelmingly rural. When a local newspaper, the *Canadian Emigrant,* was founded in Sandwich in 1831, its reports were almost exclusively oriented towards farming concerns. From instructing its readers on how to avoid the "Hessian Fly" to lectures on rural economy, the newspaper reflected the interests of an agrarian world.

Not only was it an overwhelmingly rural society, Upper Canada remained very much a hierarchical one where an elite "squirearchy" owned vast (if often unprofitable) estates and held a monopoly of government posts including the dominant one in the district, that of Magistrate. The most eminent members of the local squirearchy had their roots in the *ancien régime.* But many of them had sustained heavy losses during the war. Jacques Baby had commanded the militia in Sandwich and fought with the British until they were defeated in the west. While he was away on campaign his home in Sandwich was looted and his wife died of a fever. Tired and grief-stricken, Baby accepted a government appointment and moved to York (Toronto).[21] His brother François likewise had his property destroyed; however, he intended to rebuild his fortunes as the local seigneur. François (often anglicizing his name and calling himself Francis or signing his name as "F. Baby") still acted the part of the local overlord. Described as "Tall, ramrod straight, active in mind and body," he "possessed both personal qualities and family connections which made him a natural choice for political and civil office." First elected to the Assembly in 1792, he also occupied a seat at the Court of Quarter Sessions where as a magistrate he issued licenses and effectively controlled the townships. During the war he served as assistant quartermaster general and had seen action at numerous battles.[22] However, his devotion to the British Crown may have been viewed with suspicion by his French-Canadian compatriots. When he married an English woman, Frances Abbott, in 1795 and occupied the pew in Assumption Church reserved for the highest lord in the area, many were outraged. As one of his enemies described the scene, Baby, accompanied by "his wife and her sister, both born of Protestant parents and Protestant herself," formed a, "royal court stamping diagonally across the church and climbing into that raised and carpeted pew with a continual click-click caused distractions among the congregation during the rest of the Mass."[23] The peasants gave vent to their feelings after Mass when they detached and flung the pew out of the church. Both the presiding bishop and the colony's lieutenant governor ordered that it be reinstated. The pew was accordingly rebuilt and the Babys presided in splendor until the following Sunday when the pew was again dismantled and tossed out. The attitudes of the farmers towards their supposed lord had been registered.

The Baby family was but one element in that grander system of relations that have come down to history as the "Family Compact." While its influence was probably exaggerated, without question there existed local oligarchies that controlled offices and basked in government favour no matter which faction was successful at the election polls. These were men who had proved their loyalty during the war and usually came from the professional or bureaucratic class; they were rarely tradesmen. All magistrates belonged to the central administrative body, the Court of Quarter Sessions of the Peace, which assessed land, levied taxes, heard road petitions and granted licenses to inns. These powers made them effectively the last word in the local power structure. While members of the elite could hold an array of offices, to be a magistrate was a display of prominence. Having the right family and business connections was one of the keys to appointment. However, ethnic considerations also mattered, and of the district's sixteen magistrates with French names, four of them were members of the venerable Baby family.[24]

A new element was rising from below and increasingly throughout the 1830s, British immigrants were making themselves felt as a factor at the straits. Ever since the War of 1812, colonial authorities had been eager to encourage a greater British presence in the colony to counteract the existence of so many American settlers. While the flow of immigrants had been meager in the 1820s, after 1830 the tempo of British immigration increased.[25] Many of the tradesmen filling up Hutton's Tavern that September evening in 1836 to pick the name "Windsor" came from this recent surge of settlers. These farmers and small entrepreneurs, such as the Dougalls, bore English or Scottish surnames, and English was their language of trade. Not all of the recent arrivals were penniless refugees hoping to scratch out a living in the new world. One of the

The Jacques Baby Mansion: 1798—currently the Duff-Baby Mansion.

most prominent arrivals in 1832 was an ambitious young Englishman, John Prince. Prince had already made a lot of money practising law in England, and he used some of these funds to invest in land. These investments included 200 acres in the rear of Sandwich, which estate he called "The Park Farm." Prince, a dark, moody man who alternated between craving adulation and demanding privacy, was described as "haughty and aloof, and yet he rapidly established himself as a leading citizen..."[26] In 1836, after he was elected to the Assembly, this complex man confided to his diary, "I occasionally wish for death."

THE FERRY

Reports on the small settlements at the strait were not frequent and those that appeared were far from complimentary. One traveller, Patrick Shirreff, was not impressed by Amherstburg and was appalled by Sandwich. In 1833, he noted that the town "derives its only importance from being the county town. The houses compose an irregular street, running along the river, and chiefly occupied by the French... I do not think it has the same chance [as Amherstburg] of progressing."[27] The *Canadian Emigrant* (a Tory newspaper and an enthusiastic booster of recent British arrivals) thought that Sandwich was a poor prospect and that newcomers would do well there for the existing workers "are too lazy to earn any more at a time than suffices to purchase whiskey..."[28] In 1835, the newspaper began to notice the emerging community at the ferry and in February gave a full account of developments there. It reported that only a few months before it was simply the place across the river from Detroit. Now, a traveller found "a flourishing town... the sight of good taverns and handsome accommodations." The editor listed these establishments, including the Mansion House, the Pavilion and Stage House and "La Belaine." As a result of this growth, "merchants of capital and tradesmen are daily flocking to it [the ferry] and giving to it, the character of a place of business."[29]

All of this activity at the ferry was directly attributable to events occurring on the other side of the strait. By the 1830s, free land was increasingly unavailable in Ohio and Indiana, and settlers began to pour into Michigan's open territories. The opening of the Erie Canal in 1825 had made the export of agricultural products from the interior both possible and profitable. Easy credit enabled speculation to run riot and ships filled with hopeful settlers arrived almost daily at Detroit's docks.[30] Detroit became the hub for new developments and supplying farming implements for these recent arrivals became the city's focus. In 1837, Michigan finally became a state and Detroit, with a population of 9,763, its principal city. The little community located at the ferry on the Canadian shore across from this rising town was bound to be swept along with this growth.

One member of the local squirearchy was determined to profit from these rising fortunes. François Baby's farm was situated almost directly across the river from the centre of Detroit and was an ideal landing site for ferries. While the Baby wharf had been in use as a ferry stop since 1804, a competitor had arisen in 1820 on the neighbouring farm of Charles Ouellette. In 1825, Baby raised the stakes by scrapping his fleet of rowboats and replacing them with the horsepowered *Olive Branch*. This sidewheeler had a far greater capacity than any previous vessel and "a change of scale as well as pace came over the river connection. The heyday of the dugout canoes and flat-bottomed boats was over."[31] With this lucrative trade in the balance, the master of the *Olive Branch* applied in 1827 for an exclusive license to prohibit competitors. Baby added to the conflict by obtaining the water lots in front of his property and thereby denied his competitor, Vital Ouellette, the open use of the river. It was the beginning of a controversy over control of the crossing that would persist for a century, until the bridge and tunnel rendered the ferries obsolete. It also meant that the volume of crossings was increasing substantially, and that travellers were demanding more amenities. By 1831, there was a visible community at the ferry catering to travellers. A number of passable hotels serviced the trade and an impressive array of goods was available at the J & J Dougall Store. As Patrick Shirreff noted, by 1833 the ferry landing had "fifteen or twenty houses on the Canadian side of the river and several brick buildings were being erected…" In his view, the hamlet would soon eclipse Sandwich. He attributed this expansion to the ferry landing's proximity to "Detroit… the great market of Western Canada."[32]

In 1832, a petition was presented to realign the road that ran along the river. This river road (eventually Sandwich Street and later Riverside Drive) enabled owners such as François Baby to sell building lots on the north and south sides of the street. Two streets, Church and Assumption, were laid out with a lane (eventually called Ferry Street) leading down to Baby's wharf. Another entrepreneur, Joseph McDougall, had acquired an easterly lot of the Ouellette farm and in 1835 he laid out McDougall Street extending back from the river with cross streets attached. He called his grand project a "Plan for South Detroit." As opposed to Baby's layout of a street parallel to the river, McDougall's model of a main road extending back from the river with side streets coming off of it would be repeated constantly in Windsor's street pattern.[33] Each of these early developments was almost a village unto itself, with its own pattern of cross streets. The resulting misalignment when these streets were eventually connected created a pattern that unfortunately remains evident in Windsor's downtown.

Life remained hard on the frontier and making a living off the land was an unrelenting struggle. Added to the tedium were cholera epidemics that swept North America in 1832 and 1834. Magistrates attempted to isolate the Western District by turning back strangers, but the attempt failed and the *Canadian Emigrant* (which was forced to suspend publication for four months in 1832) reported that year that the district had 53 cases of cholera and 29 deaths, a significant toll in a sparse population.[34] The justice system could also be direct and brutal. In 1835, Robert Bird was convicted of murdering an itinerant peddler. After a brief trial at the Sandwich courthouse, Bird was convicted and sentenced to hang. As was the custom of English law, his body was publicly dissected and Dr. George Jones provided a commentary to the crowd on the "purpose of the various parts of the system."[35]

Anna Murphy Jamieson, an English gentlewoman, recorded her impressions of the area in 1837. Detroit struck her as a brisk, business-like entrepôt. Mrs. Jamieson took the ferry from Detroit to the Canadian shore (the trip took a scant ten minutes) and was struck by the contrast. The Canadian side was a tiny farming community where residents, "speaking a Norman patois, and bringing baskets of fruit to the Detroit market," lived much as their ancestors had in old France. At the hamlet across from Detroit (still called "Richmond" in her recollection), she met and chatted with an elderly French-Canadian. She was charmed to encounter "such a perfect specimen of an old-fashioned Norman peasant—all bows, courtesy and good-humour." When she mounted his cart he poured forth "a voluble speech, in which the words *enchante! honneur! and madame!* were all I could understand."[36] At Sandwich she shared the view of so many others that the town "makes no progress." She wondered why Sandwich seemed so listless when across on the American side all was bustle; "What can be the reason that all flourishes there" she asked "and all languishes here?"

The problem, at least to the squirearchy, was not the sluggish economy or outbreaks of disease, but the more fundamental problem of loyalty. Upper Canada had fallen into a near constant state of political turmoil since the War of 1812. Tories looked upon American settlers with increasing suspicion, while a faction in the colonial Assembly based largely among the American settlers was agitating for greater popular control of the government. When a prominent member of the provincial elite, such as Chief Justice John Beverley Robinson, presided over the assizes or sessions of King's Bench Court at the district courthouse in Sandwich, it was an opportunity to reassert those loyal values. Significantly, Robinson's 1836 charge to the grand jury (an address published verbatim in the *Canadian Emigrant*) focused on the question of loyalty. "Order is Heaven's first law," he intoned, and "to preserve among a people implicit and unhesitating obedience to the laws, it is necessary to take care that they grow in the habit of it," for in his view. "Submission to the laws must, where freedom is valued, be prompt and unqualified."[37]

The chief justice's address articulated a conservative reaction that reflected the widening gulf in principles that divided the communities at the strait. Americans were enthusiastically embracing Jacksonian democracy and pushing for greater authority for elected officers. After an 1838 election, the Detroit *Free Press* gushed that "The democratic republican institutions of this Union are doubtless superior to any ever known to the world." But authorities in Upper Canada did doubt it, and the editor of Sandwich's Tory newspaper, the *Western Herald*, mocked American pretensions. After the same 1838 election, the editor scorned the "lordly sovereigns turned out in all their majesty" in order to drop "a bit of printed paper into a ballot-box" as if this signified any real power.[38] Colonial governors reminded their subjects that they enjoyed the benefits of British law and institutions, of the balance between elected legislators and appointed governors. Sometimes, these reminders needed to be reinforced. In 1832, Sheriff William Hands called a meeting in Sandwich Township to forward "an address expressive of the loyalty of the people of this Township to His Majesty." The target of the meeting were the local supporters of Toronto firebrand radical William Lyon Mackenzie. According to one of Hands' allies, William Elliott, Mackenzie, and his ilk had been "disseminating discord" and had to be repudiated. Mackenzie's advocacy of popular government and securing the land rights of American-born residents was seen as seditious and disloyal. A fitting address of loyalty was unanimously passed by the Sandwich gathering and the meeting adjourned with three cheers for the King.

Matters were reaching a critical point, and during the 1836 election governor Sir Francis Bond Head became an active campaigner on behalf of the loyal cause. Bond Head, "never wavered from one simple theme: that the contest was between a loyal people and a disloyal faction."[39] All British subjects in Upper Canada, even those who had been born in the United States, should give unwavering obedience to the colonial officials sent to govern them. When word arrived in Sandwich that the governor was expected momentarily, the editor of the *Canadian Emigrant* urged that, "a number of gentlemen be prepared to escort him into Town on horseback, as soon as they are informed of his approach."[40] As a result of these efforts, the Tory faction was momentarily triumphant, but if anything, a far greater discontent was about to surface.

While political lines were being drawn, it was apparent that meetings of like-minded persons were not about to solve the differences that divided the colony. These differences were about to break out into open violence and the hamlet that had recently gained a name was about to witness a day of remarkable fury that it had never seen before and would never see again.

Chapter Two
The Battle Of Windsor: 1838

F OR ONCE, EVENTS IN TORONTO would have a greater shock on Windsor than those in Detroit. Seizing on the confusion resulting from the November 1837 nationalist uprising in Lower Canada (Quebec), Mackenzie organized a force of predominantly American settlers and marched on the capital of York (Toronto). On December 5, 1837, they were met and easily dispersed by the local militia. Mackenzie fled in panic with a few followers. Mackenzie's "rebellion" had shown that there was little popular support among Canadians for this kind of violent change, and no chance for its success. Nevertheless, it sparked an unusual reaction in the United States.

1837 had been a disastrous economic year and thousands of young, unemployed American men were eager for adventure. They easily succumbed to fiery revolutionary rhetoric that evoked past glories. The "Patriot" movement, organized in so-called "Hunter's Lodges," caught fire in the Mid-West, and demagogues proclaimed that Canadians were on the verge of striking out for their independence just as Americans had in 1776. Cities such as Cleveland became a hub for the Patriot movement, and at one typical meeting patriotic speeches stirred the crowd and "all seemed to feel for the oppressed Patriots of Canada."[41] Sympathizers subscribed money and weapons to the cause and hundreds of volunteers rushed to serve in a Patriot army to drive the redcoats out of America and perhaps annex Canada in the bargain.

The communities at the strait were the most isolated and vulnerable branch of the colony. A small British force, the Queen's Light Infantry, was dispatched to Fort Malden in Amherstburg and the local militia was called into service. John Prince, now a militia colonel, was gratified that almost 150 black residents volunteered. They were "brave and true fellows" he pronounced, most unlike the French-Canadians who were refusing to serve and who, Prince thought, "cannot be relied on."[42] In January, 1838, the militia would be called upon when the Patriot schooner *Anne* sailed past Amherstburg and a Patriot force occupied Bois Blanc Island across from Fort Malden. However, a rebel commander and former Detroit apothecary, "General" Edward Theller and twenty of his men were captured when the *Anne* ran aground near Fort Malden and the remainder returned to the United States. Patriots briefly invaded Fighting Island the following month and in March, rebels attacked and seized Pelee Island. Marching across the ice, troops under Prince drove off the invaders and captured nine of them. When the prisoners were put on trial in June, Prince was astounded that they were not charged with murder. Even though he was a sitting magistrate, Prince took on the role of prosecutor and argued at length that these nine men, the authors of the "most atrocious, unprovoked, uncalled for and unheard of villainies," deserved the death penalty. His voice breaking with emotion, Prince blamed, "that most unfriendly race (pointing to the opposite shore of Michigan) who have … attacked, robbed and murdered us." When he sat down, there was a burst of applause throughout the courtroom. However, the presiding justice, Jonas Jones, reminded him that these men had been captured after battle and that the government deemed them to be prisoners of war.[43] The prisoners would not hang, and Prince, at least for the moment, was denied the blood he thought his due.

These incursions altered attitudes along the river, as it was apparent that wealthy Detroiters were giving the Patriots financial support. This caused Henry C. Grant, an avid Tory and publisher of Sandwich's *Western Herald*, to remark that their support of this "unholy crusade" was creating "astonishment and righteous indignation" on the Canadian side.[44] Whatever the provocations, Grant promised that "English and Irish, Scotch and French, and the *enfranchised* colored people" would rise up as one and expel the invaders. As the Patriot raids continued, "the general attitude of the Canadians living along the shores of the Detroit River changed from one of friendliness, through mild resentment and suspicion, to vehement anger."[45] This anger was enhanced when three British officers were insulted and attacked on a Detroit street in May, 1838. This hardly seemed to be the relationship that should exist between two countries which were at peace. Washington finally realized the precariousness of the situation, and General Hugh Brady was dispatched to Detroit with federal troops and orders to maintain the peace along the border.

After Brady seized a Patriot ship laden with weapons, a sudden calm descended along the border. That summer the Queen's Light Infantry was withdrawn and the district defence was left to the militia and a small detachment of regular troops. However, peace remained an illusion and a force

Colonel John Prince later in life.

of several hundred Patriots, mostly Americans with a few Canadians in their ranks, were still determined to invade the colony. These men assembled a force near Detroit and by late November, 1838, an attack across the river appeared imminent. Prince recorded in his diary the constant stress on the militiamen as they waited for these "Brigands from Michigan" to descend. One of the "brigands," Friend Palmer of Buffalo, New York, later recorded his impression of the land across the Detroit River. He was struck by the three windmills that lined the Canadian shore and the horsepowered ferry (more a "cheese box on a raft" he thought) that periodically crossed from Detroit. Somewhat more ominously, he could see the red-coated militia drilling on the village green in front of Assumption Church.[46]

General Brady had successfully stopped the Patriots from seizing two vessels, and on December 3 it was reported that he had confiscated 250 weapons. This may have reassured some Canadians, but to the Patriots it made it all the more imperative for them to strike. At about two in the morning of December 4, a force of about 150 Patriots under Lucius Verus Bierce seized the steamer *Champlain* from a Detroit wharf.[47] The crew was chased off and the ship crossed the river and landed on the Canadian shore opposite Hog (later Belle Isle) Island. At about five o'clock that morning, the force moved westward to Windsor. What happened next was a morning of such violence and mayhem that it would send shock waves across America and Britain.

The Patriot's first target was the guardhouse. The advance party was challenged by a sentry; they opened fire and wounded him. The men inside returned fire so the Patriots decided to burn them out. They proceeded to the adjacent house of a black barber, William Mills, and seized some burning embers to set fire to the guardhouse. As the militiamen ran for their lives, the patriotic Mills called out, "God Save the Queen." He was fired on and killed. Bierce then sent two companies under Captains Putnam and Harvell to the orchard west of Windsor to await the expected assault from Sandwich. Three British officers from Sandwich strayed into the rebel lines and one of them, Dr. John James Hume, was captured. He was bayoneted, stuck by an axe and his body left in a hog pen. In the confusion, James Dougall hurriedly removed $20,000 from his safe and rushed off to Sandwich. The morning sun was rising, and the flag of the Republic of Canada was the only one flying over the hamlet. Windsor was in rebel hands, and hundreds of Detroiters who lined the opposite riverbank cheered encouragement.

It was not until 6:15 in the morning that alarm bells were rung in Sandwich, and two companies of Prince's Contingent Battalion of Essex Militia commanded by Captains Sparke and Bell were assembled. Sparke was too ill to march, so an avid younger officer, Ensign Arthur Rankin, led his men. These troops encountered Dougall rushing the other way and he informed them of the rebel defences along the pioneer orchard behind François Baby's house. According to Dougall's later account, the militiamen "wore a scarlet uniform, were well drilled and had all the appearance and efficiency of regular British soldiers." To many Americans they looked like British troops and in any case, they were far better trained than the Patriots. While Rankin's men engaged the Patriots in the orchard, Bell's company came up on their left and attacked the Patriot's flank. The abrupt ferocity of the militia assault overwhelmed the Patriots and groups of them ran for the woods. One of their captains, Harvell of Kentucky, tried to rally his men and waved a huge Patriot flag, a red, white, and blue tricolour with two stars (for Upper and Lower Canada) and a crescent near the staff. James Dougall called out, "A hundred dollars to whoever shoots the standard bearer!" Harvell was brought down and Ensign Rankin seized the flag. Many ordinary citizens seem to have joined the troops. In addition to Dougall, Henry Grant, the publisher of the *Western Herald*, shouldered a musket. It was a glorious day, Grant recollected, when the volunteers of

Patriot flag from a remnant in the collection of Fort Malden National Historic Site, Amherstburg, Ontario.

Sandwich sent "a few leaden messengers after the fast-footed pirates." This was the most decisive defeat the Patriots had ever endured and should have served to end their ill-considered campaign. But the morning was far from over.

As the firing died off, Colonel Prince arrived in the orchard. He cut a striking figure. Some of his own soldiers did not recognize him, for he was not wearing a uniform but rather "his hunting suit—grey coat, short coat and pants, a red-fox skin fur cap, long fur gloves and black sword belt."[48] He looked more like a sportsman on the way to the hunt than an officer engaged in a desperate battle. Instead of ordering a pursuit of the defeated enemy, Prince ordered the force to return to Sandwich and await reinforcements from Amherstburg. Before he left, Prince could see fires burning in Windsor and was told of the murder of the barber Mills and of Dr. Hume. The latter had been a friend of Prince's and he keenly felt his death. Prior to these events, Prince had despised the Patriots, but now his feelings resolved into a vengeful fury, as he later described it, "I therefore resolved upon shooting at once and without a moment's hesitation every bandit who happened to be captured and brought in."[49]

The first person to fall to the Colonel's ire was a prisoner seized in the orchard. Prince ordered him to be shot and he was instantly killed. Returning to Sandwich, where no fighting was in progress, Prince was idling in front of a tavern when a captured Detroit silversmith was brought in. Prince ordered him taken to a field for execution. As women and children watched, the man ran for his life but was caught and killed behind a haystack. A Canadian militia officer called out, "Damn you, you cowardly rascals, are you going to murder your prisoner?" Many more killings were to follow. Another wounded prisoner was killed in Sandwich, as was a wounded man who had crawled into a preacher's hut. François Baby had found the man and dragged him to the hut to be attended to; instead, he was taken out, bayoneted and an officer on horseback fired a shot into him. By eleven o'clock, the reinforcements from Fort Malden had arrived and Prince advanced on Windsor. There was no fighting to be done, merely the chasing and capture of those Patriots who remained. One final prisoner was taken out, and as hundreds of onlookers in Detroit watched and a U.S. schooner passed by, the man was executed.

The Battle of Windsor was over, but the repercussions had just begun. This brief struggle was the last spasm of the Patriot movement, for it had shown its inability to conquer Canada and Canadian determination to decide their own form of government. If the battle had been wound up with the assembly of prisoners and their delivery to lawful confinement, the matter would have been neatly resolved. However, the bloody mayhem of telling a prisoner to run for his life in a crowded street and then shooting him down, of killing a wounded man in a clergyman's hut, and "staging a shooting [of a prisoner] for the benefit of the audience on an American schooner—these were the acts not of a defender

The tombstone of Dr. John Hume in St. John's church cemetery, Sandwich: The lengthy inscription relates how his killers styled themselves as "Patriots" but "were properly styled PIRATES."

of the established order of things but of a madman."[50] Prince, of course, put a brave face on his acts and portrayed himself as the heroic defender of the province. But several of his officers and other leading men in the community were disgusted by his brutality. Sir George Arthur, the Lieutenant Governor, was shocked by Prince's conduct and wrote to Prince's superior that "To describe to you my feelings at Colonel Prince having caused four men to be shot after they were taken, or had surrendered, is not in my power."[51] The Toronto *Mirror* condemned Prince's actions as "the murderous conduct of this coward and bully." But John Prince was not the kind of man to back down, and when he resumed his seat in the Legislative Assembly, he was enthusiastically cheered. In February, 1839, a Court of Inquiry exonerated him. Newspapers across the province generally supported Prince, and the Toronto *Patriot* suggested that he had been entirely justified in his actions. His fame spread across British America, and the Halifax *Times* praised him for his "one act of decisive energy" that had put in check "the treacherous Yankees."[52] While many may have abhorred his cruelty, the Patriot raids had been a nightmare across the province, and Prince's actions had brought them to an unequivocal halt.

By May, 1839, news of the events in Windsor had reached Britain, and Lord Brougham, the radical leader in the House of Lords, raised Prince's conduct which he considered "had disgraced the name of a British Officer." According to Brougham, Prince was not only a discredit to the service; his conduct was tantamount to murder. The Colonial Secretary, Lord Normanby, was compelled to defend this obscure and distant figure, and he replied that the province's governor had already expressed his disapprobation of the Colonel's conduct.[53] By June, Normanby was able to write to Lieutenant Governor Arthur that the "awkward" affair of Colonel Prince had been officially buried.

As for the Americans, enthusiasm for the Patriot movement was limited to a diminishing few. On the morning of December 4th, when the rebels held the upper hand, the Detroit *Morning Post* editorialized that "the slumbering genius of freedom" was about to awake in Canada. However, the majority of Detroiters were opposed to these continued violations of the peace and the Detroit *Free Press* urged any remaining Patriots to give up the struggle, as it was apparent that the people of Upper Canada "would rally at the tap of a drum to defend its soil from invasion."[54] By the beginning of January, 1839, Patriot forces on the Michigan shore had vanished.

Yet there was one unfinished piece of business. Shortly after the battle, James Dougall tracked down Pierre Marentette at his gun shop. Marentette, like many French-Canadians, was an avid hunter and a fine shot, and like many of his fellows (despite Prince's disdain for them) had played a significant role in the fight in the orchard. In an editorial in the *Western Herald,* Henry Grant touched on an unarticulated but remarkable change in attitude that had been apparent during the Rebellion. While during the War of 1812 French Canadians had been indifferent as to whether their masters were English-speaking British or Americans, their attitudes during the Rebellion had been markedly different. No segment of the region, French or British, had shown any sympathy towards republicanism. Grant proudly observed that:

> ...those representing the people of Upper Canada, as a disloyal or rebellious race, have had the very opposite clearly and unequivocally demonstrated—the people have proved, by their own acts, that they are sound at the hearts core.[55]

During the heat of the battle, it was Pierre Marentette who had brought down the colour-bearer and Dougall was prepared to pay (with due Scottish reflection) the $25 reward he had promised. Despite Dougall's insistence, Marentette refused to take his money. "I was not fighting for money," he explained, "I was fighting for my country."[56]

Peace

By the summer of 1839, life began to return to normal. Federal troops in Detroit invited British and Canadian officers to join them in Detroit to celebrate the 4th of July. They did so—much to the displeasure of the *Western Herald*'s editor—and a cordial, if uneasy, peace settled along the border.

It was becoming apparent that despite Sandwich's status as the government town, Windsor would soon eclipse it. Even a Sandwich resident had to admit that the town did little trade and that business "has been entirely monopolized by the new town of Windsor, and the City of Detroit." James and John Dougall's Windsor store was supplying Hudson's Bay Company posts as far away as Sault Ste. Marie and across the Lake Superior shore. In addition to their dock and dry goods store, their operation included a warehouse and grocery storage area where "Six to eight clerks were employed at Windsor, all of them Scots."[57] The ferry business itself continued to do well, and in 1843 François Baby built a new ship, the *Alliance*. In that year he also moved his landing twenty yards to the west to put as much distance as possible between himself and the Ouellette ferry. Six years later, he stopped up the old road leading to his wharf and the new road leading down to his landing became Ferry Street.[58] To supplement the water connections, by the fall of 1840, a stagecoach operation was initiated to join Windsor and Amherstburg.

On the face of it, the diverse communities at the strait lived in harmony. In November, 1839, an announcement was made of the marriage of a Protestant militia officer to François Baby's daughter. Mass at Assumption Church was followed by another service at St. John's Anglican. This easy relationship between English and French was also exemplified by the enduring popularity of John Prince. He led the polls among French-Canadians, and one of their leaders wrote that "Colonel Prince could perhaps be considered a French-Canadian, for in every instance he has come to the defence of the Canadians of the Western District."[59]

By far the predominant ethnic group in Sandwich was the French Catholics, and they were determined to have a permanent place of worship. The cornerstone to replace the old timber church of Assumption was laid in

1842 and a Detroit architect, Robert Elliott, prepared the design. In 1846, the imposing brick structure on Huron Line was consecrated. It was a marvel of the times, both because of its impressive size and its being the first structure in the area to make extensive use of machine-made bricks. The new church also featured an enormous organ built by the Henry Erben firm of New York. Significantly, Arthur Rankin, the gallant ensign of rebellion days and an Anglican to boot, had played a prominent role in procuring this unique instrument. Rankin had his eye on challenging Colonel Prince, and "The organ was a gift calculated to gain Rankin support in anything he undertook among the Roman Catholics."[60]

In addition to French Catholics and British Protestants, there was another community at the strait that was only just coming to notice. Slavery had been legal in the colony since the beginning of European settlement, and both Indians and blacks had been held in bondage. In Sandwich, Matthew Elliott had fixed a lashing ring to a tree to be used for the flogging of recalcitrant slaves. Under the influence of Lieutenant Governor Simcoe, Upper Canada became the only British territory in the Americas to pass a statute in 1793 limiting slavery, prohibiting the importation of new slaves and hinting at its ultimate abolition. While slavery persisted in the period before the War of 1812, the institution did not flourish in the colony and there does not appear to be much, if any, evidence of slavery after 1815. Instead, fugitive slaves from the United States found the colony to be a refuge from bounty hunters who threatened to return them to the American South. By 1827, it was estimated that there were 600 black residents in Amherstburg and Colchester, making up almost one-fifth of the population. After a race riot in Detroit in 1833, several more black families crossed the river to live in Sandwich. They were not segregated, and assessment information from the 1840s indicates that they lived interspersed with whites.[61] While Canadian life may have been preferable to the alternative, blacks were still subject to dismissive comments of being "this refuse of the States" from local officials. As with the French Canadians, the church would play a central role in their lives, and in 1851 black residents in Sandwich had commenced work on a Baptist church. The Sandwich Baptist Church, with its individually handmade bricks, would exemplify the simplicity and limited resources of Sandwich's black community. With the U.S. Congress's passage of the *Fugitive Slave Act* of 1850 (which authorized the re-enslavement of persons who had escaped to the northern states), the numbers of blacks seeking refuge in the area dramatically increased.

The 1840s were witness to shifts in morality as well. Upper Canada was a drinking society and distilled beverages were a regular part of life. Public occasions such as barn raisings frequently concluded with drunken brawls.

The quality of drinking water was uncertain and it was wise to try and decontaminate it with alcohol. By the 1830s, the temperance movement had become a cornerstone of American Protestant churches. The movement spread to Canada and was particularly strong in the Methodist heartland in Niagara. No part of Canada was completely unaffected and the inaugural meeting of the "Sandwich Temperance Society," held at the Methodist Chapel that had been established earlier that year, was well attended by the leading men in the town. John Dougall, who had initiated the local temperance movement, spoke "in a short but impressive speech" about the dangers of alcohol and the benefits of abstinence. Several men, including soldiers from the local garrison, signed the "Pledge" of total abstinence.[62] Temperance did not necessarily equate to good business, and the Dougalls, who by the late 1840s were overextended at the bank, refused on principle to transport or deal in liquor. This high-minded act denied them a significant source of revenue. To add to their woes, a fire on April 16, 1849, destroyed their store. As the village was essentially a collection of wood structures, the store was easily consumed by stray sparks. Moreover, as Windsor had no firefighting force, the flames would probably have levelled the entire community had it not been for the intervention of the Detroit fire department, who took the ferry across the river and saved at least a few of the buildings. But the results were disastrous for the Dougalls and it took further bank advances to enable them to stay in business. The store was rebuilt in 1852, but the Dougalls never regained their former prosperity.[63]

By the mid-1840s, Windsor remained a quiet hamlet, the tiny offshoot of Detroit. Though it offered a ferry service, a grocery store, and several hotels, it remained a backwater, a place to pass through on the way to somewhere else. In 1845, the American historian Francis Parkman visited François Baby to learn more about the Indian chief Pontiac. He found the old seigneur in his mansion, the former American headquarters during the War of 1812 as well as the site of the battle in the orchard in 1838, and was struck by its "waste and picturesque air—books, guns, neglected tables, old clocks, chests of drawers, and garments and Indian equipment flung around." Parkman also noticed a "little Negro girl, and the strange-looking half breed who were sunning themselves among the hens and hogs in the back yard."[64] As the insects buzzed and Baby punished a brandy bottle (temperance made little headway among Catholics), the venerable aristocrat sat amidst his decaying feudal splendor regaling his American visitor with stories of the past. François Baby lived until 1852, and his death would coincide with a remarkable turn of events that would transform the land at the straits. The quiet days of the seigneur and horse travel were about to be supplanted by machines, steam, and speed.

Chapter Three
"Railroads, Railroads!" 1845–1858

THERE WAS MORE TO Colonel John Prince than simply the psychotic executioner of hapless Americans. In the summer of 1836 he had become the president and the principal moving force of the Niagara and Detroit Rivers Rail Road Company, a corporation chartered to provide a rail line from Windsor to the east. That August, the *Canadian Emigrant* reported an enthusiastic meeting of shareholders, and that a route was to be surveyed before winter set in.[65] It was not to be. The ensuing Rebellion and business downturn caused the project to be set aside. But in the mid-1840s the project would again be revived, although in a very different form.

Not for the last time, the development of Windsor was about to be overtaken by distant events. In reaction to the Irish potato famine, British trade policy was radically altered between 1846 and 1849. Prior to 1846, the "Corn Laws" effectively prevented the importation of foreign grain and had added to the misery of the famine. After that year, those laws were repealed in favour of open competition, which allowed cheaper American grains to be shipped directly to Britain. Americans also embraced free trade, and in 1845 the U.S. permitted Canadian foodstuffs to be exported in bond to American ports. As a result, the volume of wheat exported from Canada West (Ontario) exploded. Commerce was ignoring borders and was becoming concentrated on the east-west axis from the Midwest to New York, instead of the St. Lawrence route to Montreal.[66] During this "wheat boom," those parts of Canada West that exported grain flourished. Toronto and Hamilton had substantial wheat growing hinterlands, and they benefited from the transport of grain. In the west, London became the distribution hub for a rich farming area, and by

1851 it had a population over 7,000.[67] Even Chatham flourished from the trade, and its population rose from 812 in 1841 to 2,070 by 1851 (Appendix A). In dismal contrast, Windsor remained simply the hamlet of two or three hundred persons where the Detroit ferry stopped. Essex County, with its flat, swampy terrain, had missed out on the wheat boom, and its lethargic towns reflected this failure.

This did not mean that the area had to miss out on the transportation revolution. By the early 1840s, there was an array of short railways between New York City and Buffalo that were ultimately consolidated in 1853 as the New York Central Railroad. The rail link between Detroit and Chicago, the Michigan Central, was completed in 1852. There was a glaring gap in the middle of this burgeoning network and what was needed was a track that joined Buffalo and Detroit at their shortest distance. The obvious choice was a railway between Niagara and Windsor. Until that happened, the land at the strait remained isolated, and worse: a commercial dead end. In 1850, a writer in the *Detroit Daily Advertiser* worried that "Winter's approach places Detroit back twenty years—Winter shuts us up to all practical interests as thoroughly and fixes his embargo as inviolably as he did twenty years since. The telegraph alone remains to us as a connecting link with the rest of mankind..."[68]

The impetus to end this isolation and build the connecting link came from a group of Hamilton investors headed by a prominent political leader, Allan MacNab. Since 1836, MacNab had been promoting the London and Gore Railway to connect New York rail traffic to Hamilton and London. Due to the financial downturn of the late 1830s, the project had stalled, but the return of good times encouraged them to try again. MacNab and his associates called their scheme the "Great Western Railway" and considered it the essential link between the New York Central and Michigan Central Railroads. Moreover, they foresaw that this venture would become an integral part of a new American rail system capable of bringing Canadian products to New York and Boston for export. However, they faced a rival in Essex County's John Prince who still nourished hopes for his Niagara and Detroit Rivers Rail Road Company. MacNab (who had served in the provincial assembly since 1830, and was effectively the chief of the Tory faction) was a deft political hand, and in 1844 he brought forward an amendment to a railway bill to enable the Great Western to have sole access to the railway terminus in Sandwich and a generous capital subscription.[69] Not so easily outmanoeuvred, Prince and his backers sought to revive their "southern route" railway in 1847. In due course, the parties compromised and, assured that one terminal would be fixed at Windsor and that he would have stock in the joint company, Prince endorsed this "stupendous undertaking." The railways were officially amalgamated and work was begun in 1847. The Toronto *Globe* proclaimed a new era of expansion:

> Railroads, Railroads! The Canadian world is at last thoroughly alive on the subject of Railroads. Every newspaper teems with the proceedings of public meetings, with discussions as to the best routes, urgent appeals to capitalists to lend their aid…[70]

Construction began at a heated pace as the developers hoped to outdo the competing American line being built south of Lake Erie. Still, the question remained: where exactly would the railway terminus be located? Some supposed that it should have to end at the county town of Sandwich. Others felt that it would terminate at a point between Sandwich and Windsor, opposite the Michigan Central depot in Detroit. James Dougall had other plans.

From 1851 to 1852, the railway was buying riverfront lands for future use. Françoise Parent, William Hall and Daniel Goyeau willingly parted with the required frontages. One landowner would not. After François Baby died in 1852, his son-in-law Dougall had taken control of the farm lots (now comprising Dougall and Victoria Avenues) that stretched to the river, and he adamantly refused to sell any of his riverfront lands for railway purposes. This forced the rail builders to deadhead their tracks at the Ouellette properties just east of Dougall's lands. In later years, Dougall would claim that he was only saving the waterfront from development. However, the practical effect of his stubbornness was that, "Instead of going on to Sandwich, the railway stopped at Windsor, where Dougall's store and his wife's estates were located…Any urban nucleation that grew up around the railway station at the end of the line would quickly develop the family lands."[71] It further meant that the Great Western's station would be next to the ferry landing from Detroit. Daniel Goyeau, in a move almost as canny as Dougall's, sold his land to the Great Western for a nominal sum in 1851, "in consideration of their [railway] building the depot thereon." It was Goyeau's assumption "that the depot would attract business to that property thereby making property values in the area higher."[72] North of the station was a freight house, and at the foot of Aylmer Street were cattle pens to handle the enormous numbers of livestock being shipped. Thanks to Dougall's obstinacy, the centrality of Windsor as a transportation hub had been established.

January 17, 1854, was the great day when the first two trains pulled into the Windsor station (in a foretaste of things to come, three hours late) from the east. There were 400 passengers from New York and another 300 from Toronto and Hamilton. When the cars finally pulled into the flag-draped Windsor station, cannons were fired on both sides of the Detroit River. Amid the cheering throng, the passengers were ferried across the river to a gala banquet at the upper floor of the Michigan Central depot. There, distinguished guests such as Colonel Prince rubbed elbows with former "brigand" and Detroit Mayor, John Harmon. Recollections of past slaughters were put aside, and Prince proposed a toast to "The ladies of Michigan. God bless their little hearts!"[73]

Still, the Detroit River remained a barrier for incoming passengers and freight as both had to be unloaded, placed on ferries and reloaded on the opposite shore. During the winter, both commodities had to be taken by sleigh across the frozen river. Beyond this inconvenience, the coming of the railway would have a dramatic impact on the area. With its gust of soot and hot cinders and the pant and shriek of its engines, the locomotive was a powerful new force at loose in the countryside. This machine had the capacity to shrink time and space and the stupor of the past decades gave way to progress. By 1856, freight and passengers were being shipped in thirty hours between Chicago and New York. In its second year of operation, the Great Western, as part of this vast network, was doing a lucrative business and operating at almost full capacity. The Detroit press gushed that "the rush of passengers on our railroads continues. The Great Western is doing an immense business as is also the Michigan Central."[74] This commercial expansion was greatly enhanced by the Reciprocity Treaty of 1854 that allowed the free trade of natural products between the U.S. and British America.

Yet, there was a price to be paid for the rush to complete the rail line. During the winter, many of the iron rails split, and the roadbed was deficient in many places. On October 27, 1854, the evening train from London struck a car that was repairing the track bed and 52 people were killed. It was the worst rail accident in North America up to that time and a lesson that the industrial age provided not only rapid transportation, but new and previously unheard of dangers. An even more appalling incident had occurred the previous July when several freight cars bearing Norwegian emigrants pulled into Windsor's station. Likely contracting cholera in Montreal, they had been left at a siding at Baptiste Creek and in the sweltering heat, some tried to get stagnant water to alleviate their thirst. When the freight cars packed with 200 starving, dehydrated emigrants finally left Baptiste Creek and arrived in Windsor on Sunday afternoon, the town's only doctor, Alfred Dewson, described the horrific scene: "There was one person dead in the first of the freight cars... thirty-three of the emigrants fell upon the platform of the Station just after they got out of the cars..." For a village of fewer than a thousand residents, the tragedy was overwhelming. While some Windsor residents struggled heroically to save the Norwegians, or at the least comfort the dying, railway officials were largely indifferent to their plight. After a few days, the railway simply refused to supply any help and would not even contribute to the cost of burying the victims. Sixty-eight emigrants perished; none of their names were recorded and their graves were never found.[75]

A RAILWAY TOWN

Despite the railway's callous disregard for the dangers of rail travel, its impact on Windsor was enormous. The railway would dominate the area's economy after 1854 in much the same way as the automobile in the 20th century. One typical example was William Bains, whose father was drawn from England to Windsor to work on the railway. As soon as he could, William also worked on the trains. Not content with his normal duties, Bains displayed a flair for detective work and tracked down members of a gang who had been stealing railway property. This caught the attention of the town councillors of Windsor, who were looking for a new chief constable. The Council, "composed largely of railroad men" chose Bains, who would serve as Windsor's police chief from 1872 until his death in 1891.[76]

In 1854, Windsor was granted legal status as a village, and in 1858 it was elevated to that of a town. Many professionals sensed that they could do better in Windsor than in Amherstburg or Sandwich and moved their businesses to the village. Alexander Bartlet and the Noble family of Amherstburg (Scots to the man) all decamped to the new village in the 1850s. Among these new arrivals was a man of superior education and incredible business acumen. Samuel Smith Macdonell had been educated at Upper Canada College and graduated from King's College with a B.A. Called to the Ontario bar in 1847, he practised law in Sandwich and was clerk of the district council. However, a government position could not compete with business opportunity, and in 1853 he relocated to Windsor. In short order, he established himself as the pre-eminent man in the town, a leader in law, government, and business. He agitated for the community's incorporation as a village in 1854, and became its first reeve. When it became a town in 1858, he would become Windsor's first mayor.

Yet it was in real estate that Macdonell would redraw the face of Windsor. One of his first acquisitions was the Goyeau farm that lay directly across the river from downtown Detroit. He laid out building lots and straightened Sandwich Street to provide better access. He even advertised in the Detroit *Daily Advertiser* that his lots were "opposite to Woodward Avenue in the City of Detroit" and located in a village that "must soon become a large and important place."[77] The enticement to Americans was clear; here was absurdly cheap land that would soon soar in value, and it was practically right next to Detroit. Only a few weeks before the railway arrived, Macdonell laid out Registered Plan No. 91, in which he subdivided the lands along what he planned on being Windsor's main north-south street, Goyeau.[78] In 1854, he purchased the Cuthbertson farm in the eastern part of the village and began subdividing it for houses, laying out Glengarry and Aylmer streets and merging them together into Howard Avenue in the junction still known as the "Horseshoe." By 1855, the local press was proclaiming the choice lots he had for sale as "situated in the most pleasant part of Windsor." Frame houses and even pioneer log cabins were available on Goyeau Street. Yet, his most enduring achievement was the extension of Howard Avenue back into the township and connecting it to the Number 3 Highway (Talbot Road). As village reeve, (the concept of conflict of interest lay far in the future) Macdonell had signed a by-law in 1855 to authorize the "Talbot and Windsor Road Company" to create a toll road to join Windsor to the Talbot Road. In 1856, the Windsor *Herald* described Macdonell as "devoting his time and attention to the construction of the Talbot and Windsor Road."[79] It took him until 1860 to complete the road, but once finished, it enabled county farmers to ship produce directly to Windsor and bypass Sandwich entirely.

The resulting population growth was remarkable. Windsor expanded from 300 people in 1851 to 2,501 in 1861.[80] During that time, the town far outstripped Sandwich, which held a mere 988 residents. The effect of the railway boom on a town located directly on the main line was overwhelming:

> Daily trains brought in immigrants who often stayed overnight in the numerous hotels and purchased commodities from local merchants… The railroad brought in laborers to maintain its line and depot, skilled tradesmen to build new homes and ambitious business men to invest capital. Indeed the pattern remained similar to other countless small communities suddenly startled from lethargy by intimate connection with the east.[81]

This growth also led to calls for proper institutions. In his capacity as Warden of Essex County, Macdonell had lobbied for a new courthouse to replace the existing dilapidated structure in Sandwich. A committee examined other courthouses and jails and expanded the site available at the corner of Sandwich and Bedford Streets. Albert Jordan of Detroit was hired to handle the design, and the Mackenzie brothers of Port Sarnia (one of whom would become Canada's second Prime Minister) carried out the actual construction.

The cornerstone was laid in May, 1855, in a blaze of patriotic fervor on the Queen's birthday and as her Empire was engaged in war in the Crimea. Construction would take more than a year and a half, but would result in a magnificent classical revival building that would become a landmark in the area.[82]

Other accomplishments were not as imposing. Until the coming of the railway, Windsor had no churches. As the last stop on the rail line, many Irish Catholic rail workers took up residence in the town and they sought their own place of worship. In 1852, the Bishop of Toronto, whose diocese included Windsor, promised them a church. In 1857, St. Alphonsus, only three blocks up Goyeau Street from the train station, was dedicated.[83] This simple, wood frame structure, built on land donated by S.S. Macdonell, would later become a hub for other Catholic institutions on the block. In the early years, it provided only weekly masses and the parish church remained Assumption in Sandwich. In 1855, the Congregationalists opened "a very comfortable frame building on Ferry Street." Anglicans also hoped for a place of worship in the new railway centre, and they had more resources at their disposal than either the Catholics or the Congregationalists. In May, 1855, barely a year after the arrival of the Great Western, a construction committee was formed. Calling on the aid of the mother church in England and friends in Detroit, they amassed an impressive sum of more than £500. The selected site fronted the barracks "on the corner of Windsor Ave., and London St., and therefore was the very centre of the village."[84] The congregation hired Albert Jordan to design a handsome brick structure, and All Saints' Anglican Church held its first service on September 10, 1857.

The village also needed a public hall, and in one of its first acts on May 1, 1854, Windsor enacted a by-law "To purchase land for a Town Hall and for a Lock-up House" to accommodate politicians and criminals.[85] While not as commanding as the Sandwich courthouse, the town hall completed on Sandwich Street in 1856 was intended to have a wider array of functions. In addition to providing space for the municipal council, it would eventually serve as a market, opera house, police station, and jail. During the American Civil War it was requisitioned as a military barracks and, on several occasions, the upper floor was converted into a saloon.[86]

As a railway terminus, Windsor was attracting workers and their families; schools became a pressing need. A small brick primary school had existed in the hamlet in the 1840s, and during the 1850s, two schools were built: one for Protestants, and one for Catholics. While a grammar school for post-primary students had been opened in Sandwich in 1853, it became apparent that there were more children in Windsor that needed the school. In 1857, the school

All Saints' Anglican Church of Canada, Windsor, Ontario.

board moved the grammar school to Windsor, and in the process exposed a raw nerve. As early as 1853, Sandwich residents had been circulating a petition in favour of the amalgamation of Windsor and Sandwich. A "greater Sandwich," it was argued, would be able to benefit from the coming railway boom instead of being bypassed by it.[87] However, there was no appetite for municipal union and the proposal was shelved for 82 years. The removal of the grammar school to Windsor deeply rankled Sandwich residents, and their newspaper, the *Oak*, denounced it. In response, the Windsor *Herald* pointed out that the board trustees were only making a logical decision based upon the location of the children. The newspaper felt that the county had always hindered Windsor, to the extent that it had opposed the village's removal from the Township of Sandwich and that, "When our young village was first incorporated the Township Council protested against it."[88] The rivalry between town and county was well under way.

Windsor, the hamlet of a few saloons and hotels, was most definitely evolving into an identifiable community. The fashionable young blades of the town belonged to the "Windsor Cricket Club" and took on their counterparts from Chatham and Tilbury. A Mechanics Institute was formed to enable the literate to share books. A lower order of amusement was available at Howrigan's Saloon, which supplied, "agreeable recreation to many who have too much leisure time at their command." The Anglican vicar of Windsor and Sandwich, the Reverend E.H. Dewar, thought there was too much drinking in the border towns already. He was shocked that the liquor laws went largely unenforced and that taverns were allowed to operate on Sundays, leading to "a lamentable profanation of the Sabbath, and much drunkenness." He ruefully admitted that when the saloons were open, this drastically reduced the numbers at his services.[89]

Despite the new churches and schools, there were glaring deficiencies in the village infrastructure. Roads were largely unpaved, and to remedy the situation, by-laws were enacted to allow private companies to gravel roads and collect tolls on them. The "Grand Coulee" remained an open ditch that flowed across the town just south of Pitt Street. A clergyman visiting All Saints' remarked that even foot travel was hazardous, and that in order to approach the church from Sandwich Street, one had to "cross over quite a gully via a foot bridge." Water was supplied by men who filled a large barrel on a cart and hauled it up from the river. In 1856, the village council approved a town pump which enabled the barrels to be filled more rapidly. The *Herald* felt that "The water used in the village, during summer, is execrable," and it was unlikely that merely pumping the water faster would solve the problem.[90] In many ways, Windsor remained a village of the 18th century. Grain was still being milled by the windmills that had been a quaint feature of the French regime. The technology of the industrial age that had just arrived at the Goyeau Street train depot seemed to elude those who were processing the area's produce for market. However, one keen-eyed individual had taken note.

WALKER'S TOWN

Hiram Walker, a Massachusetts man, arrived in Detroit in 1838 at the age of twenty. He worked in the grocery business, and by 1850 had his own general store. One of his products, cider vinegar, was so lucrative that he began to manufacture and retail it himself. This one insignificant item set the standard that Walker would follow throughout his incredible career. He had an intuitive sense for a product that would sell, and once he had identified it, he was determined to control all aspects of it from manufacture to market. It involved only a slight change in process from manufacturing vinegar to distilling spirits, and soon whisky was available in Walker's store. However, the temperance movement that had raised its head cautiously in Windsor in the 1840s was a positive maelstrom in Michigan. The first law banning the sale of liquor went into effect in that state in 1853. While it was declared unconstitutional, abstemious Michiganders persevered and passed an "Ironclad Maine" law in 1854 outlawing the liquor traffic.

Walker began to cast around for a more welcome venue to continue his alcohol production. As a grocer, he was already familiar with the Canadian side and knew the resources available there. The closer he looked at it, the more the advantages on the other shore became apparent. The Great Western offered a connection to the eastern section of Canada West, and from there to New York City. Thanks to the recent Reciprocity Treaty, any natural products he generated could be sold across the border without tariffs. Moreover, land and building materials in Canada were cheap in comparison to Detroit. There were no significant competitive distilleries, and the Canadians had not fallen prey to the forces of temperance. Walker looked at the curious windmills that ground the local grain and knew that if he introduced steam-driven mills, he could vastly increase output and profits.[91]

In 1856, he bought his first lands on the Canadian side to the east of Windsor and introduced the technology that would make the "Windsor Distillery and Flouring Mill," a huge producer of whisky and foodstuffs. Always on the lookout for a way to maximize profits, Walker discovered that distilling wastes could be used as cattle feed, and he added a thriving livestock business to his exports. Walker briefly moved his family to the Canadian side in 1859, but he returned to Detroit around 1864 and lived there for the rest of his life. By the 1860s, his operations had become a small community known as "Walker's Town" (soon to become "Walkerville") in which all the inhabitants both worked for Walker and lived in his cottages. The County of Essex *Gazeteer* of 1867 described it as:

> A small village, situated on the riverside, about a mile above Windsor. It contains a distillery, carried on by Hiram Walker and Company, a hotel... store etc., and several tenements built by Walker and Co. for the convenience of their employees, which number from eighty to one hundred.[92]

By the 1860s, there were three distinct border communities spaced at intervals along the Canadian side of the Detroit River. Unlike Detroit, which had a strong central focus and major roads radiating out like spokes from the centre, Sandwich, Windsor, and Walkerville were separate entities unto themselves. The independent growth of these communities would set the pattern for the uncoordinated development that was to mark the coming decades. In addition to an increasing sense of rivalry among the towns was friction with the recent arrivals who had sought refuge in the fledgling communities.

There had been a growing black presence in Essex County since the 1820s, and in the Battle of Windsor black residents had demonstrated their enthusiastic loyalty to their country. The black presence was so substantial that at one of their August celebrations of British Emancipation (attended by many white notables), Colonel Prince counted "not less than 12 or 1500 persons."[93] For many of the refugees, the border communities along the Detroit River were their final destinations, and some estimates put the number of black residents of North Essex at twenty to thirty percent of the total population. One of the new arrivals was Henry Bibb. Born a slave in Kentucky, he had escaped, gained an education, and worked in the abolitionist movement.[94] Once he and his wife Mary had located in Sandwich, Bibb started publishing a newspaper describing the state of the blacks in Canada and advocating on their behalf. The *Voice of the Fugitive* was first printed in Sandwich on January 1, 1851, and in its defining editorial proclaimed that it advocated, "the cause of human liberty in the true meaning of the term." The newspaper intended to be "a mouthpiece for the refugees in Canada... We shall make no compromise with the wrong."[95] While Bibb felt that the best solution to the problems facing the refugees was their integration into Canadian society, until that was possible he directed the Refugee Home Society to settle incoming blacks in a separate settlement, the Sandwich Mission just north of Amherstburg. However, as a result of infighting and poor financial planning, the project floundered. Still, Bibb had succeeded in establishing an independent black press that circulated through the northern states and gave a voice to the small community of black Canadians. In October, 1852, he was elected president of the Windsor Anti-Slavery Society. A year later, his press was lost in a fire and Bibb's premature death in Windsor in August, 1854, silenced a great voice for equality and integration.

If anything, the community at the straits was moving towards greater separation between the races during the 1850s. Black residents in Sandwich complained that they had only one inadequate school. The province's *Common School Act* of 1850 provided for religious denominational schools and for schools for "coloured people." Bibb's wife had attempted to open a private school in her home in Sandwich in 1850. However, as her husband confided to a friend, Lewis Tappan, "she has a large school, but has not a suppy [*sic*] of books for the children."[96] Mary Bibb also opened a school in Windsor that was open to all races. By 1855, seven of her forty-six students were white.[97]

The provision of schools was a key indicator of the racial divide for another teacher, Mary Ann Shadd, who noted that the public schools were more racially divided than the private ones. Windsor had planned for a separate coloured school in 1854, but none was built until 1858. The resulting structure was described as a "coop," just 16 feet by 24 feet for forty-five students. One black Windsor resident, Clayborn Harris, was appalled by this inadequate structure and wanted his son to go to the common school. He wrote to his lawyer that he feared that black children would be barred from opportunities, and that "The question that we wish settled is, 'Shall the Trustees use the government money to support a prejudice of one class of Her Majesty's Subjects against another?'" It would not be until 1862 that black children had a more suitable, but still separate, school available to them.[98]

The school issue was only one indication of a growing white enmity towards black arrivals. Colonel Prince, who had previously been partial towards black residents, gave a speech in 1857 in which he held that the kindness whites had demonstrated towards blacks had "been met with the basest ingratitude, the recipients rewarding their benefactors by robbing, pilfering and plunder." In 1841, the Windsor *Herald* published the account of a Montreal agent who was recruiting local blacks to go to Jamaica, and the newspaper hoped that many of them would take the inducement and leave. The reaction of the area's embattled black community was to take comfort in their church. The Sandwich Baptist Church was already the centre of their neighbourhood in 1851. In Windsor, the black community would come together, the men carrying bricks while the women brought up water from the river to mix in the mortar, to build the

British Methodist Episcopal church (originally an African Methodist Episcopal congregation) on McDougall Street in 1856.[99] The presence of a significant black population along the strait would become an emotional and sometimes divisive factor over the coming decades.

It would be a decade dominated by a rising political star. Arthur Rankin, the gallant ensign of the Battle of Windsor, had been unable to obtain a permanent commission as an officer. Casting about for something out of the ordinary, he enlisted some of the Indians he had served with during the Rebellion and formed a Wild West troupe that toured Britain, and even performed before Queen Victoria. He then invested his show business profits into various mining ventures, and by 1849 returned to Essex County a wealthy man. His first public venture was to chair the committee to present a silver trumpet to the Detroit Fire Department for their help in extinguishing the Dougall warehouse fire of 1849. In 1854, he had the temerity to challenge Colonel Prince by standing against Prince's son Albert for the Essex assembly seat. Rankin won and was carried in celebration through Sandwich's streets. "Such Vain Costs & expences!" the Colonel sniffed.[100]

The following year the Crimean war broke out, and Rankin wrote to the British commander Lord Raglan offering the services of a battalion of Essex men to fight the Russians. "The gallant member for Essex," as Rankin was

Sandwich Baptist Church, built in 1851.

proclaimed, stood behind the mother country in her moment of peril.[101] A petulant John Prince pointed out that he had proposed raising local troops before Rankin had thought of it. While Rankin and Prince tried to outdo the other by wrapping themselves in the Union Jack, there seemed to be no realistic possibility of Essex militiamen being sent to the far side of the world in this dubious conflict. After the war, one of the cannons seized at the victory at Sebastopol was donated to Windsor. Captured cannons were being distributed throughout the Empire as symbols of imperial unity, and the "Russian cannon" would be used in ceremonial events for decades to come.

The 1850s had been a decade of remarkable technological advances. Windsor was now a day's travel from New York City and far less than that to Chicago. In 1854, the telegraph system accompanied the railway and in 1857 the ferry boat *Windsor* was used to lay a telegraph cable across the Detroit River. A web of communication had come into being across North America and Windsor was a part of the network. The value of the Great Western's shipping had gone from £132,000 in the first half-year of 1854 to £345,000 two years later, and dividends were running at over eight percent. [102] These huge advances had spurred new industries, including a major distillery. Yet, in other ways, the town seemed to be timeless. Its muddy streets often remained impassable. Its drinking water was hazardous and the development of public utilities was in its infancy. Yet, the waterfront was alive with wind- and machine-driven craft and the rhythms of river life remained a constant at the straits. On May 5, 1855, the Windsor *Herald* announced that the ice was gone from the river and that "A number of sailing vessels and some few propellers" were on their way, "the shipping business commenced."[103] The *Detroit Daily Advertiser* noted in 1853 that "The river has swarmed all day with vessels trying to make a little headway upstream against wind and tide," oblivious to the fact that there is no tide in the Great Lakes. Somewhat more accurately, the same newspaper waxed enthusiastically in 1854, "What a fine picture was presented yesterday at noon! The whole reach of the river from the Fort to Belle Isle, was crowded with sail vessels going up. Taking advantage of a favourable breeze, nearly fifty craft were spreading their white wings 'obsequious to the gale.'"[104]

Enormous changes had occurred at the straits. Even more momentous events were about to happen, and Windsor, the tiny hamlet that had so recently been merely "The Ferry," was about to be touched by Royalty.

Chapter Four
Copperhead Capital: 1860–1867

A	T EIGHT O'CLOCK on the evening of September 20, 1860, Albert Edward, the Prince of Wales, stepped off a Great Western train and set foot in Windsor. The town was, for a few moments, about to host the most celebrated man in the world. Windsor was the final Canadian stop on a royal tour that had stirred unexpected controversies. While in many ways it was a triumphal progress, with the Prince being welcomed by native groups, church and political officials, one group was barred from participation. The Orange Lodges, while militantly loyal, were seen as a divisive presence by the Prince's advisors, and his entourage firmly insisted that they be given no recognition. During the Toronto visit, the Prince's carriage was forced to careen through side streets to avoid passing under an Orange arch. No such unpleasantries would occur in Windsor.

On the day of the royal visit, the "loyal little town of Windsor" (as the Detroit *Free Press* called it) was alive with excitement. The newspaper went on to describe the fever pitch that seized the community:

> Flags were thrust out from windows, housetops and flagstaffs, the window-panes of every window in every building were decorated with candles; busy committee men bustled about conspicuously displaying their insignia of brief authority; children ran the streets crying "God save the Queen" and "Long live the Prince of Wales" and with true spirit firing their crackers…[105]

According to the *Free Press,* "Windsor made a demonstration of which they had no occasion to feel ashamed," and none of which the Prince would see, since his train arrived during the evening and his time in the town was brief. The official party was welcomed by Mayor Dougall, County Warden O'Connor, Sandwich's Mayor Charles Baby and Arthur Rankin. The Windsor stop was perfunctory, and the Prince was bundled onto a ferry and taken across the river to Detroit where a riotous celebration was already in progress.[106] While the Windsor stop was brief enough, one local group had been specifically excluded. Black Canadians were enthusiastic royalists and a community leader, A.G. Green, had written an address in fulsome praise of British liberties and freedoms and had hoped to present it to the Prince on behalf of "the colored people of Windsor and Sandwich." His request was denied. The reasons are unclear, but it may have been thought that such sentiments might be seen as antagonistic to Americans. Whatever the reason, black Canadians would be relegated to the position of spectators and, much like the fractious Orangemen, would play no official role.[107]

Another major presence from Essex County was conspicuously absent. John Prince would have been expected to have been in the forefront of any royal reception. However in February 1860, he accepted a judgeship in Sault Ste. Marie and left the (as he called it) "ungrateful Soil of ungrateful Essex" behind him. In so doing, he left the political field open to his rival, Arthur Rankin.[108] While he was eager to step into the Colonel's shoes, Rankin's roller-coaster political career would be constantly marred by controversy. He had become deeply enmeshed in the "Southern Scandal" of 1857, in which he had been charged with bribing various railway promoters. The subsequent election of 1858 was one of the most riotous in memory. When it appeared that Amherstburg businessman John McLeod had won, 800 Rankin supporters from Windsor and Sandwich seized the courthouse, imprisoned Sheriff John McEwan and forbade him from declaring McLeod the victor. A short time later, several hundred McLeod partisans arrived from Amherstburg and demanded to see the sheriff. When he was not forthcoming, "A wagon load of hickory clubs was drawn in… and the brave Kanucks armed themselves and awaited the onset." A bloodbath was avoided when McEwan jumped out a back door, made his way to Windsor and escaped to Detroit. Before his departure, he had signed the papers declaring McLeod elected and left it to braver folk, such as Reeve Macdonell and a poll clerk, to make the public announcement. They were both, "thrown down stairs in attempting to save the poll books." If anything, the tumult of 1858 showed that elections were still largely personal contests rather than party affairs. A strong personality such as Rankin did not accept defeat lightly and he inspired his followers to (as the Toronto *Globe* called it) "a display of brutality which we hope has no parallel in any other county." Detroit reporters were amazed at the proceedings which "were perfectly lawless and riotous, and the wonder is that no collision of the opposing parties took place" for "both were armed to the teeth." The depredations of the Kansas border ruffians seemed tame next to the conduct of a Canadian election.[109]

Rankin was nothing if not resilient, and in 1861 he again ran for the assembly as a supporter of John A. Macdonald's government. However, he had a new opponent to reckon with. Ever since the potato famine of the 1840s, Irish Catholics had been moving into northern Essex County, and they had become a powerful presence in Maidstone Township. Naturally, they looked for political leadership from among their own, and found their champion in John O'Connor. Born in Boston of Irish immigrants, O'Connor's family had purchased land and moved to Essex County in 1828. After losing a leg in a farming accident, O'Connor took up the law, was called to the bar in 1854, and had a moderately successful practice with Charles Baby. He also dabbled in journalism and local politics, becoming reeve of Windsor and a county councillor. In the 1861 election, Rankin narrowly beat out O'Connor, and the virulently anti-Catholic Toronto *Globe* boasted that Rankin had won the support of liberals and French-Canadians, "against the Irish Roman Catholics, their clergy, and the Ministerialists."[110] Even though O'Connor challenged the results, for the moment Rankin reigned as the dominant political force in the area. The assembly was, however, not scheduled to sit until the following year, and Rankin had time on his hands. That time would be consumed by the dramatic events unfolding on the other side of the river.

COLONEL RANKIN'S LANCERS

The outbreak of the American Civil War in April 1861, brought the issue of slavery to the forefront. This complex struggle was characterized (to men such as Rankin) as a straightforward fight between freedom and servitude, and he was eager to be a part of it. While yet a young man in 1837, he had rescued an escaped slave in Ohio and given him an armed escort to Canada. Denied a military life after his taste of glory in 1838 and kept out of the Crimean War, Rankin was now anxious to step forward and play a part in this monumental conflict. And perhaps the North needed him, for after the defeat at Bull Run in July 1861, it was apparent that the Union Army could use trained men. Oblivious to the British declaration of neutrality, Rankin met with a group of Detroiters in the summer of 1861 and proposed raising a regiment of lancers to be officered by British veterans. Americans were intrigued, and in August 1861, Rankin and Michigan Senator Kinsley Bingham met with President Abraham Lincoln to discuss the idea. The President authorized a warrant on

September 11 to raise "The First Michigan Regiment of Lancers," and Rankin was commissioned a Colonel in the U.S. army. By October, more than 500 Americans and Canadians had joined the Michigan Lancers. While many Canadians supported the anti-slavery struggle and applauded Rankin's efforts, others questioned the propriety of a member of the assembly and a militia colonel taking part in a foreign war.

Rankin's political opponents seized on his questionable activities and had him arrested in Toronto in October 1861, for having breached the *Foreign Enlistment Act* by having recruited British subjects for a foreign conflict. While there was no direct proof that he had recruited Canadians, he was nevertheless bound over for trial for having joined the U.S. army.[111] However much goodwill Rankin's enthusiasm had generated across the border, it was all undone by an international incident that threatened to once again bring war to the peoples of the strait. On November 8, 1861, a U.S. naval vessel seized two Confederate agents from the British mail packet, R.M.S. *Trent*. This flagrant breach of British sovereignty brought an exchange of diplomatic notes, and it appeared as if war between the U.S. and Britain was imminent. Rankin now faced the prospect of having to fight the same troops he had so recently been training. In December 1861, he resigned his U.S. commission and returned to Windsor. As for his men, the loyalty of the Lancer Regiment was put into question and it was disbanded. The previous friendly feelings that had existed between Detroit and Windsor were, as a result of the *Trent* affair, replaced with suspicion and watchfulness.

The situation became so precarious that Mayor Dougall wrote to the Governor General in December 1861, requesting that regular troops and artillery be sent to Windsor, and shortly thereafter soldiers of the Royal Canadian Rifles were billeted in the town hall.[112] Peace along the border was made all the more precarious by the presence of so many "skedaddlers," as American military deserters and draft evaders were called, or by escaped Confederate prisoners who were now serving as spies. The Detroit *Tribune* reported that the "Skedaddle Guard" in Windsor was an unruly lot who made life miserable among the people who gave them refuge. There were enough southerners in the town to push up real estate prices and the *Tribune* reported that a Nashville man had bought four acres of the Dougall farm. In August 1863, the same newspaper ran an extended editorial on "The Secesh Element at Windsor," in which it inferred that there were so many pro-southerners in the town that they had all but taken it over, and that "Their lawless character is becoming every day more and more manifest, and as a consequence our Canadian friends will, one of these days, wake up to a real sense of their danger." The editorial went on to describe how a Kentucky family had walked into the middle of a service at All Saints' Church and the family's matron had ostentatiously pulled out a large fan in the colours of the Confederate flag and waved it before the rest of the congregation.[113] Any display of the rebel flag was severely frowned upon in Windsor as a provocative act, so the little drama in the church set the town on edge. The following year the town hired a night watchman and the *Tribune* reported that the appointment was "necessary owing to the great influx of rebels into the town lately."[114]

Inevitably, the war also brought profits and opportunities and Windsor businesses were making money shipping wheat and livestock to northern states. In May 1863, it was reported that over twenty horses a day were being shipped through Windsor for the federal cavalry. As grain was needed for the war effort, distilling was discouraged. Of course, this did not mean that American thirsts had abated, and Hiram Walker filled the void by increasing production. Walker was supplying so much whisky to Detroit that it was widely (but incorrectly) believed that he had installed a pipeline under the river to his facility at 35 Atwater Street in Detroit.[115] As a result of this war-driven prosperity, the town was steadily growing, and in 1864 the council resolved to confront one of its most pressing needs by approving a $25,000 loan to construct a waterworks. For the first time, water would be siphoned out of the river and provided by pipe to the town's inhabitants. The ready availability of water would also (hopefully) limit the number of fires that regularly swept through the wooden structures of the town.[116]

The People of Windsor

In February 1864, Mayor Macdonell and the town council authorized the completion of a census. Why this was done remains a bit of a mystery as a national census was usually carried out at the end of each decade. But for whatever reason, the council wished to have a complete demographic record as of that date (see Appendix B). The result provides a remarkable snapshot of a mid-Victorian Canadian town. Most of the residents were labourers, with a few persons specializing in trades such as butchery or shoemaking. A substantial number of residents in the eastern part of the town, the Second Ward, worked for the Great Western Railway. Of the 2,579 residents, three-quarters were Protestants; the rest were Roman Catholics. This was not unusual: as a result of the Irish Famine, the number of Catholics in the province had been rising steadily. Toronto's population, in comparison, was also a quarter Catholic, and "these mounting Irish Catholic numbers made mid-century Toronto more than a little uncomfortable. They represented a change to its ruling Protestant patterns and presumptions."[117]

In contrast, Windsor seemed to be entirely comfortable with its religious divisions. While many of its residents were Irish Catholics, and St. Patrick's Day was celebrated in Windsor with green flags and parades, much of the Catholic population was still made up of French-Canadians who had lived in the area for generations. Protestant and Catholic children had long attended the same schools, and intermarriage was still common. The census reported that Mayor Macdonell was a Catholic and his wife Ellen an Anglican. Their daughters were being raised as Protestants and their sons as Catholics, a compromise that had been a common family arrangement since the early 1800s. Throughout the 1860s, Windsor's mayoralty passed regularly between the Scots Presbyterian Dougall and the Scots Catholic Macdonell. Apparently religion was not a factor in politics so long as one was Scottish. But in other ways, the census revealed that Windsor was a very unusual place.[118]

Many communities in Canada West were composed of recent immigrants. In Kingston, for example, almost 40% of the population was Irish and more than half the population of that city was British-born. In Toronto as well, the Irish-born, whether they be Protestant or Catholic, were the dominant ethnic group in the city.[119] In Windsor, however, 35% of the town had been born in the United States. Americans were by far the largest ethnic group, to the extent that while the rest of the province may have been largely British, Windsor effectively constituted a small American enclave. There was also a close connection between those of American origins and the town's racial composition. While across Canada West the black population was miniscule, composing perhaps one or two percent of the total, some townships in the southwest had become magnets for blacks fleeing slavery. Amherstburg was certainly the main port-of-entry, but Sandwich and Windsor were, as a result of their proximity to Detroit, not far behind in offering a place of refuge. Thirty percent of Windsor's densely populated Second Ward, which held 60% of the town's citizens, were black. All of the homes along stretches of McDougall Street were owned by blacks, who effectively formed entire neighbourhoods. Overall, 570 blacks lived in Windsor, making up 22 percent of the town. Windsor had become such a prominent haven for black refugees that it had even attained international recognition. In 1861, a mass meeting was held in Hull, England, for the express purpose of letting citizens know about Windsor, Canada West, a town where "of about 3,000 souls... about 800 are coloured"[120] and who were badly in need of a church. In many cases, it seemed families kept one foot in Canada and the other in the States, for in many black families some children were born in Detroit and others in Windsor. Black residents were overwhelmingly Methodists, while a strong minority, perhaps a quarter of the total, were Baptists.

In contrast, Windsor's Third Ward, which stretched east along the river, held a thinly populated community composed largely of French-Canadian farmers. The numerous Langlois and Marentette families (who would lend their names to the streets) dominated an area that was racially and culturally more county than town. While the central town was dominated by Protestants, Catholics comprised more than 60% of the Third Ward. Even though Windsor was predominantly English-speaking, there remained a strong French presence and several of the area's leading figures were French-Canadians. François Caron, the town's first police magistrate, was a former Quebec lumber merchant who owned the Jeanette farm on the town's west side. His wealth and position gained him the magistracy even though on occasion he felt it necessary to apologize for his limited use of English.[121] Dr. Charles Casgrain, another Quebecker, had originally settled in Detroit in 1851. Five years later he crossed the river to serve the predominantly French-speaking community in Sandwich. The 1864 census was a remarkable document and it provided a picture of a border town that was quite different from its provincial contemporaries and was itself divided along religious and racial lines.

The presence of such a long-established Catholic community would have an impact on the religious organization of the southern part of the province. Sandwich and the northern half of Essex County had such a concentration of Catholics that the first bishop of the Diocese of London, Pierre-Adolphe Pinsoneault, had the episcopal see transferred from London to Sandwich in 1859. The bishop concluded that London had barely enough parishioners to support one priest, while Sandwich already had a fine church and a significant number of Catholics. However, Pinsoneault seemed incapable of administering his charge and he was constantly quarrelling with his priests and staff. To enable him to travel about his diocese, he ordered that an ornate barge be built. However, "the barge sank at its launching in the Detroit River. With it sank $1,500 and, moreover, the reputation of the bishop of Sandwich."[122] One of his most ill-considered projects was the construction of a bishop's palace (dubbed "Pinsoneault's Folly") next to Assumption Church. Built to resemble a French chateau, it was both enormously expensive and poorly constructed. It generated even more discontent as it required the removal of the existing cemetery and the reburial of the dead near the location now adjacent to the Ambassador Bridge. As a final embellishment, the bishop ordered rows of chestnut trees planted to resemble a cloister. Pinsoneault resigned in 1866 and the diocesan see was restored to London in 1869. It was later noted that, "The palace was demolished in 1896. Only the chestnut trees remain."

ALEXANDER BARTLET'S DIARIES

Windsor's growth in twenty years from a hamlet of a couple of hundred persons to a town of over 2,500 was encouraging. Yet, compared to its neighbour across the river, it remained a modest place. Detroit had 21,000 residents before the completion of the railways in 1850. The 1860 census showed that it had more than doubled to 45,620, all but dwarfing its Canadian counterpart and establishing itself as the dominant presence at the strait. While it was very much the junior partner in economic affairs, Windsor remained attached to Detroit by bonds of family and commerce. As the war years wore on it was also apparent that Windsor was also inextricably woven into the drama that was resolving itself in the adjacent states.

Town clerk Alexander Bartlet kept a detailed diary during the Civil War years, and it reveals a town that was in many ways a microcosm of the conflict. He lamented the number of "skedaddlers" and that, "our streets are lined with a very promiscuous population, all running away from the draft." In August 1864, Bartlet attended the "Secesh Pic-Nic" at Turk's Grove near Windsor, where about fifty Confederate exiles and curious Canadians gathered for slap-jacks, hoe-cakes "and other similar products of rebeldom." As the evening wore on, a rebel flag was produced and attempts were made to raise it. However, the property owner ordered that no such display be made. Bartlet (who counted himself among the curious and not a Confederate sympathizer) recorded that the attempted flag raising was "to the great discouragement of the Northern or Northern feeling people who were on the grounds." A frustrated rebel spokesman literally wrapped himself in the flag and delivered a denunciation of Lincoln and his administration.[123] Yet Windsor was more than just a refuge for a few malcontents, and it was about to play a role in the political resolution of the conflict.

As the casualty lists mounted, a widespread anti-war movement emerged in the United States, and the "peace Democrats" or "Copperheads" (a reptilian reference applied to them by their enemies) sought an end to the hostilities. Far from being on the fringe, "the peace movement was so influential by August 1864, that it very nearly took over the Democratic party."[124] The movement's leader was an Ohio congressman, Clement Vallandigham, an unwavering opponent of the Lincoln administration who considered the president's war-time edicts to be affronts to the American constitution. Seized by a military court in May 1863, Vallandigham was banished to the Confederacy. From there he made his way to Canada and became the Democratic candidate for governor of Ohio. He cast about for a secure location to run his campaign and decided on Windsor. "An ordinary looking fellow" was the way one Canadian editor described Vallandigham as he stepped off the train at the Great Western station on the evening of August 24 1863, and walked down the block to the Hirons Hotel. In subsequent days he would be welcomed by several leading Democrats, including a Detroit delegation headed by Judge Cornelius Flynn and Acting Mayor Phelps. The Detroit *Free Press*, whose editorial views coincided with the peace Democrats, welcomed Vallandigham and his "hosts of friends who stand firm for the Union and constitution."[125]

As his political allies crossed the Detroit River to consult with him, there was no question that Vallandigham was a force in American politics. Should the Union armies have had another disastrous campaigning season, he would almost certainly have become Ohio's governor, and from there he would have been a favourite to defeat Lincoln in the 1864 election. Understandably, his opponents were uneasy at having him in such close proximity. The pro-Lincoln Detroit *Tribune* sneered at his arrival in Windsor and hinted that his associates were mostly Confederate sympathizers. The gunboat *U.S.S. Michigan* patrolled the Detroit River and kept its batteries trained on the suite of rooms at the Hirons Hotel. The *Cleveland Leader*, a staunch Union newspaper, was shocked to discover that Windsor had been overrun by skedaddlers and rebel spies, and that it was "Probably the society of these scoundrels [that] attracts the banished convict [Vallandigham] to Windsor."[126] To loyal Americans, the town had become a nest of Copperheads, and their leader was plotting to dismantle the Union from this safe haven.

Yet, a string of Union victories in the spring and summer of 1864 stole the momentum from the peace Democrats. While Vallandigham polled strongly for the Ohio governorship, he lost the election and faded into obscurity. He lingered in Windsor for a few months (with the *Michigan* still anchored outside his hotel window) until in June 1864, he returned to Ohio. His departure did not mean that tranquility returned to the border. To the contrary, the closing months of the Civil War would feature some of the most dramatic events ever to occur along the strait. As the Confederate cause became more desperate, southern agents contemplated an exploit along the border which would infuriate Americans and might escalate into reprisals that could bring Britain into the war on the side of the South.

Confederate Pirates of the Great Lakes

On the evening of September 18, 1864, a conventional-looking young man with a Scottish brogue left the wharf at Windsor and took the ferry across to Detroit. Like so many British residents, his appearance raised no suspicions.

He booked a passage for the next day on the *Philo Parsons*, a passenger and freight ship that ran a regular route between Detroit and Sandusky, Ohio. In addition to booking his own passage, the young man inquired if the ship would stop at Sandwich and pick up three of his friends. The following morning, the young Scot boarded the *Parsons* and reminded the captain to stop at Sandwich. The ship did slow down at the Sandwich pier and three men gingerly hopped on board. At Amherstburg, another twenty roughly dressed men also boarded. After the ship had passed Kelly's Island in Lake Erie and entered U.S. waters, one of the men who had boarded at Sandwich suddenly appeared on the top deck brandishing a gun and proclaiming that he was in charge and that the *Parsons* was now a ship of the Confederate States Navy.

The new captain was John Yates Beall, an implacable Virginian rebel who, despite severe wounds and imprisonment, had made his way to Canada and devised a plan to seize a ship and raid the Confederate prisoner of war camp at Johnson's Island near Sandusky and free hundreds of rebel prisoners.[127] In this he was aided by the young Scot Bennet Burleigh, who was also an officer in the Confederate Navy. Burleigh had travelled from Glasgow to Richmond in order to persuade the South to invest in his family's torpedo invention. Instead, he became caught up in the romance of "the cause" and enlisted in the Confederate navy. He was captured and later escaped to Canada, where he joined up with Beall and became engaged in this dramatic, if far-fetched, plot. Burleigh, with his accent, would draw no attention in Detroit, but could have the ship slow down at Sandwich so that Beall (whose drawl would instantly arouse suspicion) and his fellow conspirators could safely board. However, the plan quickly unravelled when the *U.S.S. Michigan* appeared outside Sandusky Bay and forced the ship to turn back into Canadian waters. The rebels retreated, the Confederate flag flying at their masthead as they sailed up the Detroit River to Sandwich. Once they got there, they scuttled the *Parsons* and the band dispersed.[128]

Americans were outraged. "Piracy on the Lakes" was the next day's headline in the Detroit *Tribune*, and it reported that Detroit police were in Windsor with arrest warrants for the culprits. Needless to say they had fled, but still the *Tribune* editorialists grumbled that Windsor folk were colluding with the pirates and that "the bitter and senseless prejudice [that] has warped their feelings has also blunted every sense of honor and propriety." More generously, the Detroit *Free Press* trusted that the "reputation of our friends across the river" would not be tarnished by harbouring "thieves and pirates."[129] For their part, Windsor authorities were unsure just what was expected of them. S.S. Macdonell, the County Crown Attorney (among his many other offices), telegraphed the provincial government in Quebec City seeking instructions.

Alexander Bartlet recorded in his diary that the raid "makes a good deal of noise and disturbance the other side people [Detroit] are very much exercised about it."[130] But as Beall and his band had vanished, there was little that Windsor authorities could do.

The raid had alerted the provincial government to the dangers that existed along the border, and that "While border tensions increased as a result of the affair… imperial and local authorities in British North America were aroused sufficiently by the violation of British neutrality involved in the *Philo Parsons* incident" to take vigorous action.[131] The situation along the border was made all the more precarious a month later when Confederate agents from Canada East (Quebec) attacked St. Albans, Vermont, robbed a bank, and left one man dead. Americans had to be reassured that the northern border was not a threat, and a special meeting of Windsor's town council was called for the evening of December 15, 1864. The purpose was to address "the raids which have already been committed from our borders by strangers who came into our midst" and to assure Detroiters that Windsor "has no sympathy whatever with those who have contrived… marauding or hostile expeditions from Canada." The Detroit *Free Press* thought that the meeting manifested "a most friendly spirit on the part of our neighbor over the river." Friendly spirit was one thing, but posting a few guards at the border was unlikely to deter the raiders. The *Free Press* also noted that a Gilbert McMicken of Windsor had been appointed a magistrate "to see that the proclamation of neutrality is strictly enforced," and that he has been empowered to create a police force "to protect the border from the excursion of raiding parties."[132]

McMicken was an unlikely border agent. A failed politician and a faltering businessman, he had hoped to improve his prospects by moving to Windsor from the Niagara area sometime between 1860 and 1864. During more prosperous times he had served in the provincial assembly, and had gotten to know the provincial attorney general John A. Macdonald. The latter considered McMicken to be a "shrewd, cool and determined man who won't easily lose his head, and who will fearlessly perform his duty."[133] In the final year of the Civil War, as tensions mounted along the border, Macdonald would increasingly rely on this fearlessness. In December 1864, McMicken was named a stipendiary magistrate in Canada West and was authorized to hire constables to work as undercover agents to uproot clandestine plots and halt any further border incursions. McMicken's men became the "Western Frontier Constabulary," who worked on both sides of the border to ferret out information on fresh plots.

American Secretary of State William Seward did not think the Canadians sufficiently contrite, and on December 17, 1864, an executive order went into effect requiring all persons entering the United States to have a passport. The documents were expensive, not easily obtained, and while they did little for security they did succeed in stifling trade. Even the Detroit newspapers were alive to the reality that border restrictions would hurt American business as well as Canadian. The Detroit *Tribune* noted that since the completion of the railway in 1854, the commercial bond between Detroit and Windsor had been growing ever stronger and that the war had generated greater demands for raw materials. The *Tribune* protested that "This passport order, so far as passenger traffic is concerned, restricts as to one, and will almost completely paralyze two of the leading railroads of our State."[134] There was some small comfort in the understanding that the passport order would be lifted as soon as the war was over.

In his diaries, Alexander Bartlet recorded the mounting euphoria across the river as a string of Union triumphs culminated in the final victory at Appomattox. On April 10, 1865, he marked Lee's surrender and that, "The people of Detroit have had a gay old time today by their rejoicing." The joy was short-lived when news arrived of Abraham Lincoln's assassination. Windsor's reaction to the event would have a huge impact in eliminating the animosity aroused by the *Philo Parsons* incident. Arriving at Windsor's town hall, Bartlet hoisted the flag to half-staff. Like most townsfolk, he was infuriated that "The Southerners were elated over it and seemed as though they would go on a Drunk... They are most horrible fiends these fellows and at every turn are stopped by Mr. McMicken who declared he would arrest any of them who do such a thing." On the day of Lincoln's funeral, the mayor ordered Windsor's stores to be closed and the local militia asked for permission to cross the river to take part in the funeral pageant. To preserve neutrality they were not allowed to go. Nevertheless, many did attend in civilian dress. Detroiters were impressed that so many Windsor residents sympathized with them and that the majority of Windsorites were "united with us in paying the last tribute to the noble dead."[135]

By May, escaped rebels and deserters were drifting out of Windsor and returning home. As the *Free Press* noted, "The camps over the waters have been nearly broken up, and the town deserted by a very interesting class of people."[136] While the skedaddlers would not be missed, another more formidable faction was just beginning to stir up trouble along the border.

FENIANS

Unknown to the American authorities who were assisting McMicken, his activities also served another purpose. A significant minority of Irish-Canadian

Catholics belonged to the Fenian movement, which supported the struggle to create an independent Ireland through revolutionary means. They were joined by a powerful Fenian organization in the United States that had both the money and men (from the recently discharged armies) to present a military threat to Canada. At their meetings, Fenian leaders proclaimed their intention to invade Canada and use it as a base to gain Ireland's freedom. In December 1864, Macdonald drafted a memorandum on the Fenian menace and instructed McMicken to use his men not only to monitor Confederate activity, but also to report on any Fenian plans which might be directed against Canada.[137]

By February 1866, there were reports of armed Fenians in Detroit, and the frozen Detroit River presented a ready-made route for them to invade Canada. Alexander Bartlet feared that it was "a very good time for the Fenian to come across if they are coming…the Fenians are still giving us a good deal of trouble and anxiety." In March, he observed that money and men were flowing into the Fenian organization, and that the threat to an outlying community such as Windsor was palpable. On Saturday, March 10, 1866, he entered into his diary: "Great excitement this morning. Five companies of volunteers came in or rather five skeleton companies… They left so early and were hurried to the frontier so quick." The troops had arrived so hurriedly that they had no barracks and had to be housed by civilians. Volunteers from Chatham marched into town, and their newspaper boasted that "the best dwellings in town were everywhere thrown open to them." More realistically, Bartlet noted that "Some [townsfolk] were very bitter and did not like the idea of having men billeted upon them."[138] Once again Gilbert McMicken stepped forward and ordered that civilians take in the soldiers.

As St. Patrick's Day, 1866, approached, the anxiety grew. In Toronto, Thomas D'Arcy McGee asked the Catholic bishop to withdraw Church support from the annual parade to spare the city from "blood and rapine." In Windsor, Mayor Macdonell called a mass meeting and begged the government to distribute 300 rifles among the townspeople "to enable them to render efficient assistance to the military." This mass meeting was the result of information McMicken had obtained (and shown to Bartlet) to the effect "that there will surely be an invasion of our country on the 17 March next." McMicken had urged Macdonell to take all necessary steps including "forming a home guard this afternoon… and the Mayor was authorized to telegraph for muskets for the Home Guard." It was a measure of the prevailing hysteria that no one questioned the wisdom of arming an utterly untrained mob of civilians. Alexander Bartlet wrote on March 16 that people, "feel that something is to take place tomorrow. Many families are moving across the river indeed the ferry boats are crowded with people and horses." There was some satisfaction in

Detroit that the shoe was now on the other foot and that it was the Canadians who were in imminent dread of a raid across the river. "Two years ago it was just the reverse," chuckled the Detroit *Tribune*. "They [Canadians] were then in high glee, but today there is little glee about it."

The end result however, was anti-climactic. "The great Fenian Demonstration came off today in Detroit," Bartlet recorded on St. Patrick's Day, "but it was rather a failure." Fewer than 500 men who "did not amount to much they were a ragamuffin looking set of men of no standing nor of any weight" gathered in the city.[139] The Fenian threat had utterly fizzled, or at least so the authorities thought. Spring turned to summer and the only threat to the peace came from the cocky red-coated boys from Chatham and London who prowled Windsor's streets.

Then, with no forewarning, on Friday, June 1, 1866, a Fenian force crossed the Niagara River, and on the following day they faced and defeated a force of Canadian militiamen. In Windsor there was some relief that the long-awaited invasion had finally come and that the fighting was somewhere else. It was a measure of how unexpected was the attack that McMicken was in Windsor when the blow fell, and that he had to cross over to Detroit to telegraph the British consul in Buffalo to get details. A Detroit reporter felt the edginess on the streets, and he wrote that the "excitement at Windsor yesterday was very great and the most wild and improbable rumors were afloat." That Sunday, Church services were curtailed as the militia was put on alert to repel Fenian raiders. In the middle of the service at All Saints', the rector, John Hurst, noticed that soldiers were being tapped on the shoulder and ordered to leave. He then announced that the Fenians were believed to have landed just above Walkerville and that the congregation should prepare for the worst. Parishioners at Assumption Church in Sandwich were about to celebrate the feast of Corpus Christi and, in the French tradition, were going to "Shoot the Devil" and fire volleys in the air. A magistrate asked the Vicar-General to forgo the ceremony as the population was edgy enough without adding random gunfire. The priests concurred, and after an abbreviated Mass the congregants were told by the officiating priest to "go home and prepare to defend their firesides."[140] For once the border was closed and the ferry service across the river was suspended.

Despite the panic, no attempt was made to cross the Detroit River, and the stories of enemy landings were pure rumour. Even the Fenian invaders in Niagara had no reinforcements and were compelled to return to the United States. Federal troops were sent to Michigan and insured that there would be no further cross-border incursions. In a few days the hysteria subsided. While the immediate threat waned, Bartlet wrote at the end of October 1866, that "The Fenians are very boisterous and threatening all sorts of vengeance on us poor Canadians."[141] One effect of the Fenian menace was to encourage Canadians to create a larger, more secure political union that could repel a foreign threat. The prospect of invasion had started a process that was about to lead to the creation of a new nation, and one of the area's leaders desperately wanted to play a part in these events.

Arthur Rankin had overcome the embarrassment of his arrest and the questions concerning his loyalty in raising the Lancer Regiment for the American army. However, John O'Connor remained a persistent political irritation. While O'Connor's challenge of the 1861 election results had succeeded and the results had been voided by the Courts, Rankin ran again and was elected (by a mere two votes) in 1863. While he had cast himself as a George Brown Reformer, he ultimately chose to side with John A. Macdonald's "Great Coalition" in the drive to unite the British North American colonies. As a vocal member of that coalition, Rankin may have hoped to play a leading role. But he had become too much of a political maverick to be depended on. Despite an impassioned speech on March 10, 1865, in which he wholeheartedly supported Confederation and the "establishment of a nationality for ourselves," he was not included in any of the delegations that negotiated the creation of the new country. In the end, his many indiscretions had denied him the starring role he had cherished, that of a Father of Confederation.[142]

CONFEDERATION DAY: JULY 1, 1867

The first celebration of Canada's Confederation was observed in most communities with patriotic speeches, picnics and parades. In Windsor it was marked by a full-fledged race riot.

The day started innocently enough with a salute fired from the "Russian gun," the cannon captured in the Crimea. Colourful flags and pennants were hung on every building, and one of the most notable proclaimed "Our Union, Four Chips of the Old Block," in reference to the four united provinces. With so many visitors from Detroit, the town's population had almost doubled, and it was estimated that 5,000 people turned out to watch the militia parade through the streets. The soldiers were followed by a band of "callithumpians" men wearing bizarre clothing, some of them on stilts and playing discordant music. They were "a society famed for the ridiculous character of their dress, and whose turnout created no little amusement among the townspeople." The parade was followed by a picnic and a cricket match between Windsor and the Phoenix or Detroit & Milwaukee Club. In the spirit of the day, the Canadian team won. As the afternoon wore on, the whisky that was being freely drunk began to take effect. One drunken soldier accosted a black man and struck him. The black man, seeing that he was surrounded by whites, retreated. However he returned with several companions and confronted the soldier and his comrades. A crowd assembled beside a small shanty in which an elderly woman was selling peanuts and candy and, "as a rolling ball gathers snow, so did the small number gradually become increased until not less than 600 or 700 people, black and white, were assembled." A bloody collision ensued and the lady's peanut stand was dismantled to provide boards and cudgels for the combatants:

> Then followed a riot in earnest. The colored people seized stools, chairs, etc. and dealt their opponents some fearful blows. The whites stood up to the work they had undertaken to prosecute and retaliated with clubs, stones, fists, boots etc. for fully 15 minutes the miniature war raged...[143]

It was only broken off when the blacks, noticing that they were outnumbered, tried to disengage. They were pursued by militiamen. Then, finding a cache of stones, the blacks began to pelt their red-coated pursuers. Finally, armed troops under the command of officers restored a semblance of order. Bartlet recorded that the affair was "a regular row between the toughs and the blacks—dishes were broken, heads were broken." In Police Court the following day many of the combatants were "exhibited to dry out the extraordinary splurges of last night."

The day ended on a more predictable note with fireworks and bonfires set along the river. A Detroit reporter felt that there were so many bonfires that it provided a "total illumination of the town." This was ironic, for fire and illumination was one phenomenon the town had hoped to avoid.

Chapter Five
Fire, Growth And Panic: 1870–1879

THE DETROIT RIVER was often illuminated, though these fires usually had nothing to do with celebrations. On April 16, 1849, sparks from a passing ferry set fire to a wharf on the Canadian side and the flames quickly spread to Dougall's warehouse. The Detroit Volunteer Fire Department had agreed to assist Windsor, but when the fire broke out a one o'clock in the morning there was no way to cross the river with their equipment. It took more than an hour before two companies could cross, and despite the "hurricane of cinders and flame" they contained the fire that threatened to completely destroy the town. The riverfront was again alight in April 1859, when the Great Western Railway depot burned down. By the time the Detroit pumpers crossed the river, the depot was a flaming mass of embers. Still, the Windsor *Herald* credited the Detroiters with saving the engine house, and that if this had been lost then "the little town of Windsor might have been numbered with 'the things that were.'"[144]

Depending upon Detroit volunteers to sail to the rescue was not a long-term solution to Windsor's fire problem. The first local firefighting attempts were modest and consisted of horse-drawn hose reels that depended upon drawing river water. In 1866, the first hook and ladder was purchased, and the next year a volunteer fire company was organized.[145] But their effectiveness was questionable: before the end of the year, a major fire consumed the Western Hotel, rendering it "a mass of roaring flames which brilliantly illuminated both Windsor and this city [Detroit]." Despite the élan of its volunteers, Windsor, a town made up of highly combustible wood frame buildings, remained vulnerable to uncontrolled blazes. The town councillors appreciated this danger and had debated the erection of a waterworks in 1866. In 1867, they passed a by-law forbidding the erection of new wooden buildings, as they were "a source of great danger from fire." But nothing was done to remedy the existing threats.

The summer of 1871 was a particularly dry one, and in October high winds fed infernos that engulfed many communities in the Midwest. On Sunday, October 8th, a monstrous fire destroyed nine square kilometres of Chicago and killed more than 200 people. Major fires broke out in Wisconsin and Michigan and, on October 10th, nearly half of Sandwich was destroyed. Two days later it was Windsor's turn. Early in the morning of October 12th, a fire started in McGregor's livery stable and quickly spread to the bank, the post office and the offices of the *Record* newspaper. Flames swept away most of the business district and consumed twenty-five buildings. Compared to the devastation in Chicago, the loss was minor, but considering the municipality's size, the impact was enormous. The Town Hall became a temporary residence as survivors with nowhere to go moved in and stored their possessions. Crowds of Detroiters crossed the river to stare at scenes of desolation that seemed reminiscent of Sherman's destructive march through Georgia.[146]

REBIRTH

Days after the event, the photographer Gorst was selling panoramic views of the blasted remains of the town. Retailers were hurriedly arranging for the mass sale of fire damaged goods. The Detroit *Free Press* reported that Windsor merchants were optimistic that they could replace their losses, and that instead of wood-frame

Gorst's photograph of a devastated Windsor (corner of Sandwich and Ouellette, 1871).

structures, "it is expected that four new brick ones will be ready for occupancy this fall." One of these merchants emerged as the leader to rebuild a new brick town. A former Scottish draper's apprentice, Donald Cameron was a founder of "Cameron and Thorburn," one of the stores that had been destroyed in the disaster. He understood that the great fire had brought to the forefront an issue that, while not often debated, was at the heart of the town's future: water. Ironically, for an area that was practically surrounded by the Great Lakes, most of the town had limited access to water, and none of it was readily available to fight fires.

Only days after the fire had been extinguished, Cameron brought forward plans to construct a waterworks. As mayor from 1870 to 1874, he became the main proponent for the construction of a pumping station and the installation of a series of water pipes under the city's streets. It would not be cheap, and a proposed by-law called for the issuance of a debenture for $60,000. This was a significant expense for a small community, but the fire had shown "the primitive method hereto resorted to for supplying the people with water" could no longer be tolerated. The by-law was put to a public vote and passed 149-1. In the wake of the destruction of so many businesses, it was questionable how such a major project could be financed. But Cameron had business contacts in Britain, and he satisfied them that Windsor could be counted on to repay the debenture. Even when the cost of the pipe installation and waterworks grew and eventually doubled the initial estimate, Cameron insisted that the works proceed. The Waterous company of Brantford supplied the pumps, while the iron pipes were cast in Scotland. When the pipe shipments were held up in Montreal, Cameron personally went to that city and reported to the town clerk, Bartlet, that he had contacted a number of shipping companies to see if they would guarantee the pipe shipment to Windsor. He promised Bartlet: "I will exhaust all means within my reach to get them shipped through by water to Windsor… If they can be moved at all, I will have them shipped."[147]

Construction began on the pumping station at the foot of Langlois Avenue in 1872, and a 16-inch steel intake was projected a short distance into the Detroit River. Significantly, the town had taken the step of insuring that the water supply would be under public ownership and "under the absolute control of the corporation, in order to protect consumers against the invariable imposition of monopolists."[148] The waterworks were such a unique project that the town had to petition for a special act of the Ontario legislature to sanction the arrangement. This 1874 Act provided that the Water Commissioners appointed by the town would be responsible for the management of the system, and that the works themselves would remain the property of the municipality.[149] The waterworks were such a success that Hiram Walker asked that the pipes be extended to Walkerville.

Now that it had a dependable source of water to retard the spread of fires, Windsor took on a more permanent shape, with rows of brick structures lining Sandwich Street. One of these was the resurrected retail store of Cameron and Thorburn. In some ways, the fire had had a cleansing effect, ridding the town of many slapdash frame structures, and leading to their replacement by permanent brick stores and houses. The town's growth in the decade after the Civil War was remarkable. By 1874, it had almost tripled its population to 6,043, and its assessed property was worth $1.5 million. This growth could no longer be contained within the town's borders. In August 1874, John Curry, a banker and real estate speculator, purchased the Mailloux farm to the west of Windsor for the enormous price of $25,000.[150] It was the largest single purchase in the area's history, and marked the start of the urbanization of the farm lands between Windsor and Sandwich. By that fall, Crawford Avenue was laid out; Curry and McKay Avenues soon followed. Without question, these achievements were attributable to Windsor's role as a subsidiary of Detroit. William McGregor, a rising figure in the town, thought that its first concern should be to improve the ferry service across the river, for "we should at once see the merchants and mechanics of Detroit flocking hither to reside." The *Essex Record* noted that hundreds of Detroit mechanics and clerks already found it far more convenient to live in Windsor and take the ferry across the river to work, and that "circumstances have combined to force this town into a position of great prominence with Detroit and made it as it were a suburb of the city."[151]

Even with these developments, Windsor remained very much dependent on its rural hinterland, even hosting the County Fair in 1865. Farming remained

Remains of the waterworks begun in 1872—the intake pump house at the foot of Langlois Avenue, built in 1914.

the basis of Ontario's economy and farmers were the dominant class in society. Rural businesses occupied many of the townsfolk. Alexander Cameron, a rising young lawyer in the town, also operated a bank and lumber mill in the county. One of his most lucrative operations was the gravelling of the toll roads that led into the town from the countryside. Maintaining travelled roads was very much a private, and not a public, concern. It was also highly lucrative: Cameron's investment in the Windsor and Sandwich Gravel Road yielded a dividend of 28%.[152] Having to pay for what seemed to be a public right led to a growing resentment of privately owned utilities. When Cameron tried to extend his toll road into Sandwich, residents protested at being "barred in with toll gates and compelled to pay tribute for traversing their own street."[153] Toll booths were occasionally sabotaged and even burned down.

Not only were they subject to corporate toll roads, Sandwich residents understood that so long as their community remained disconnected from the railway system, growth would be unlikely. Then, in 1864, John B. Gauthier, a grocer and brick-maker, noticed odd substances oozing out of his land at the southern end of town. Oil was being discovered in many parts of southern Ontario, and Gauthier suspected that he was sitting on a potential fortune. The "Sandwich Petroleum Company" was formed by the town's leading men, and plans were made to procure drilling equipment. When drilling finally began in 1866, speculators across Ontario were intrigued; the London *Free Press* reported in November that a depth of 144 feet had been reached when the unexpected happened: "A fine stream of sulphur water is the principal show at present." The drillers nevertheless remained optimistic, and it was reported that "the company intends to continue the work." Yet, none of the coveted oil appeared.

Gauthier was determined to exploit what he had found. He advertised his sulphur springs as having marvellous beneficial effects, including curing rheumatism, neuralgia and asthma. Commodious bathhouses were built along the spring, and a canal was dug from the Detroit River to Albert Street. By the summer of 1868, Detroiters were taking note and flocking to the Sandwich Mineral Springs to take the baths and carry away bottles of the semi-miraculous liquid. While carriages were available from Windsor, impatient Midwesterners took a special ferry service directly from Detroit to the Sandwich wharf. A large brick hotel was built to accommodate those health-seekers who wished to tarry and enjoy the medicinal effects of the springs.[154] By the early 1870s, the Mineral Springs and Gauthier's hotel-resort were Sandwich's most prominent attractions.

PUBLIC VERSUS PRIVATE

While Windsor had made a sound decision by placing the waterworks under public control, there was no escaping the financial reality that, in the wake of the great fire, much of Windsor's rebirth would have to be financed with private capital. Street lights and gas for houses would be provided by private companies. In 1872, the Windsor Gas Light Company was granted a monopoly to install gas pipes under the town streets. It seemed that they might not be provided at all, as the gas company had difficulty obtaining financing, and it was not until May 1877, that the pipes were laid. By the end of August it was reported that "The rays of the gas lamps will now in a few days be shedding their cheering light throughout the town."[155]

Private capital was also necessary to encourage public transport. Even if the land at the straits was composed of three distinct communities, the reality was that people and businesses needed a regular mode of transportation between them. Iron rails offered a faster and more reliable service than stagecoaches, and in early 1872 Albert Prince (son of the Colonel) proposed a bill in the provincial legislature to enable a private company, the *Sandwich and Windsor Passenger Railway Company,* to operate a street railway between the towns. By the following year, plans for the street railway were well advanced and crews were fencing in

Horse drawn streetcar on Sandwich street, looking east between Mill and Detroit, 1880. The Dominion Tavern is on the left.

the "rear line" to the south of the river. As the river road (later Riverside Drive) was controlled by the toll road company, the street railway would have to operate along a separate public right of way along the lands that, in due course, became London Street and eventually University Avenue. When completed, the street railway would connect the ferry landing at Brock Street in Windsor to the Sandwich Mineral Springs by horse-drawn trolleys. It was suggested that once the street railway was extended to Walkerville, "steam will certainly be used."[156] By the summer of 1874, six horse-drawn cars were making the six mile run from Windsor to Sandwich in three-quarters of an hour. A reporter travelling on one of the initial runs wrote of the breaking-in period that "the horses [were being] made familiar with the to them extraordinarily strange work."

KNITTING TOGETHER A COMMUNITY—CHURCHES AND SCHOOLS

The construction of the waterworks would do nothing to foster protection against fires until a dependable firefighting force was created. In 1876, twelve-man hose companies were established in each ward and one central hook and ladder company serviced the entire town.[157] Membership in the volunteer firefighting force was a prestigious position, and even though the volunteers came from ordinary walks of life, they faced danger to protect the public and thereby earned the respect of the community. At least they were more highly regarded than the police. Windsor's handful of constables were regarded as corrupt, and in the fall of 1871 they were discovered not only frequenting taverns during duty, hours but "making the taverns the headquarters."[158] They were all fired and new constables were hired. In 1876, the police force was reorganized with Chief Constable Bains in command of five policemen. Strict new rules of conduct were laid down, prohibiting the officers from dabbling in politics, drinking in taverns, or smoking while on duty.[159]

As Windsor coalesced as a town, other organizations were coming together that cemented the relationships between individuals and their neighbourhood, most often through the churches. Anglicans and Presbyterians had been well established in the town since the 1850s. Maintaining fine structures such as All Saints' Anglican in a small community was not easy, and in the 1860s it was feared that the church might close. The Rev. John Hurst was called in to raise the funds to reinstate its solvency. He was so successful that the congregation was able to build an addition to the original structure. However, his focus on fundraising had its price, and by November 1873 the "occasional whispers" that some in his congregation had grown weary of his appeals caused him to abruptly hand in his resignation.[160]

The Wesleyan Methodists had had a place of worship in Sandwich since 1804. In due course the Sandwich circuit took in Windsor, and a small frame church was erected on Ferry Street. By the 1870s, the Methodists were prosperous enough to build their own brick structure at Windsor and Chatham Street, and young Methodists established their own group, the "Epworth League," as the vibrant forefront of their Church. [161]

On a similar but reduced scale, Walkerville was also knitting together the fabric of a community. The Walkerville Fire Brigade, organized in 1877, not only brought a measure of protection to the residents and the distillery, but also became socially "the most important group in the village." Hiram Walker kept a paternal eye on the brigade, and his nephew, H.A. Walker, became fire chief. All of the firemen worked for the Walker distillery, and while the men elected their officers, their appointment had to be approved by Walker. Not only did Walker control most facets of his workers' earthly existence, he was also concerned about their hereafter. In 1870, he erected a handsome brick church off of Sandwich Street, and in accordance with the wishes of the majority denomination of his workers, it became a Methodist chapel. A student minister was appointed, though he was warned that "no reference was to be made to the liquor traffic…" Hiram Walker appreciated the spiritual life, but he was not about to tolerate any interference with the lifeblood of his distillery. A succeeding minister disregarded this edict, and after a sermon warning of the perils of drink, Walker closed the church. When it reopened in 1874, it was given to the Anglicans and rededicated as St. Mary's in memory of Walker's wife. [162]

Shortly after the end of the Civil War, in June of 1865, a clergyman arrived in Windsor who was to have a profound effect on the community. James Wagner was a young Catholic priest from French Lorraine who recognized the need for a church to serve the spiritual needs of the Irish navies who worked on the railways. Since 1857, they had been worshipping in a crude wood frame structure, and Wagner was determined that they have a permanent place of worship. In order to accomplish this, he exhibited an extraordinary entrepreneurial flair; venturing to Europe in 1869, he sought support from Napoleon III and Pope Pius IX for his Windsor projects. Gaining the support of both men, he received a series of pictures from the Pope and a set of steel engravings from the Emperor. Upon his return to Windsor, he auctioned off or sold the engravings and pictures to raise the necessary funds. The cornerstone for a brick church, on land donated by S.S. Macdonell on Goyeau Street, was laid on September 3, 1871, and it opened for worship two years later. In 1877, in recognition of his organizational abilities, Wagner was named the Dean of Windsor. In a confrontational age, he was renowned for his selfless devotion to his Church and his ability to harness various groups and interests to a cause. His biographer concluded that he was "something of an administrative genius with a strong penchant for showmanship."[163]

Options for Victorian women in Windsor rarely varied from becoming a wife and mother. However, small groups of women were to leave a decisive mark in education and medicine. In 1859, two Grey nuns commuted from Sandwich to Windsor to teach at the small school across from St. Alphonsus Church. They were succeeded by sisters from the Montreal order of the Holy Names of Jesus and Mary, who arrived in Windsor in 1864 and established a Catholic mission in the town. When Mother Jean Baptiste stepped off the train in October 1864, she was in effect the founder of Windsor's Catholic community before the appointment of a priest or the organization of a parish. Her successor would convince Vital Ouellette of the desirability of donating two acres of his centrally located farmland for the purposes of a Catholic girls' school. Construction on St. Mary's Academy commenced in 1865, and it opened as a boarding school in November 1866. The school attracted so many students that an annex was completed in 1870; the structure was so visible from Detroit that it was known across the river as "Windsor Castle." Another large addition was added in 1904. Over the decades, the sisters educated hundreds of young women from across Canada and the U.S.[164]

The construction of schools was considered one of the most vital requirements in creating an enduring community. The *School Improvement Act* of 1871 provided that the public schools were to be maintained by the community, and that high schools should also be established to offer classical courses. While the area had had small brick primary schools since the 1850s, it was not until November 1871—barely a month after the great fire—that construction began on a major new educational institution, the Windsor Central School. The site selected, the "Barracks Square," was a curious one. In 1839, it had been sold to the Crown for military purposes, and a wooden barracks and a medical facility was constructed for 106 troops. With the press of fugitive slaves arriving in the town in the late 1850s, some of the barracks was set aside as a shelter for these refugees. But even at this time it was apparent that the municipality had their eye on the square, and in 1855, S.S. Macdonell registered a plan of survey showing this four-acre plot as the town park. The site was apparently acquired by the town in 1859, but nothing was ever done to turn it into a park.[165] Now the decision was made to allow a completely different use; the Board of Education took control and erected a fine two-storey brick school. In November 1871, ragged lines of "children of the several Protestant schools" marched down Windsor Avenue to the site of the new Central School where James Dougall, the man who had played such a major role in the town's history, dedicated the cornerstone.[166] The ceremony was an entirely Protestant affair, with the Masonic Lodges of Windsor and Detroit leading the way and Dean Hurst of All Saints' giving the invocation.

While the *British North America Act* of 1867 had specifically contemplated the creation of separate school boards for Roman Catholics in Ontario, this step was not followed in much of Essex County. Education remained under the auspices of one public board, which provided schools for both Protestants and Catholics. The public board had constructed the "Catholic School" (St. Alphonsus) in 1873 at the corner of Park and Pelissier Street, and Ursuline nuns provided instruction. Windsor had even developed a unique way of allocating school board positions to reflect religious and ethnic groups. There was a general agreement to continue "the custom of apportioning seats at the School Board to the respective denominations according to their strength in the Town." Dr. Charles Casgrain, the highly respected French-Canadian physician, represented Catholic interests, while Prest (Methodist) and Stephen Lusted (Anglican) represented their respective denominations.[167] As James Dougall remarked, Windsor was unique in that it had one public board that provided for Protestant and Catholic schools, and that "this arrangement although it was not exactly in accordance with school law, has been the source of great harmony, and has worked very satisfactorily..."[168]

As far as providing a high-school education with an introduction to Latin and algebra, those few (almost all male) students who sought higher education attended the two classrooms on the second floor of the Central School. When this proved to be inadequate, the high school was moved in 1874 to the red-brick building on Goyeau Street that had formerly been the Catholic primary school. This small, block structure, under the direction of Thomas Smellie and later Angus Sinclair, was derogatorily known locally as the "soup kitchen."[169] In order to accommodate students, the basement was deepened and wood planks were laid over the clay with no provision for drainage or ventilation.[170] The structure was so unsanitary it was eventually condemned by the medical health officer.

Catholics had grander ambitions. In 1857, the Jesuits, under Rev. Pierre Point, had opened Assumption College as a school for young men. Thereafter, its administration had been shifted between diocesan and Benedictine clergy. On July 20, 1870, a young Basilian priest, Denis O'Connor, arrived in Sandwich. He had been unwell with tuberculosis prior to his 1863 ordination, but he had already proved himself an able administrator, and in 1870 he became the superior of Assumption. O'Connor had helped negotiate the Basilian takeover of the school, although when he arrived "the college building was in disrepair, few students were registered for September, the teaching staff was nearly non-existent and the initial budget was only $300."[171] Over the next twenty years he would triple the number of students, refine the curriculum and enlarge the buildings. When he left in 1890 to become Bishop of London, O'Connor left behind a vibrant educational institution which was the pride of Sandwich, and which attracted students from southern Ontario and the adjacent states.[172]

These churches and schools were enduring institutions that made the land at the strait more than a collection of border hotels, or a brief transit point on the way to the United States. When combined with community groups such as the volunteer firemen and the Masonic Lodges, they were part of the social glue that was making the area a distinct community. As well, new leisure activities spawned new clubs. Young men formed the Windsor Cricket Club, and on Windsor's second Dominion Day in 1868 (held without any riots), they upset a heavily favoured London squad. However, cricket was quickly being superseded by baseball in popularity, and it was the new baseball club, the "Auroras," that attracted the town's young bloods. By the late 1870s, football was all the rage and Ouellette Square in front of St. Mary's Academy featured contests between the Catholic and Protestant schools. In 1879, it was reported that "Scarcely an afternoon passes that Ouellette square is not crowded" with football players and spectators.

Social opportunities for women were more limited, but the Ladies Association of All Saints' Church presented its *tableaux vivants* to local acclaim.[173] Women also participated in the Windsor Dramatic Society, which regularly presented shows ("Ten Nights in a Bar-Room" being the 1873 offering) at the Town Hall. The other public hall in the town was the old frame church of St. Alphonsus. This structure had been turned into an auditorium, and there the young ladies of St. Mary's Academy presented spectacular productions.

There were other, more simple pleasures as well. The boys of the town still swam in the nude in the Detroit River. In true Victorian fashion, the Council had enacted a by-law to regulate public morals, which prohibited public drunkenness and indecency and specifically forbade bathing in the river. But the law was usually ignored (two boys would be arrested in 1880 for nude bathing), and it remained the rule in hot summer months. Older males frequented the Williams brothel on Mercer Street. The Madam in charge was occasionally charged when the house's activities disturbed the neighbourhood.[174]

As the 1864 census had shown, Windsor was much more ethnically diverse than its Anglo-Saxon compatriots such as Chatham or London. For that matter, the town remained almost surrounded by a traditional French-Canadian community. One boy, whose family had moved to the First Concession (Tecumseh Road) in 1879, recalled that "we were almost the only English-speaking family on that road… they [French-Canadians] followed the pattern of their old homes in France, using wood in place of stone." The French settlers still raised sheep and "Washing, carding, spinning and weaving were the women's jobs." Almost in the shadow of Detroit, these settlers next to Windsor lived a rustic life that had not changed significantly since the *ancien régime*. During long winter months, they would weave straw and "drink cider, sing songs, swap stories and turn work into pleasure."[175] Another boy growing up in the town recalled that "Windsor in the early [1870s] was by all accounts a lively and picturesque community—not unlike New Orleans in social complexity. It had a considerable negro population… French Canadians, the earliest settlers, were numerous… and there was an active and numerous English-speaking commercial class who had made a great deal of money during the Civil War." One of the lad's first recollections was the sight of two women wearing long dark robes and mysterious headdresses, talking in a strange language and harvesting grapes. They were French-speaking nuns from a local convent.[176]

War of the Gauges—the Great Western in Peril

Even if, thanks to the resourcefulness of Donald Cameron, Windsor had recovered from the losses of the great fire, it remained vulnerable to economic forces that would inevitably have an impact on its growth. When the Reciprocity Treaty lapsed in 1866, Americans were seized by protectionist sentiment which greatly alarmed the Windsor Board of Trade.[177] Of even greater importance, however, were the difficulties endured by Windsor's premier employer, the Great Western Railway. Before it was constructed, the railway's builders had

The Great Western yard, looking west, 1871. The third rail to provide the narrow gauge is apparent on the tracks.

hoped that the rails would be set at the standard gauge of 4 feet, 8 ½ inches, the measure used in the connecting railways in both New York and Michigan. Parliament, however, influenced by the Great Western's rival the Grand Trunk, required the Great Western to build the British wide gauge of 5 feet, 6 inches. The result was that in addition to crossing the waterways at Niagara and Detroit, the Great Western had to "break bulk" and transfer goods and passengers at both entry and exit points. As the Detroit *Tribune* observed, "it consumes on an average as much time to break bulk and transfer freight at the two ends of the Great Western, as it does to run the trains."[178] This placed the Great Western at a huge economic disadvantage, especially when compared to the new American lines being built south of Lake Erie.

Beginning in 1864, the Great Western began to construct a third rail within the wide gauge in order to give it the capacity to carry narrow gauge cars. By 1867, there were celebrations to mark the completion of the narrow gauge track as well as the launching of an iron ferry boat which could transport cars across the Detroit River. These improvements caused the railway's directors to proclaim that:

> The produce of the West and the merchandise of the East will be shipped across Canada under custom-house seals without the vexatious and costly changes of cars at the Detroit and Niagara rivers. The "Blue Line" will be loaded on the banks of the Mississippi and in four or five days unloaded at the wharves of Boston or New York.[179]

Unfortunately, the challenges facing the Great Western were far from over. Beginning in 1871, the Canada Southern Railway planned an entirely new line to run north of Lake Erie which would present a challenge to the Great Western as the most cost-effective link between New York and Chicago. The Canadian extension of the Canada Southern would extend from Fort Erie to Amherstburg and cross the Detroit River just north of that town. When the Canada Southern was completed in 1873, a substantial portion of rail traffic now bypassed Windsor and the community had lost its pre-eminence as a major transportation hub.[180]

In the years following the Civil War, the Detroit River remained very much at the heart of the community. One boy growing up in Windsor recalled that "Sailing vessels outnumbered steam craft ten to one." The river was a constant show of "Schooners, sloops, flat scows, catboats..." and to "see a square-rigged vessel with all canvas set, bearing down under a strong breeze and leaning away from the wind, was a sight to delight the heart of anyone."[181] However delightful the prospect, in the age of rail transport, the river had become an enormous barrier to transcontinental commerce. During the winter, lake ports would have to put grain into storage as ice could block the river for days or weeks at a time. James Joy, the president of the Michigan Central, came up with a plan in 1869 to dig a tunnel under the Detroit River. Trains would leave from St. Antoine Street in Detroit and emerge on Parent Avenue in Windsor. But without ventilation or modern excavating equipment, the project was doomed, and it was abandoned in 1872.

Perhaps the solution was to go over the river. In 1873, there were public hearings in Detroit on the possibility of a rail bridge. However, a determined opposition was mounted by the shipping interests who thought that any piers or structures in the river would be a threat to vessels. These arguments won out and despite the obvious economic necessity for a more reliable crossing (by 1887, more than a thousand railway cars were being ferried across the river each day),[182] no project had the financial or political backing to go forward. The only method of cross-river transit remained the ferry.

Between 1854 and 1867, there were no facilities to take railway cars across the river. Freight and passengers were unloaded and packed onto ferries such as the *Windsor* to be reloaded in Detroit. The main ferry running this operation was the *Union*, built at the Jenking shipyard in Walkerville. The *Union* commenced the river run in 1857, and its powerful, coal-burning engines enabled it to act as an ice-crusher and clear the river. During the winter, it was frequently the only ship capable of making the crossing. Still, it was neither convenient nor economical to ship only cargo, and the railway commissioned a car ferry, the *Great Western,* in 1866. Built in Scotland, the ¾-inch thick plates were shipped to Walkerville and assembled at the Jenking shipyard. For a time it seemed as if shipbuilding might become one of the area's prime industries, as both the *Transit No. 2* and the *Michigan* were built at the Jenking shipyard in 1872 and 1873 respectively. The *Great Western* was one of the Jenking shipyard's greatest projects and became the first iron-hulled boat to haul freight cars directly from the Windsor depot to the Detroit loading dock. When the *Great Western* was first launched from the foot of Glengarry Street in January 1867, a crowd of curious Windsor residents gathered to see if a ship made of iron could actually float.[183]

Throughout the 1860s and 1870s, a small navy of commuter ferries—the festively named *Gem,* the *Argo No. 2,* the *Mohawk,* the *Essex* and the *Detroit*—enabled people and cargo to cross the river. These sidewheelers competed with each other and generally served local needs. But they were not large craft, and during the winter months the river was often frozen. When the land at the strait was joined by ice, traffic had to resort to horse-drawn sleds. During one winter, an entrepreneur threw up a frame shanty midway on the river and sold liquor without paying license fees to either country. It was reputed to be "the first Duty Free shop on the U.S.-Canadian border." In 1870, George N. Brady of Detroit brought a new, larger ferry, the *Hope*, into service. Brady understood just how vital the ferry service had become to the growing town, and in 1873 he brought an application to Windsor's town council to obtain an exclusive license to operate the ferry service. Up to that point, the provincial government had granted to the municipality the right to lease ferries and it was entitled to license as many or as few as it pleased. Council decided to retain this situation and was unwilling to part with its control over the ferry business. Two of Brady's ships and three other ferries were granted licenses. The result was five vessels (the previous year there had only been three) jostling on the figure-eight course across the river to the Detroit dock. One commuter asked, "If you can go to Detroit and return in fifteen minutes when three boats are running, how long will it take when five boats are pretending to run?"[184]

The following year, Brady renewed his application and pointed out that he had brought into operation an icebreaker, the propeller driven *Victoria*, which provided cross-river service even during the winter. An editorial in the *Essex Record* argued that Council should seriously consider the Brady proposal. Windsor had effectively become one economic unit with Detroit, and it depended on easy transit across the river. Brady's *Victoria* had proven that a small ferry could provide year-round service, and the newspaper felt that "the people will ratify no agreement that fails to secure a certain means of communication with Detroit every day in the year."

In the meantime, however, a rival had sprung up, consisting of a consortium of smaller ferries called the Detroit & Windsor International Ferry Company. While the council committee on the ferry license question recommended Brady, the town council could not make up its mind. The ferries were left in a state of ongoing conflict with almost daily struggles over who had the rights to land at which docks. Ferry boats "would land alongside of each other two or three at a time, much to the inconvenience of the travelling public."[185] Ferries would race across the river to head off a rival. On one occasion, the ferry *Excelsior* actually rammed the *Erie Belle* in a contest for priority at the wharf. Adding to the confusion was the question of where they would dock. While Detroit had one central pier, most ferries to Windsor used the wharf at the foot of Brock Street next to the Great Western depot. However, the dock at the end of Lower Ferry Street was still in use and west-end residents favoured it as being more convenient. One solution was to have the ferries run from both docks on alternate weeks.[186] The confusion and inefficiency could not have been more complete.

NEW DIRECTIONS

By 1874, it was apparent that there was sufficient discontent in the local political scene for a new direction. John O'Connor had proven himself to be a lacklustre member of Parliament who had accomplished little for Essex. Nevertheless, he became the leading Irish Catholic figure in Sir John A. Macdonald's government, and in 1872 entered his cabinet.[187] To that extent, he was the first figure from Essex County who played a leading role on the national stage. O'Connor was re-elected in 1872, much to the disgust of the *Essex Record*, who attributed his success to "the power of the Roman Church and the power of money."[188] But in the wake of the Pacific Scandal and the bribery charges that stained Macdonald's government, O'Connor's days in government were numbered.

He was about to be succeeded by William McGregor, a rising figure in the Liberal party. The grandson of Scottish emigrants, McGregor had grown up in Amherstburg and had been a dealer in horses and a supplier of mounts to the federal army during the Civil War. He was one of the founders and later the manager of the street railway between Windsor and Sandwich. But it was in public life that he made his mark, and from 1868 to 1874 he served as reeve of Windsor, and from 1869 to 1873 as warden of Essex County.[189] In 1874, he ran for Parliament as one of the Liberals who had pledged to crush that "consummate trickster," Sir John A. Significantly, McGregor ran on a platform of free trade with the U.S.

The wisdom of such a policy in regard to Windsor was becoming questionable by the late 1870s, for the economies in both the United States and Canada were about to be severely tested. A series of financial panics that had their origins in far off and seemingly remote events (including inflation caused by the Franco-Prussian war) led to the Panic of 1873. In addition to the global downturn, in North America reckless speculation in railways and factories in the years after the Civil War had enriched a few, but had spurred many to take huge risks in the stock market. Speculators were wiped out, railways went bankrupt, and a depression settled over North America for the remainder of the decade.[190] Windsor had been spared the early years of the depression and had continued the upward trajectory it had enjoyed since the Civil War years. Yet eventually even the giant across the river was affected by the depression, and "Wages, jobs and prices plummeted after the Panic of 1873."[191] Windsor, as an appendage of Detroit's economy, would inevitably be influenced by any slump. Moreover, by the late 1870s, Windsor was beginning to feel the loss of trade due to the diversion of rail traffic to the Canada Southern. It was also beginning to appreciate the absence of a solid base for future growth.

As an editorial in the *Essex Record* observed, "Windsor is singularly devoid of manufactories, there being fewer establishments of that kind here than in any town half its size in Ontario."[192]

By December 1875, the "prevailing complaint of hard times" had set in, and the Ladies Benevolent Association set up a soup kitchen in an unused school to provide meals for the indigent. "District Visitors" descended upon applicants for relief in order to determine if they were truly deserving "objects of charity." Not quite as hard up, but equally anxious, was Hiram Walker. Still basking in the profits acquired during the Civil War, he had taken his son Edward Chandler into the firm in 1871, and the company became "Hiram Walker & Son." Throughout the early 1870s, he had continued to expand his holdings until it became clear that he was overextended and "For two years he was in the balance, one month on the edge of ruin, the next bringing a gleam of hope."[193] No one was immune from the Panic, and even Member of Parliament William McGregor's livery business failed in 1877. That year the town council cancelled a plan to extend streets and opted instead for "a policy of retrenchment," arguing that it was inadvisable to "unnecessarily legislate away the people's money in these hard times."[194]

In 1872, the town had not thought to use the trenches created by the water pipe project to install any sewers. An editorial in the *Essex Record* condemned this lapse, for "in the absence of common sewers, private individuals are compelled to live in filth and suffer from disease." In 1877, when they decided to invest a modest $7,000 in building the first brick sewers, the intent was to not only provide an outlet for waste, but to alleviate the depression by "giving employment to the people of the town." The jobs were welcome. However, the brick used was the cheapest available and the poor quality of the works would come back to haunt the municipality.[195] By the late 1870s, the town had effectively stopped growing. According to *Bradstreet's Commercial Register*, Windsor had 34 men worth over $10,000 in 1876. By 1878, 18 of them "had come to grief" and business failures were mounting. If anything, Windsor's population had stagnated at around 6,500 residents and had not grown significantly since 1874.[196] Sandwich had not even shared in the Civil War boom, and from 1860 to 1880, its population hovered at a modest 1,000.

Building a livable, growing town with passable streets and a healthy environment would depend upon the development of a productive commercial base. Based upon the grim experiences of the late 1870s, no one knew when, or if, this would be possible.

Chapter Six
Recovery: 1879–1886
"Bully for Windsor, Hurrah for Tringham!"

I
N THE EARLY 1880S, Windsor would take steps to recover its confidence. During these years, the stagnation of depression would pass and the town would initiate its first tentative experiments in the new technologies that would spark the modern world.

But first the economy had to recover its dynamism, and it would take two unrelated interventions from different levels of government to breathe new life into commerce. The first came at the local level, with the town deciding to grant bonuses (either in the form of cash grants, tax exemptions, or free utilities) to persuade factories to locate in the municipality. "Bonusing" was a common phenomenon in late 19th-century Ontario, where scores of communities bid against each other to lure potential employers. While dismissed as a "vicious system of intercommunal warfare"[197] that benefited businesses at the expense of property owners, bonusing was the way the game was played and Windsor was willing to take the risks. A cash grant was approved to induce a line of steamers to operate from Windsor to Lake Superior, and a by-law was considered to forgive taxes on a pork packing house. All of these paled to insignificance when, in 1879, the town was asked to make a major donation to a project that promised to reinstate its pivotal position in the continental transportation system.

The Canada Southern Railway had never been satisfied with its river crossing north of Amherstburg, for in the winter the shallow waters caused ice to pile up and block the passage. The winter of 1875 was particularly harsh, and ice made it impossible for rail ferries to cross for an entire month. The *Essex Record* reported that "The Company had better build their branch line to Windsor and avoid this difficulty, which will recur every winter, no doubt."[198]

Deeper water at the Detroit-Windsor crossing largely alleviated this problem and offered prospects of reliable, year-round service. But the Canada Southern had other problems. It had tried desperately to expand and offer a competitive route across southern Ontario and Michigan to Chicago; however, it had become overextended, and Cornelius "Commodore" Vanderbilt, the owner of the New York Central and the railway mogul of his day, had been quietly buying up the railway's stock. In June 1876, he formally took over the Canada Southern which became part of his empire, a middle link between his New York and Michigan Central lines.[199] Commodore Vanderbilt was not about to tolerate extended delays due to weather conditions, and he expected a smooth running operation. The natural solution was to build a cut-off from the town of Essex to Windsor. But before proceeding, Vanderbilt's companies expected the communities in their path to smooth the way with money.

In 1879, a group of Windsor and Detroit businessmen organized the "Windsor and Essex Centre Railway" to build the cut-off and, as an added incentive, they proposed that Windsor provide a bonus of $30,000. As this grant would have to be repaid over a number of years, it would have to be approved by the voters. To encourage the public, businessmen organized a public meeting at the American Hotel (chaired by the timeless James Dougall), where speaker after speaker hailed the project as both a godsend to Windsor and the assurance of its future prosperity. Lawyer Alexander Cameron (who denied that he had any profit motive in the scheme) warned that Vanderbilt could easily go elsewhere if the money was not forthcoming. S.S. Macdonell, another distinguished figure from Windsor's past, recounted the town's history and reminded voters that its lifeblood had always been the railway system. Not everyone was convinced. Some wondered why working men who put in ten-hour days at factories should be giving money to Cornelius Vanderbilt, one of the wealthiest men on the planet. "Investigator" wrote a letter to the *Essex Record* and protested that: "With nearly $300,000 indebtedness, streets almost impassable in wet weather, and many other important and expensive improvements absolutely needed" that it was folly to impose this additional burden. If the cut-off was a viable business project, then Vanderbilt would build it—he needed no financial support from Windsor.[200]

Notwithstanding these qualms, formidable forces backed the bonus, and both Conservatives and Liberals allied in urging the measure. The *Essex Record* campaigned tenaciously for the grant and reminded its readers that in 1870 voters had turned down a bonus to the Canada Southern. Now it was "Windsor's last chance of regaining what was so foolishly sacrificed" back then. The final tally was close, but in the end a majority of Windsor residents supported the bonus. On the day after the vote, the Detroit *Free Press* praised "the spirit of enterprise which has been dead in Windsor for many years [and which] has been revived." The Detroit *Post and Tribune* concluded that "the result cannot fail to be highly advantageous to Windsor," and further, that "The Detroit capitalists who have interested themselves in the scheme will furnish the necessary capital to put the work through with all possible speed and Windsor can expect to see the Canada Southern cars in town early in the spring."[201]

Spring passed without a hint of the cut-off's construction. The Vanderbilts were apparently holding out for more contributions from Detroit businessmen and were pressuring them to provide a free terminal in Windsor. New developments eventually galvanized the Canada Southern into action. The Great Western Railway had been ailing since the Panic of 1873, and it could not compete with its eastern rival, the Grand Trunk. In August 1882, the Grand Trunk absorbed the Great Western and emerged with a powerful web of tracks across central Canada and the only year-round Detroit River crossing. Determined not to lose a step to a rival, the Vanderbilt companies sprung into action and in three months had completed the 16-mile-long cut-off. Not by chance, it was built across the lands owned by Windsor bonus proponents John Curry and Alexander Cameron, and both men profited handsomely. By December of 1882, Canada Southern trains were running to Windsor, and cars were crossing at a new rail wharf. The cut-off provided an essential link between the Michigan Central and New York Central main lines and placed Windsor back in the hub of the North American transportation network.

Inevitably, there was a price to be paid for this improvement. In the year after the bonus, the town was forced to go to the provincial assembly and seek financial relief. The waterworks had cost double the initial estimate and the town had borrowed heavily for its sewers, the market, and bonuses. As a result, its "debt has been so irregularly arranged as to become at times oppressive to the ratepayers." In March 1881, a private statute was passed enabling Windsor to consolidate its $270,000 debt, but not discharging it from its liabilities.[202] This close encounter with bankruptcy might have been a lesson to the municipality, but in decades to come Windsor would repeat its flirtation with financial ruin. One way to increase the town's revenue and pay down the debt was to encourage new industry to move in. But where was fresh capital to be found?

National Policy

During the Civil War, Americans had established high tariffs and used them to protect and foster young industries. After the war, American industry continued to expand and Canada was seen as a useful dumping ground for unsold products. By 1876, Sir John A. Macdonald had seized on this imbalance and argued that Canada needed its own system of tariffs to build a more solid industrial base.[203] The prospect of creating a "National Policy," as it was known, was hotly debated during the federal election of 1878, with the Liberal member William McGregor closely adhering to the free trade policies that dominated his party. Unfortunately for him, by 1878 the voters were weary of the depression and receptive to Macdonald's plan to aid national manufacturing.

During the 1878 election, McGregor would face a stellar Conservative candidate in James Colebrooke Patterson. Born in Ireland, Patterson was 18 when he emigrated in 1857 with his family to Canada. Establishing himself in Windsor, he became a schoolteacher and then inspector of the local high school. Being a civil servant in no way inhibited him from seeking elected office, and for ten years he served as reeve of Windsor and, after 1874, as member for North Essex in the provincial legislature. Patterson served on the town council through the 1870s and there was rarely an issue on which he did not voice an extended opinion. Moreover, he felt sure there were few problems that could not be addressed by government action. In 1875, he advocated for a bonus to the steamship company that promised to open up the Lake Superior lands to Essex County's produce. At the same meeting, he fought against any additional tavern licenses, arguing at length that there was already too much drinking.[204] It was up to the government, Patterson believed, to bring prosperity and to make men holy.

For his part, McGregor stuck to the free trade line that protectionism was uncalled for and not needed by local industries. But the people wanted it: Patterson won the election and McGregor was "engulphed by a great Protection wave," as the Liberal organ the *Essex Record* called it.[205] In early 1879, Macdonald put his plan into action and raised tariffs on manufactured goods and lowered tariffs on the raw materials used by factories. The incentive for American firms to open branch plants in Canada could not have been clearer. Furthermore, "In Ontario, where most of the branch plants located, there was a tendency for the Americans to try to straddle the border, which made Windsor a prime location for Detroit firms."[206]

While American investors did not come storming in overnight, they eventually realized that establishing branch plants enabled them to reach a wider market. By 1882, the town received a tentative enquiry from two Detroit hardware manufacturers asking "as to the encouragement" that would be given to them to establish a factory in the town. Under the National Policy, the Canadian tariff on pharmaceuticals was so prohibitive that in 1887 the Parke Davis Company of Detroit established a laboratory in Walkerville. Hiram Walker encouraged this investment and built the initial brick building, which was quickly followed by additions. Ten years later, 125 staff worked for Parke Davis in Walkerville.[207] By 1896, it was estimated that "more than three-fourths of the business in Essex county is carried on under the auspices of American citizens."[208]

One Detroiter, attracted by the favourable tariffs and easy access to rail transport, was Louis Griesinger Jr. As a young man helping his father build breweries in Michigan, it became apparent to Griesinger that there were over twenty breweries in the Detroit area and none in Windsor. Small breweries had operated in Windsor for brief periods, but none had established an ongoing presence. In 1882, Griesinger crossed the river and founded the British American Brewery. The Detroit entrepreneurs who were becoming so prominent in the town had no hesitation in cloaking their businesses with patriotic Canadian names. The British American became so successful that the original frame structure was replaced by a four-storey brick building that could produce 40,000 barrels of beer a year. In 1887, the brewery's trademark brand, the famous "Cincinnati Cream Lager," was introduced.[209] Hiram Walker, never one to miss a chance, joined in and by 1890 his Walkerville Brewery also began to supply lager and ale across the city. Detroit connections remained the rule, and most of the principal firms and employers in Windsor had their head offices in Detroit. Penberthy Injection, Globe Tobacco Works, Seeley Manufacturing and Canadian Typograph were all American-based firms with substantial operations and employment in Windsor or its environs. While the *Essex Record* would continue to rail against Macdonald and his policies, J.C. Patterson would be overwhelmingly re-elected in 1882, a confirmation of the popularity of the national tariffs.

The British American Brewing Company, founded in 1882 by Louis Griesinger Jr.

INFRASTRUCTURE

Despite the heavy debt burden on the town and the passage of a by-law to add a special rate on property owners, the community remained badly in need of physical improvements. As of 1880, streets were unpaved and their condition— muddy in the spring and fall, choked with dust in summer—was a source of derision to Detroit visitors. The sewer system was still in a rudimentary state, with few laterals between the streets and many areas where waste and garbage accumulated.[210] As James Dougall and S.S. Macdonell passed from the local scene and town clerk Alexander Bartlet became the police magistrate, their places were taken by men who appreciated the difficulties facing the community.

One individual who had a thorough knowledge of the problems and the political finesse to deal with them was a local physician, Dr. John Coventry. Born near Edinburgh, Scotland, in 1836, Coventry emigrated to Canada in 1854 and graduated from the University of Toronto Medical School in 1860. He had served as a surgeon in the U.S. army during the Civil War, and thereafter established a practice in Windsor. As a town councillor in the 1870s, he was an advocate for a more aggressive approach to public health and under his guidance "Windsor soon acquired a reputation among professionals as an activist public health city."[211] He was so widely respected that he was asked by the town's leading businessmen to assume the mayor's position in 1880. He agreed to do so, and while he acknowledged the need to economize, "he could not bind himself to oppose any required improvements. They must go on improving."[212] So capable was Coventry in handling the town's debt and issuing new debentures that when he wished to retire from the mayoralty in 1881, there was a public outcry demanding that he continue in office. Coventry would be aided by the new town clerk, Stephen Lusted. A prolific newspaperman, Lusted had reported for Windsor's *The Record and Journal*, Detroit's *Tribune*, and the Windsor *Essex Record*. The *Essex Record* gave Lusted an introduction to everyone great and small in the town, and upon his appointment to civic office he became an efficient and popular town clerk.[213]

One of the first things Mayor Coventry had to address was the ferry service fiasco. It was his opinion that Windsor needed a central ferry just to the west of the railway depot, which he believed should satisfy merchants on either side of the commercial core and put an end to the bickering. The problem was that this space was already occupied by the Medbury block of shops. Coventry went hat in hand to Detroit to discuss the problem with Mrs. Lucetta Medbury, the property's owner, and asked her to consider dedicating that portion of her lands that extended northwards from Ouellette Street to the river to the town. He was assisted by her lawyer, Francis Cleary, and together, they convinced Mrs. Medbury to make the donation. The by-law to "Promote the establishment of a Central Ferry" was passed on October 26, 1882, and the two upper and lower docks on either side of Ouellette were abandoned.[214]

Streets and sewers were the other two mundane, but essential, services facing the town council in the 1880s. Ouellette Street, the road that led up from the central ferry and which was quickly establishing itself as the town's main street, was still a mud track. In February 1883, the abutting owners petitioned for a by-law to pave it from Sandwich to London Street. Three years later, the pavement was extended to Wyandotte. The Ledbeter & Stewart Company of Detroit was put in charge of Windsor's paving projects and they used a combination of cedar blocks and cobblestones to pave the way. In 1884, the town council decided that, "Now that a good sewer had been constructed," Sandwich Street could be paved.[215] However, the project did not go smoothly. The street railway occupied a portion of the highway and its turntable, where the cars were reversed for the trip back to Sandwich, occupied a good portion of the right of way. Henry Kennedy, a prominent liquor wholesaler and operator of the street railway, was not willing to see any infringement on his operations. Persons unknown took matters into their own hands and removed the turntable and deposited it elsewhere. In August 1884, Kennedy's men attempted to re-lay the rails and were confronted by the town police. A pitched battle almost ensued until Kennedy wisely decided to take his case to the courts. The presiding judge suggested that the parties should resolve their differences, and an agreement was entered into whereby the street was paved and the company agreed not to block the traffic. The town had to pay the costs of re-laying the tracks. As a local newspaper observed, "Mr. Kennedy has thus gained his point." Still, by the end of 1884, most of the town's principal streets were paved, and as town clerk Lusted observed, in this way, "most of the unimproved thoroughfares were lifted out of the mud."[216]

Underneath the mud lay another problem: disposing of the town's waste. The first sewers had been built as part of the make-work projects of the late 1870s. However, it was not until 1883, that John Coventry, concerned with the continuing unsanitary state of the town, proposed the construction of four main sewers on Sandwich, Victoria, Church and Ouellette Streets. One of the town's primary health concerns was the lack of drainage from the main "Coulie," the open drain running along the south of the town (roughly along the current route of Giles boulevard), which was reputed to be the source of the "miasma that arises during the summer season." The process of getting tenders and financing for sewer projects was not easy and Coventry's successor as mayor, Francis Cleary, noted in his inaugural address of January 1884 that,

"The principal legacy left by the outgoing board was the sewer by-laws."[217] Cleary was determined to see that the town persevered in its construction.

In the coming months, the main trunk sewers were completed and were soon flushing their burden directly into the Detroit River. Some of the older versions, such as the Parent drain, were four-foot diameter square brick structures, while the 1885 Ouellette Street sewer was an elliptical six-foot cast iron tube. This project to take sewage from the "Coulie" (now under Giles Boulevard) down Ouellette Street was a daunting and expensive undertaking. To ensure that they got their money's worth, the town councillors carried out a personal inspection and walked the length of the sewer. Councillor Giles was six-feet tall and could walk it without bending over. Francis Cleary recalled it as something of an unnerving walk and furthermore, "there was nothing to see but blank walls on top, bottom and sides, and he was only too glad to get out when the inspection was completed."[218] Lateral sewers, many of them fragile wood-box structures, carried sewage from the residential streets to the mains.

All of these new works needed a floating supply of unskilled labour, and this led to what was probably Windsor's first labour confrontation. In 1882, the "Dockwollopers" at the ferry, who were unloading stone for the road projects, were being paid twenty-five cents an hour. Agitators thought they should be getting thirty. Alerted to the impending strike, Chief Constable Bains intervened and "raked in three of their [strikers] number, and quiet was restored."[219]

Sandwich had even more limited means to build any kind of modern services. Water was still pumped up from the river and the streets lay unpaved. After a particularly hot summer, the "dust in town is something unbearable,"

An unpaved Sandwich Street West, looking east from Church Street, 1878.

92

and it was difficult even to pump water to sprinkle down the dusty streets.[220] Walkerville, on the other hand, still basked in the untiring largesse of its patron. Hiram Walker had gas lamps installed at his expense, and by 1876 the village had its own waterworks. His distillery occupied the riverbank between Sandwich Street and the river. By the mid-1880s, four streets extended southward from Sandwich and Walker Road (or Fifth Street) was likely the first one to be laid out about 1860. On the south side of Sandwich Street, Walker built a three-storey structure in 1882, the first floor being stores, the second the "Walkerville Music Hall" the town's community centre, and on the third, various lodge rooms. [221] All the structures in the community, from the reading room to the fire-engine house to the brick church, were owned by Walker.

PEST HOUSES AND EPIDEMICS—PUBLIC HEALTH

"Red death." Smallpox was still one of the most dreaded diseases to sweep the congested, dirty cities of North America. When it struck, the victim's skin turned hot, developed puss-filled blisters, and "in malign cases the skin seemed burned and in places scorched to a purple blackness. Sometimes the whole body began to hemorrhage..."[222] There was no treatment other than to let the disease take its awful course. It was already known that universal vaccination and the isolation of infected persons could effectively halt the disease. Ontario had laws, although seldom enforced, mandating vaccination and municipal public health regulations required isolation. Despite the advances in sanitation, including the waterworks and sewers, towns and cities still saw a massive accumulation of unsanitary filth. In Windsor, the streetcars ran on horse power and manure piled up in the streets, froze into huge clumps during the winter, and had to be shovelled into the river in the spring.

In 1877, smallpox appeared in Windsor and three cases were isolated in the pest house. As the town had no hospital, this simple frame structure on the town's outskirts served to isolate those persons who appeared most likely to infect the rest of the community. Dr. Coventry, on behalf of the town's Health Committee, advised that there was no cause for panic and that keeping the victims in isolation had prevented any spread of the disease. The medical profession played a dominant role on the local political scene, and in 1877, of ten councillors, three were doctors.[223] Despite this, public health was not a priority, and the town's health resources were rudimentary. In 1880, it was reported that the County Court House in Sandwich "serves the purpose of a poor house, a lunatic asylum, a hospital, and a place for the confinement of criminals."[224]

Smallpox struck again in April 1882, and local businessman Henry Askew, and his daughter were sent to the pest house. Askew died a few days later, and six more cases, most of them blacks and railway workers, were also diagnosed. The headline in the *Essex Record* attempted to be reassuring and declared that there was "No Necessity for a Scare." But there was a necessity for decisive action, and Dr. Coventry called a special meeting of the town council on May 10th to lay out an immediate program to curb the epidemic. It was decided that all Windsor residents who had not received a vaccination within the past five years were to be vaccinated. A publicly funded doctor would be on duty at the Town Hall to vaccinate the poor. But that was not enough. Coventry reported that there were now eight smallpox cases in the pest house, but that six other infected persons refused to go into isolation, and that "we have met with determined opposition in removing [these cases] and the neighbourhood in which they are respectively situated is greatly endangered by their presence." It was so serious that, "In some instances armed resistance has been threatened if the attempt should be made to remove them."[225]

Remarkably, the main resistance to the quarantine of smallpox carriers came from the town's chief law enforcer. The young daughter of Police Magistrate Alexander Bartlet had contracted the disease. When Bartlet refused to let her be taken off to the pest house, Coventry had tried to coax him to let her be taken to a separate building "built for better accommodation of the afflicted ones." Bartlet adamantly refused. Apparently, drastic measures could be applied to the poor, but when it came to the town's elite, the pest house was not an option. This defiance was a keen humiliation to Coventry, who told his fellow councillors that:

> When the head of the police force defied the Board of Health, how could the latter employ the police to enforce the law? If the Board of Health had no authority to remove the patient in this case, they certainly had not in any other...

In Coventry's view, "Mr. Bartlet allowed his sympathies in this matter to warp his better judgment," and as a result the doctor was considering:

> ...finding that he was the head of a Board which was neither useful nor ornamental, to tender his resignation at once; but subsequently a powerful reason for his not doing so presented itself, which was this: it would look as if he was fleeing from the face of an enemy that threatened the people of Windsor, a small-pox epidemic. He would therefore withhold his resignation for the present.[226]

For their part, the Councillors backed up Coventry and considered it absurd that the Board of Health did not have the power to enforce its orders. In response to public fears that the pest house was a death trap where the inmates were "indiscriminately huddled together," Coventry showed that while the isolation space "was not carpeted, neither were there lace curtains," it was perfectly clean and that each patient had a small apartment. One newspaper felt that the food provided was first-rate and that confinement at the pest house was equal to a stay at Sandwich's Mineral Springs Hotel.

The failure to isolate smallpox cases would have fatal consequences as the disease continued to infect new victims. The Amherstburg *Echo* reported by mid-June that "The smallpox does not seem to be decreasing much in Windsor." There were eleven cases in the pest house at this time, and one child died. The failure to control the disease could also have a major economic impact. In the face of an uncontrolled contagion, it was likely that Americans would close the border to goods and passengers and effectively bring trade to a halt. In light of that, the Windsor epidemic was a provincial concern. However, the intervention of the newly created Provincial Board of Health to enforce the isolation order kept the disease from spreading, and by late summer it had died out. In 1883, the town enacted a new Public Health by-law which replaced the previous Board of Health, which had consisted of three doctors, with one composed of a single doctor, the Chief Constable, the Mayor and the head of the Board of Works. This new board had greater powers to order the clean-up of any properties that might harbour disease and the isolation of infected persons.[227]

The Windsor epidemic would have province-wide repercussions. The incident "confirmed the [provincial] Board's corporate opinion that compulsory vaccination of all citizens coupled with rigorous isolation of victims was necessary to control and eventually stamp out smallpox."[228] Ontario's *Public Health Act* would be amended shortly thereafter to make local Boards of Health mandatory, with emergency powers stripped from public officials and granted to professional health authorities. Flowing from the events surrounding the Windsor epidemic was a state-directed determination to enforce public health regulations. Ontario's response to defiance such as Magistrate Bartlet's stood in direct contrast to the tragedy that overwhelmed Montreal three years later in 1885, where stiff resistance to universal vaccination resulted in the loss of more than 3,000 lives to smallpox.

Respectable Society—and others

For the most part, Windsor was a town of church goers. The churches had devoted congregations who regularly appeared not only for services, but for communal outings. On Dominion Day, 1880, it was reported that the town had almost emptied as various church groups left on excursions. Chartering a ship for a short trip in the lakes was the preferred way to pass a day off. The entire congregation of All Saints' Church had spent Dominion Day sailing to Sarnia and back. The members of St. John's parish in Sandwich preferred to sail to and picnic on Walpole Island. In 1885, Andrew Buchanan of Kentucky had opened up the Brighton Beach Hotel in Sandwich, and his brother George constructed an amusement park just south of the Sulphur Springs. The Buchanan brothers had made a fortune in the liquor business in their native state, but "revenue trouble" had caused them to cross over to Sandwich.[229] Now excursionists could take a short ferry ride to experience one of the first roller coasters. These summer excursions were one of the rare opportunities for land-bound residents to get onto the lakes and explore the inland seas that surrounded them.

Perhaps the most impressive gathering during the summer was one that occurred on land. The "Societé de St. Jean Baptiste d'Essex" regularly held their annual get-together in Windsor at the end of June. It was the occasion for French-Canadians in the county, as well as many in Michigan, to worship, socialize, and renew their sense of a distinct French community. At the St. Jean Baptiste celebration of 1883, an estimated 20,000 people flooded into the town for the day. Overnight the population tripled, and for the moment French was the language that dominated the streets and shops. An elaborate *arc-de-triomphe* was erected on Ouellette Street and festooned with French flags and a banner that proclaimed "*O Canada, Mon Pays, Mes Amours.*"[230]

While religious and patriotic services were well-attended by the majority of residents, the town remained in many ways the rough frontier village of the early years of the century. Through the 1880s, Magistrate Bartlet presided over a Police Court that daily dispensed justice to a motley variety of offenders. After vagrancy, the most common offence in the town was drunk and disorderly: in a typical year this made up twenty percent of all convictions. A less common offence was a conviction in 1879 for "driving without sleighbells."[231] If the offender was an American, a frequent way of disposing of the case was simply to order him back across the border. If the offender was a female, in lieu of jail time she could be remanded to a parent or male guardian.

While the towns at the strait had their fair share of churchgoers, there was another branch of society that had no use for respectability. In Sandwich it was reported that a class of persons regularly desecrated the Sabbath, "indulging in fast driving, bathing and other nuisances within the limits of Sandwich until the evil has become unbearable." Women were particularly vulnerable, and it was reported in 1878 that "Wife beating is becoming very prevalent in

Windsor." Several wife beaters were brought up before Magistrate Bartlet and one had been "rolling [his wife] in the mud and tearing her clothes almost off." He was sent to jail for fifty days. One Saturday evening in 1880, a gang of "drunken rowdies" took over Windsor's main street and began beating passers-by with pickets torn from a fence. A black man who had just gotten off the evening train was almost murdered.[232]

THE DEFIANT JANE ANN DUNN

The beating of one man was an indication of the precarious situation of black residents in the city. It was reported in 1877 that of the 885 children who attended the primary schools, 130 of that number (almost half the Catholic total) were in the segregated black school on Mercer Street. While he was a school trustee, J.C. Patterson had visited that school in 1876 and found it "greatly over-crowded. Indeed an additional room was imperatively necessary." When parents of the children in the black school complained about one of the teachers, they had no representative on the school board to advance their complaint. Instead, "The matter was referred to the Colored School Committee."[233] One member of the black community was not prepared to wait for his child to get access to a regular school.

On the first day of the new term on September 3, 1883, Jane Ann Dunn stood in the yard of the Central School while her father argued for her admission. It is difficult to imagine this young, black girl alone and surrounded by curious, or possibly hostile, white faces while adults debated her future. In previous years, Jane Ann had gone to the segregated school, but her father claimed that Central was the closest school to their house and he demanded that she be admitted. The headmaster, James Duncan, refused, claiming that there was not enough room for her. James Dunn instructed "his child to remain in the school till expelled." She was.

He then brought a lawsuit against the Board of Education, claiming that his daughter had been barred from the school because of her race. On the face of it, this was apparent. Moreover, it was illegal, because Windsor's coloured school had not been established as a "separate" school for black children in the same manner that Catholics were entitled to have separate schools. It was simply another public school, and the Board had no right to segregate pupils according to race. The Dunn case began to attract widespread attention; the Detroit *Evening News* covered the case and felt that "The privilege the colored people ask is not a social but a civil right." The press was generally sympathetic to Dunn's cause, with another newspaper reporting that one school board member was in favour of a compromise whereby senior black students could go to the Central School. This was instantly rejected as "Some of the other trustees were shocked at the idea of having their kids sitting beside colored children."[234] When Dunn's case came up for a hearing before Justice Ferguson in October 1883, the Court ruled that there were valid accommodation issues. The school was already overcrowded and the case was dismissed. But having lost the battle, Jane Ann's stand in the schoolyard effectively won the war. In his decision, Justice Ferguson inferred that if the refusal had been based on race it would have been illegal.[235] Within five years, black and white children would be attending their neighbourhood schools together.

SPARKS

While social change was coming, albeit slowly, Windsor also contained the seeds of technological innovations that were on the verge of making it into a modern, industrial centre. The individual who carried the spark of these new ideas more than any other was John W. Tringham.

Born in England in 1844, Tringham came to Windsor in 1866 and worked at the railway freight depot. In 1872, he struck out on his own and opened a brick and pottery business in Sandwich. This enterprising spirit earned him a laudatory editorial in the *Essex Record*, which not only praised his initiative but noted as well that he had never required the financial encouragement of a government bonus. Two years later he sublet a ferry to the Sulphur Springs. While neither the pottery business nor the ferry prospered, Tringham had other ideas. In 1876, Alexander Graham Bell had conducted the world's first one-way telephone exchange between Brantford and Paris, Ontario. Barely three years later, Tringham organized the "Windsor Telephone Exchange" to bring this marvellous new mode of communication to the area. Tringham had a natural flair for electrical devices and was an inveterate tinkerer in the same mould as Thomas Edison. In 1879, his exchange began stringing telephone wires between Windsor and Sandwich and projecting an underwater line to Detroit. He made an arrangement with the Dominion Telegraph Company who held the leases and patent rights from Bell to operate the exchange as a private enterprise and lease the equipment from Bell.[236] By March 1880, there were twenty telephones in Tringham's exchange.

Taking advantage of Dominion Telegraph's offices and the existing telegraph cable across the Detroit River, a "telephonic communication" was established in January 1880. Two years later it was reported that "Mr. Tringham has completed the telephone line to Leamington, and the communication between that place and Windsor is as clear and distinct as if only a mile separated the two towns."

Communication by telephone was such a promising field that the Montreal Telegraph Company (using disputed patents) also erected a telephone line between Windsor and Sandwich in 1879. However, the new communication network had no room for competing companies or local operators, and in July 1880, Tringham sold his private exchange to Dominion Telegraph. The following year, Bell Telephone selected Tringham to take charge of their Windsor operations. But Tringham was not content to simply run a business. In 1883, the prestigious *Electrical World* journal, the source of the very latest information on inventions, reported that J.W. Tringham of Windsor, Ontario, had devised a significant improvement to telephone lines. He had invented a new system of insulators that dispensed with glass cups and instead used wires laid in a wood block and secured by rubber. It was far cheaper than previous methods and improved the clarity of the transmission.[237]

The first few subscribers to the telephone service of the 1880s had to crank a ringing generator which connected them with a central switchboard. The operator would then plug in the caller's line and inquire, "Well?" When the caller said who he wished to speak to, the operator then plugged the line into the name requested. Sixteen-year-old Walter Griffith became a night operator at the Windsor switchboard in the late 1880s. In addition to connecting calls and sweeping the exchange, he had to run out into the streets and advise people they had an incoming message. It was a measure of the rowdiness of the town that young Griffith had to keep a shotgun in the telephone exchange to ward off robbers.[238] The telephone nevertheless remained something of a curiosity, and by 1894, there were still only 290 in use in Windsor.

Electricity was also becoming a regular feature of Windsor life. An electric light and power company had been authorized to install street lights. Drawing power from a small generating plant, the company began stringing street lights in a few parts of the town in November of 1884. By the following February, they had thirty lights casting a modern glow on the town's recently paved streets.[239]

On a Streak of Lightning

On May 24 1886, an unusual collection of four men assembled at a rough barn in Walkerville near the Peabody Bridge, where Sandwich Street crossed the Grand Trunk rail line.

The first man was Richard Bangham, a Windsor town councillor. In 1885, he had been back to visit his native town, the seaside resort of Brighton, England. While there, he was amazed to see a car powered by electricity running along the beach and giving short rides to vacationers. He bought a picture of it with a brief description on the back and brought it back to Windsor to show to his fellow Englishman, J.W. Tringham. Together they spent an evening going over the picture and wondering if a commercial electric streetcar was feasible. While horse-drawn cars had long connected Windsor to Sandwich, there was no comparable service between Windsor and Walkerville. Tringham sat up all night thinking about it and eventually came up with a plan. The first step was to get a franchise along Sandwich Street to enable the rails to be laid. This was not a given, for Hiram Walker proved suspicious of any new development in his town that was not under his direct control. But with Bangham leading the way, a by-law was enacted on March 15, 1886, allowing the Windsor Electric Street Railway Company to build its tracks on the north side of Sandwich Street.[240]

However adept Tringham was with electrical devices, he did not have the background in dynamos and generators that would be needed to power a streetcar. Bangham and Tringham therefore contacted the third man who was present at the barn that morning. Charles Van Depoele was a Belgian engineer who was fascinated by the potential of electric motors. After he moved to Detroit in the 1870s, he did not have the means to continue experimentation but worked in furniture manufacturing. However, he did not give up building dynamos and electrical lights. In 1883, he had built his first electric car for a Chicago

Tringham's electric streetcar after its first run, May 24, 1886.

exposition. The potential of electricity replacing the horse remained merely a possibility until, in 1885, Van Depoele invented a trolley pole whereby a streetcar could collect current from an overhead wire. Such an overhead wire was installed on a Van Depoele car at the Toronto Industrial Exposition in 1885. Tringham had grander plans for these cars than just passing exhibits at a fair. In his view, there was no reason why electricity could not supply fast, clean transportation between the growing towns. Van Depoele was contracted to supply the ten horsepower dynamo and generators to power the Windsor streetcar. In the barn, Tringham and his men assembled the trolley, which was later described as "resembling nothing quite so much as an unusually long milk wagon."

The fourth man present that day was perhaps the most unexpected. One of the business partners in the enterprise, P.C. Ponting, had loaned one of his workmen to Tringham. The worker was Lindon Brooks, a black man originally from Kent County. For two months, Brooks worked with Tringham assembling and installing the motor, as well as laying the steel rails along Sandwich Street. On May 24, Van Depoele was in Windsor, and Tringham felt that a trial run was in order. Lindon Brooks thoroughly understood the machine and would act as motorman. He took up his position at the middle of the trolley car, where the throttles were located, and was joined by Van Depoele and Richard Bangham. The levers were eased over and the car moved out of the barn and slid quietly down the tracks. It was their original intention to see if the engines worked, but Van Depoele was so pleased with its performance that he turned and asked Bangham "if he should run the car down to Windsor." He agreed that they should give it a go. Van Depoele then asked if they should wait for Tringham, who was anxiously standing alongside watching the test run. "No," Bangham replied, "let's run away with his car." They proceeded to do so and, followed by a shouting gang of men headed by Tringham, finished the mile and a quarter trip in front of the British American Hotel. A breathless Tringham arrived a few minutes later and was so elated at the trolley's performance that he treated all present to beverages in the hotel.[241]

The first official run of the electric streetcar was held on Wednesday, June 3, 1886. It was an historic occasion, the first commercial electric streetcar operation in North America, and it created a sensation. Nothing of the kind had been seen on the American side and "All Detroit visited Windsor and Walkerville during the first few days after the car was placed in operation, to see this new wonder." No fares were charged for the first three days, as first government dignitaries and then ordinary folk were allowed to experience electric transport. Perhaps it was even more remarkable that the first man to operate this glimpse of the future was a black Canadian, the son of former slaves. Lindon Brooks had such an intimate knowledge of the dynamo that he had to be present at six o'clock when the runs began and at midnight when the service ended. In later years he would install the first electric fire alarm in Windsor and assist in the installation of the first powerhouse. But for the moment, dressed in his natty blue serge suit, he was in charge of the technical marvel of the age.

This innovation created an international stir, and New York's *Electrical World* took note that a "permanent electric railway" had been built in Windsor using the Van Depoele system by "J.W. Tringham, a well-known electrician of that city." The magazine felt that, "The prosperous and enterprising town is to be congratulated upon this recent increase in its attractions and conveniences which already included telephones and electric lights."[242] The local press was, naturally, even more gushing in its praise. To the *Record*, Windsor had outdone its neighbour, for "Detroit has been dreaming about such an enterprise for some time, but the slow people of that place hadn't the nerve to tackle such an enterprise…" But now the problem had been confronted and solved:

> The railway is a reality and we can now 'scoot' away up to Walkerville
> on a streak of lightning, and we'll soon have the same motive power for
> our trips to Sandwich and beyond. Whoop! Go away, old world, you're
> too slow for Windsor. 'Bully for Windsor.' 'Hurrah for Tringham.'[243]

After the euphoria of the opening, a regular streetcar service ensued and riders paid their five cents (less than half of what the horse-drawn service charged) for the trip. Travelling at twenty miles an hour, commuters could now make quick and clean trips from Windsor to Walkerville. Electric traction would have an impact on urban geography as it became apparent that labourers no longer had to take lodgings within walking distance of their factories. Especially in an area as spread out as the towns along the Detroit River, the street railway would alter the method of land use. It was said of Toronto, but could also be applied to Windsor, that the streetcars "made for greater spatial separation since considerably longer journeys to work were feasible in the streetcar city than in its walking predecessor."[244] But in contrast to Toronto, where the street railway would become a means for the well-to-do residents to commute to the city centre, in Windsor the system became a means to unite the towns along the Detroit River and enable ordinary workers to travel to their factories.

The streetcars became the impetus to fill in the intervening rural spaces, since residential areas could now develop along the rail line and their residents could travel with ease to the town centre. Moreover, it was now possible to separate residential areas from more obnoxious uses. In June 1886, two ladies, Miss Dewson and Mrs. Grant, spoke before the town council, objecting to the "dangerous manufactories within those portions of the town occupied by private residences," and asking the council to restrain the building of a planing mill on Dougall Street.[245] In addition to the novelty of women taking part in public affairs, their comments revealed concern with a dangerous situation to which there was now an obvious remedy. Thanks to the streetcars, it was now possible to separate the construction of new residences from factory areas. This was just as well, for due to the impact of the National Policy, American businesses had been spilling across the river and there was a huge pent-up demand for housing. In 1884 alone, "Detroiters opened up produce stores, a spice manufactory and a cigar factory in Windsor." In 1886, the L.H. Thomas Company of Chicago opened up a glue plant in Windsor "for the Canadian trade."[246] The return to prosperity was reflected in the scarcity of housing as all available space was taken up by families moving into the town or by Detroiters taking advantage of the cheaper, convenient accommodations just across the river.

The scarcity of available buildings also hampered retailing, and Donald Cameron, out of municipal politics but still very much the town's leading businessman, was compelled to rent additional store space to display the latest European fashions. Each year, Cameron would travel to Britain and return with "Piles upon piles of new goods."[247] In 1880, he took into partnership the debonair George Bartlet, and together they made Cameron, Bartlet of Windsor, the prime shopping location on Sandwich Street. Thanks to the National Policy and the commuter transportation provided by the streetcars, there was no scarcity of customers.

Two other businessmen were also determined to capitalize on the impact of the streetcars. Alexander Cameron, the lawyer and land dealer who had founded the town of Essex, had an intimate knowledge of which lands looked ripe for development. John Curry operated a lumber and charcoal business with his brothers William and James. The Curry brothers' main interest was in finances, and in 1874 they formed the Curry Brothers Bank of Windsor. John Curry first partnered with Cameron in 1879 to create the Essex County Bank. Together, they would acquire and then subdivide the lands that lay along the London streetcar route. The two businessmen had grasped that the horse-drawn cars going between Windsor and Sandwich had opened up the potential for urban expansion beyond the town's westerly limit of Crawford Street. Three of their major subdivisions would be in Sandwich West Township, adjacent to the west side of the town. In 1882, Curry laid out 85 lots along Curry Avenue, and in the following years the pair would sell over a hundred lots along Salter and Caron Streets.

Aware of the intimate connection between the streetcars and land development, Cameron and Curry tried to buy the service in 1885. They were rebuffed, but that did not prevent them from profiting from the effects of the streetcars. "They were the owners or part owners of five out of the nine largest developments in Windsor in the period 1880 to 1892. In partnership alone or with others, they subdivided 1,287 lots; whereas in the four major subdivisions in which they were not involved only 860 lots were subdivided." [248] Cameron and Curry acquired almost legendary status, and there were rumours that they owned tens of thousands of acres in the western states. Locally, it was reported that their "town lots are selling at from $40 to $250," and that "It is expected that the whole country around Windsor will quickly become settled."[249]

With Tringham's electric rail service operating between Windsor and Walkerville, prospects also opened up for expansion to the east. Cameron and Curry prepared a 461 lot subdivision between Elsmere and Louis Streets, registering it in 1890.[250] This subdivision was composed of thirty-foot lots, which was a standard size for a compact neighbourhood of working-class houses. The density of such neighbourhoods remains apparent in these areas in modern Windsor. In 1884, the two men also laid out the Windsor Fair Grounds at the southern extremity of Ouellette Avenue (as it was now known) and Tecumseh Road. In so doing, Cameron and Curry had effectively laid out a ring of development around the core of the old town that had first been established by James Dougall and S.S. Macdonell in the 1850s and 1860s. A "core-ring configuration" of a residential halo surrounding a commercial core was not an unusual form of urban development in Canada.[251] What was unique in Windsor's case was that the development had been so dominated by just two individuals. The impact of their developments on the town was enormous as the rural area between the towns shrank and was replaced by a burgeoning urban space. By April 1886, it was apparent that:

> The building boom on Jennette avenue still continues and Caron avenue has been opened 70 feet wide and extends back as far as Elliott street, the farms on each side being sold, divided into building lots. If arrangements can be made, Caron avenue will be continued to the river. The time is not far distant when it will be necessary to take in that portion of Sandwich West lying between Crawford and Campbell avenues, thus giving the town of Windsor sufficient population to incorporate as a city.[252]

It was a measure of the growing sentiment that Windsor was a distinct urban community, a potential city, that the town had withdrawn from the jurisdiction of the County of Essex. When the proposal to separate was put to a vote in 1879, there was not a great deal of interest, but a small majority felt that it was time for the town to go its own way. Windsor was still required to reimburse the county for the administration of justice, which was occasionally a point of friction. In 1885, Windsor objected to a significant rate increase and argued that it should only be assessed on a *per capita* basis. County officials pointed out that "85 per cent of the criminals in the county came from Windsor," and that the town should pay for the expenses its criminals generated.[253]

By the mid-1880s, residents began to seriously consider that Windsor had a greater future than simply being the town across the river from Detroit. The increase in production, employment, and population during the 1880s enabled the community to explore the possibility that it might emerge as one of Ontario's main urban centres. J.W. Tringham had even grander plans in store for his electric streetcars. Barely a month after the successful launch of his Windsor-Walkerville route, he proposed the creation of an electric railway connecting all the communities of Essex County, whereby people and products would be able to move rapidly and cheaply across the county to markets. Essex County had already seen the installation of the first commercial electric streetcar system in North America, and there was reason to build on this innovation, for Tringham could see that "in the near future, electricity will take the place of steam on all our railways, both on account of its economy and greater adaptability to the requirements of modern transportation."[254]

It was not to be. On August 1, 1886, Tringham suddenly fell ill and died. Without his direction the service could not long continue, and in April of 1888, the company no longer had the resources or expertise to keep the dynamos running. Later that year the trolley was being pulled by horses. Progress by no means followed a straight trajectory; the following decades would see some unfortunate reversals and several spectacular achievements.

Chapter Seven
Incorporation: 1887–1892

B

Y THE LATE 1870s, Hiram Walker had grown weary of braving the uncertainties of the ferry crossing and the mud of Sandwich Street to commute from his Detroit mansion to his Walkerville office. He decided to remedy the situation by building his own cross-river service, and in 1880 he leased the steamer *Essex*. But relying on others was not Walker's way, and in 1881 he purchased the *Ariel* and began a regular commercial ferry run between east Detroit and Walkerville. During the summer, the *Ariel* also stopped at Belle Isle Park. This ferry service was incorporated in 1888, but despite its convenience it was never one of Walker's profitable ventures. Of far more significance was an enterprise arising out of a near disastrous fire in 1882.

That fire had destroyed Walker's stockyard at the riverfront, and he was determined to move south and rebuild his cattle barns. At the corner of what would become Walker and Tecumseh Roads, he reconstructed the livestock operation and built eight brick barns for the accommodation of 1,600 head of cattle. A short railway already existed from these stockyards to the Grand Trunk tracks near the riverfront. If he could operate this miniature railway, why not something grander? Whisky was made from grain and Walker already had extensive grain growing operations in Colchester Township. He decided to go into the railway business, and in 1885 he had the Lake Erie, Essex and Detroit River Railway Company incorporated. However, it was not until 1888 that construction got under way, and by 1889 it spanned Essex County from Walkerville to Leamington. Not only would this railway fill Walker's needs by supplying his distillery and stockyard, it would give a huge impetus to county agricultural production by enabling farmers to supply the Detroit market. Perishable fruit, vegetables and fish were shipped overnight from southern

Essex County and were on Detroit breakfast tables by the morning. As well, timber could be harvested from the southern county and shipped to markets in Michigan. Less vital, but just as civilizing, was the impact of Walker's ferry and train service in opening up Detroit's theatres and opera to county folk in southern Essex County who rarely had the chance to see something of the wider world.[255] While the L.E.E. & D.R. railway provided another important communication link between the towns at the strait and the surrounding countryside, an even greater innovation was on the way.

By 1880, the Grand Trunk Railway had lost out to the Canadian Pacific in the race to build the transcontinental railway to the west. At least the Grand Trunk retained its pre-eminence in Ontario; that is, until the Canadian Pacific discovered that there were rich new fields it could exploit. By May 1888, the Canadian Pacific had constructed a new line from Montreal to St. Thomas, and it was prepared to extend farther west to connect to American lines. This news brought members of Windsor's town council to exclaim that:

> the establishment at this point of the terminus of the Western branch of so important a railway as the Canadian Pacific, marks an era in the history of Windsor fraught with promises of eminently gratifying results… the bringing to our doors of a third competitive line of communication will not fail to prove a boon to our Merchants.[256]

Then the problems arose. Thanks to Cameron and Curry's efforts, the western part of the town had recently been developed and residential streets were about to be extended. This would directly interfere with the Canadian Pacific's projected rail lines and prohibit them from having an efficient rail yard to ferry cars across the river. While the town had been founded by the railways, a railway expansion now threatened to block further development. At the council meeting of October 15th, 1888, a Canadian Pacific lawyer outlined the company's preferred route and warned that they would not be able to build their train yard if the town streets protruded through it. In defiance of the railway, the committee on street openings moved to pave and extend the streets to the west. The matter was put over to a special meeting of the town council held on October 24th. The railway's representative offered to build and maintain bridges over the major streets, Wyandotte, London and Sandwich. However, it could not permit the smaller streets such as Chatham and Pitt to cross its yard. A heated debate followed, and there were motions and countermotions for and against the railway's proposal. While a few members supported the Canadian Pacific as a boon to the town, the majority fiercely opposed the railway's blocking of any street expansion. An extended council session ensued, until the members finally resolved to permit the railway to bridge and maintain the crossings of the main streets, while the town retained a right (never invoked) to bridge the smaller ones.[257] Despite the acrimony aroused by the railway's extension through the town, it had indelibly established Windsor as a part of the major rail system in North America. As a Windsor newspaper observed a few years later, "Already Windsor is the western Canadian terminus of three transcontinental railways, and will, in all probability, have another added in the near future by the Lake Erie Road."[258] But, as events would show, Windsor was by no means on the main line of industrial commerce.

While the rail network was expanding and connecting Windsor to greater markets, the ferry crossing of the Detroit River, a service that had existed for over half a century, remained maddeningly inadequate. Since 1863, Windsor had been authorized by the Province of Canada to issue a cross-river license, and in 1884 the town had issued that license to the Detroit, Belle Isle & Windsor Ferry Company. However, their operation of the service generated continual unrest, and as their lease neared its end, the press noted that "the company managed its boats in a way very unsatisfactory to the residents of Windsor" and that the regulation providing for regular crossing times "was grossly violated."[259] This discontent moved the town council to approach the federal government (since Confederation, Ottawa had assumed control of all cross-border regulation) to impose controls on the new license operator. There were rumours that the ferry company would lose their monopoly and that a newcomer, the Detroit Navigation Company, a group headed by Hiram Walker, would capture this valuable license. Capt. John Pridgeon, the owner of the existing ferry operation, dismissed this and pointed out that he owned all the wharves and almost all of the existing ferries. It was his monopoly and he intended to continue operating it despite any grumblings.

The ferry license question was the one issue that could generate deep passions, and at the meeting of November 12th, 1888, there was a sudden, fierce confrontation between Councillors T. Mercer Morton and J.W. Drake. Morton was incensed by Drake's opposition to his suggestion to refer the ferry question to a legal authority for an opinion and thundered:

"You are a coward, sir,"

To which Drake retorted:

"The man who says I am a coward lies!"

Morton looked around wildly and seizing upon an ink pot, "hurled it with all his manly power at the head of his municipal colleague. The world stood still for a moment to hear Drake drop with a dull and sickly thud." But it was not to be, as Morton missed but did succeed in spraying his opponent, several other council members, and the fastidious town clerk Stephen Lusted with ink. Lusted was compelled to explain that a large ink blot defacing the Council Minute Book was "the work of an unfriendly altercation between Members."[260] Yet, mayhem in the council chambers did nothing to resolve the ferry dilemma. J.C. Patterson, the Council's advocate in Ottawa, urged the federal government to allow the Council to control the terms and conditions of any future license. However, Ottawa was disinterested in Windsor's ongoing ferry disputes and it issued a license to the existing operator for a further five years.

The other major problem affecting the town, the lack of a proper high school, was within its ability to remedy. In 1885, the provincial education inspector had condemned the "soup kitchen" on Goyeau Street and ordered the town to build a proper facility. Both the western and eastern ends of the town vied to have the site, and the controversy was only remedied when J.C. Patterson, in gratitude for his many years as the school inspector, donated the lands at Ann (Elliott) Street and Goyeau to the school board. In 1888, construction was started on the Windsor Collegiate Institute, and the following year the turreted building took in its first students.[261]

Collegiate Institute, Windsor, Canada

A postcard of Windsor Collegiate Institute.

RED HOT METHODISM

By the late 1880s, Victorian morality had descended in full force at the strait. When the young men of the county arranged for a championship baseball match against players from Windsor and Detroit, more than two hundred spectators gathered on the Forrest Common on Huron Line one Sunday. The area was baseball mad, and contests between Windsor and Detroit teams and between Assumption College students and any challengers were well attended and widely reported. This championship game had caused an even greater stir than usual, but was interrupted by a zealous Christian who stepped forward and reminded the players that this was the Lord's Day. He then summoned a magistrate who ordered the players and spectators to disperse forthwith. The offended observer was glad to have stopped this abomination, but somewhat put out that some ministers, who must have known of such a major event, had not taken any steps to stop it.[262]

Victorianism in its full judgmental force was on the loose and Windsor constables were dispatched to the barber shops to remind proprietors that no hair could be shorn on the Sabbath. By 1888, it was observed that, "Windsor is so moral as to seize the works of Zola when found on sale."[263] Moral arbiters had decided that the minds of Windsor readers should not be tainted by the French writer Émile Zola, perhaps the greatest social commentator of his day. The embodiment of this morality was the local Police Magistrate, Alexander Bartlet. Since his days as clerk during the Fenian times, Bartlet had grown an imposing beard and become an almost biblical figure, handing down justice from on high. Public drunkenness or fighting got stiff fines or several days in jail. In addition to his judicial duties, Bartlet was also a mainstay of St. Andrew's Presbyterian Church and an instructor in its Sabbath School. In 1890, he addressed the failure of so many parents to send their children to the school and blamed the evil influence of Detroit. Detroiters read newspapers on Sundays, went on Sunday excursions and, in Bartlet's view, "the moral condition of the people of Detroit, which permitted and approved of paving streets on Sunday, was not brought about in a day," but had been a gradual deterioration. "Windsor was warned of the consequences of allowing such things to exist."[264]

Protestant churches were the mainstay of this movement towards a more rigorous morality, but even they had their ups and downs. In early 1880, Windsor's Methodist Church was on the brink of financial ruin and the congregation was forced to worship in a hired room. Thanks to a few generous supporters, it soon regained its momentum. The Baptist community owed its very existence to J.P. Molasky, who had come to Windsor in 1884 to open a music store. In the course of his business he located a dozen families who expressed their desire to have a Baptist Church, and by 1885 they had a modest structure in use.

The Anglican community of the 1880s was deeply divided by liturgical controversies. In 1883, low church members of All Saints' Church were put out by the introduction of a surpliced choir and a proposal to introduce candles on the communion table. Only a meeting of the vestry prevented "an open rupture." One member of All Saints' congregation was so incensed that he refused to pay his pew rent and had his seat boarded up. When the females of the family attempted to regain their position one Sunday they had to climb over the back of the pew, "apparently oblivious of the fact that they were the observed of all observers."[265] At the close of the service the boards were removed so that they might exit more decorously. These disputes soon passed, and by 1885 All Saints' was united again and able to open a new Sunday School building with a capacity for 800 persons.

Windsor's black community continued to find solace in the British Methodist Episcopal, the American Methodist Episcopal (established in September, 1888) and the Baptist church. In March, 1888, Bishop Lennox, the "colored prelate of Windsor," presided over a hundred persons who attended mass baptisms in the Detroit River. A London newspaper reported that:

> On Sunday morning nearly the entire colored population of Windsor gathered at the foot of McDougall Street. There was also a sprinkling of whites in the crowd, drawn there by the announcement that some fifty colored persons were to be baptized. Elder Hawkins and Elder Washington... grasped each candidate and with a firm hold, recited the usual formula and in twenty-two minutes forty-two converts had been baptized.[266]

A month later, Pastor Marsh at the Mercer Street Baptist Church conducted a revival meeting that brought in 100 new members. In August 1889, Windsor's black community lost one of its most noteworthy members when James L. Dunn died. In addition to fighting for the rights of black children to attend the Central School, he had operated a successful varnish business and regularly ran for town council. In January 1887, he was elected and served two terms as an active and vocal member of council. In a time when black citizens were denied basic civil rights in most parts of North America, James Dunn's life was a testament that blacks could be an integral part of a larger community. Happily, he had lived just long enough to see Windsor's schools integrated the previous year. Dunn's funeral was one of the largest ever seen in Windsor, and the entire board of education and town council attended and followed the hearse to the B.M.E. Church for the service by Elder Washington.[267]

In addition to these congregations who had lived along the Detroit River for decades, entirely new religious groups were springing up. The peddler and fur trader Moses David had been the first Jew to live in the area before the War of 1812. Notwithstanding the restrictions against non-Christians, David had become a major land speculator and even a captain in the militia. However, the first Jewish community did not begin to form until the arrival of a handful of Russian Jews in the 1880s. Unlike arrivals from the British Isles, these newcomers had customs and manners that set them apart, and to many of the established residents their religion and language was a huge curiosity. But there was no denying their work ethic, and the Meretskys, Weingardens and Kovinskys became the successful forerunners for a larger influx of Jewish families. In the summer of 1888, local Jews purchased a black church, "Bishop Lennox's modest Christian cathedral on Pitt street," and turned it into a synagogue. Its dedication on August 17th was a major public event and the band of the 21st Fusiliers "headed a procession of Hebrews, male and female" who paraded solemnly to their new place of worship. Rabbi Eger of Detroit addressed the congregation and urged them to live in "peace and harmony with their gentile neighbours."[268]

Other newcomers were more rambunctious. The Salvation Army had arrived in Canada in 1882, and by 1885 there were two Windsor barracks, one American and the other English. Every evening during the week and twice on Sundays, the American Salvationists, led by their fourteen-piece brass band, paraded through the town's streets. The English Army made its presence known at "Hosannah Meetings" and aroused the ire of Magistrate Bartlet, whose house lay across from their barracks. "That gentleman [Bartlet] has at different times called on the police to make them stop beating the drum and yelling, a practice they are in the habit of doing all day Sunday." These exuberant forms of worship attracted disparaging comments in the local press, and some tried to break up their parades and meetings. But there was no denying their enthusiasm, and when Captain Dyman led an Army service that "rolled out the terrors of the law, of damnation and eternal fire, in a way that made some of the soldiers shout with religious fervor," it made even the non-soldiers tremble. That Captain Dyman was a woman of "delicate features and feminine voice" only added to the drama of the scene.[269]

People expected excitement from their churches, and Methodist clergy were eager to oblige. In 1881, the Rev. J.V. Smith preached a "Red Hot Sermon" that "quickened the pulse of the Methodist denomination in Windsor, and few empty seats are to be found in his church." Itinerant preachers could inflame the indifferent with religious zeal, and even John Bains, known as "cheap John," who ran the second-hand furniture store on Sandwich Street, was not immune. John belonged to no church, and both his merchandise and children were typically covered with a thick coat of dust from Sandwich Street. As a retailer, he "catered to the very poor, of which there were many in Windsor." But after attending a revival meeting put on by the evangelists Crossley and Hunter, "John became a changed man," and he and his family became regulars at St. Andrew's.[270] Methodists in particular had seized upon the reformist ideology of temperance and the anti-saloon crusade. When the famed lecturer Sam Jones preached at the Methodist Church, ushers had to lock the doors to prevent overcrowding. Jones did not disappoint and gave a sermon that dwelt on the evils of drink, of the poor mother weeping "over the grave of a drunken son." Positive action was needed, for "You can't pray whisky out of the country. You must toss it out."[271]

While the temperance movement was very much alive among a segment of Windsor's population, it was by no means predominant. In the counties north of Lake Ontario, known as the "womb of Methodism," and in the Niagara Peninsula, temperance was preached loudly to receptive congregations. In Windsor it was a different matter. The "Scott Act" that sought to limit the number of distilleries and allow a municipality to enact local prohibition was largely rejected. Instead of limiting the number of alcohol producing facilities, Windsor resisted the provincial trend and was actually increasing the number of distilleries and breweries. The Amherstburg *Echo* observed in 1886 that "Windsor liquor men think that two new breweries in Windsor in a year means that the sentiment in favour of the Scott prohibition act in the county is not increasing."[272] Moreover, it was difficult to advance temperance in a place where the livelihood of so many people depended on the consumption of alcohol. When provincial government ordered a plebiscite on prohibition in 1894, Windsor was the only city in Ontario where the male electors voted to keep drinking. There was something of a gender split on the issue, as Windsor's female voters tended to favour prohibition. The *Evening Record* regretted Windsor's anti-prohibition stance and attributed it to the influence of "Walkerville, which is a product of the liquor manufacture."[273] In addition to Hiram Walker's distillery, the county had an active viniculture industry, and the manufacture of wines and brandies brought in much employment and revenue. This was especially true of the French-Canadian portion of the county, who since the days of the Jesuits had produced and consumed ciders and "eau-de-vie" as a way of life.

French-Canadians distinguished themselves from their neighbours in other ways besides their fondness for alcohol. French speakers were becoming increasingly concerned about assaults on their heritage in a province that was so overwhelmingly English-speaking and Protestant. When Lowe's store on Ouellette Avenue featured an effigy of Louis Riel hanging in their front window in 1885, French-Canadians understood that it was their loyalty that was under suspicion.[274] Those marchers who filled the ranks during the St. Jean Baptiste parade were displaying more than a momentary enthusiasm; they were a tangible sign that French-Canadians would resist any mass absorption into the dominant culture. All they needed was a champion.

Jean-Baptiste-Napoléon-Gaspard Pacaud was born in Quebec, but had moved to the Detroit River region. With his brother Aurèle, he founded the newspaper *Le Progrès* in 1881. Fiercely protective of language rights, the brothers' newspaper was a voice for French-Canadians in southern Ontario and Michigan. In an 1881 editorial, "Notre Langue," the Pacauds acknowledged those parents who gave their children some English education, but they insisted that their first study must be their native French.[275] In December 1886, Gaspard Pacaud ran for the Liberals in the provincial riding of North Essex against the incumbent Conservative, Solomon White. The election had already been raised to an emotional pitch by controversy over the "Ross Bible." George Ross, the Minister of Education, had selected scriptural readings for use in the common schools, and to the horror of many Protestants he had asked Archbishop Lynch, the Roman Catholic Bishop of Toronto, to review the selections. This was perceived as a direct infringement on Protestant rights, and the Orange Lodge threatened reprisals. It was not surprising that when federal Liberal leader Wilfrid Laurier attended a Pacaud rally in Windsor that French-Canadians from across the county jammed the meeting in solidarity. An energized population gave Pacaud the victory, and a procession of sleighs, one of which was "a canoe upon runners, filled with men who sang the characteristic songs of the habitant," carried Pacaud in triumph. But the election left some residual bitterness and the Windsor *Clarion*, a newspaper unsympathetic to Catholics or French-Canadians, alleged that participants in the victory procession had carried a British ensign upside-down as a mark of disrespect.[276]

These petty slights were put aside and French-Canadian pride expressed itself in actions such as the construction of the new church of *"Notre Dame du Lac"* to the east of Walkerville in 1884, and especially in major works that would profoundly benefit the entire community. The medical profession in Windsor, both Protestant and Catholic, saw the need for a functioning hospital. In the earlier part of the century, a hospital stay was a last resort, as the likelihood of infection, painful treatment and death dissuaded all but the most desperate. In 1880, there were only eleven general hospitals for the two million people of Ontario.[277] As the decade progressed, the medical acceptance of asepsis made treatment in a hospital safer and more likely to cure the patients than kill them. However desirable it was to have a hospital in Windsor, no one seemed to have the ability to raise the funds or to cajole contractors and workers to contribute to such an undertaking. Dr. Richard Carney, one of the most public-spirited physicians in the town and the organizer of the Medical Society of Windsor, turned to the community's leading fundraiser, the Catholic Dean of Essex, Father Wagner. Carney, a Protestant, appreciated that only Wagner could mobilize the Catholic community's considerable resources in this most worthwhile cause.

Over the years he had led St. Alphonsus parish, Dean Wagner had shown his administrative skill in raising money through bazaars and art auctions. Now he seized upon the hospital project with the same gusto. Ladies' socials and bazaars were organized to help raise funds for the hospital. Money was even obtained by selling cancelled Canadian postage stamps to European collectors. When the public found out about this aspect of the project, the Dean was deluged with used stamps. His years at St. Alphonus had given him many connections and by the time construction began, he began to call them in. Hypolite Reaume agreed to do the work on the stone, while the Robinet company supplied the bricks. Wagner inspired the entire community to do whatever they could, and one French-Canadian, Émile Chauvin, later recalled eagerly joining a team of men hauling stone up from the wharf at the river and carting brick and sand to the hospital construction site. As for staffing the institution, Wagner called upon the Religious Hospitallers of St. Joseph, a Montreal religious order. Five nursing sisters under the direction of Mother Joséphine Paquet arrived in September 1888, and began to assist Wagner in fundraising. Sometimes that assistance amounted to the sisters simply going from door to door begging for contributions. However demeaning the task, the funds were acquired and a year after the initial groundbreaking, the hospital was completed.

The formal opening of Hôtel-Dieu hospital on Sunday, October 13th, 1889, was an indelibly Catholic affair, with every Catholic fraternal order in Windsor and Detroit on parade as Archbishop Walsh of Toronto blessed the building. The construction of Hôtel-Dieu, while largely under the control of Catholic leaders, had been undertaken for the benefit of a wider community. A Protestant reporter toured the hospital two years after its opening and

Hôtel-Dieu Hospital.

found that it was being efficiently operated by the "Sisters of Charity." There was no religious distinction in the service provided to the patients and many were given medicine and care without charge. The reporter concluded that the nursing sisters were a "devoted, self-denying band… giving their lives to this work."[278]

Dean Wagner also had plans to reach out to Windsor's black community. As the 1864 census had shown, twenty-two percent of Windsor's residents were black. Moreover, they lived in a cohesive and self-reliant community in which the Methodist and Baptist churches played central roles in their lives. Wagner hoped to make some headway and acquire at least some of this community for the Catholic Church. Since 1886, Wagner and another priest, a Father McManus, had been proselytizing among Windsor's blacks, and by early 1887 they reported that they had a few converts, as well as enough children to found a school. In 1887, Wagner opened up a short-lived mission at the back of St. Alphonsus. The priests concluded that their black converts would have to be kept separate from white Catholics, and that in due time "they [black converts] will need a chapel of their own." Until this was available, a number of pews were reserved for them at St. Alphonsus.[279] Wagner also envisaged a more substantial Mission for Coloured Children which would provide a school for poor black children and an orphanage for the destitute as an adjunct to Hôtel-Dieu. The Mission was founded in 1890, and the Hôtel-Dieu Sisters were also charged with providing education for the children. Wagner employed a black woman known as "Aunt Christian" to circulate through the neighbourhood around McDougall Street to encourage indigent children to attend. As the sisters later explained to the Bishop of London, Wagner had amassed substantial funds "for a two-fold purpose of founding a Catholic hospital and for assisting the colored children whom he wanted to convert to the Catholic Faith."[280] While a Vatican Cardinal lauded Wagner for his efforts, the mission did not attract many children or converts and was discontinued after 1894. Of Windsor's 886 black residents in 1899, only 24 were Catholics.

INDUSTRIAL LEVIATHAN NEXT DOOR

While French was still spoken on Windsor's streets and predominated in the villages of the northern part of Essex County, there were few vestiges of the French heritage left in Detroit. In contrast to Windsor, entire neighbourhoods in Detroit were German or Polish-speaking as immigrants from central Europe flooded in to man the growing number of factories. After the Civil War, Detroit was described as "a rapidly growing medium-sized industrial city" whose population had risen from 79,577 in 1870 to 205,876 in 1890.[281] At more than twenty times Windsor's size, Detroit was the industrial and commercial giant of the region. And it was a city that made things. The Michigan Stove Works was a major employer, as was the technically advanced Pingree and Smith shoe factory. One of the largest enterprises was the Eureka Iron and Steel Works in nearby Wyandotte, Michigan. Eureka's operator, Eber Ward, was a hard-driving steel man, and at the time of his death in 1875 he was reputed to be Detroit's first millionaire. In an ironic union of the cross-border *nouveau riche*, Ward's widow Catharine married Windsor's land mogul (described by the press as "Western Ontario's Croesus") Alexander Cameron in 1878.[282]

The animosities of the Rebellion of 1838 had long been set aside, if not completely forgotten by the 1880s. Hundreds of commuters sailed across the Detroit River daily, almost as if an international border did not exist. The housing market reacted and prices were exorbitant. By 1881, it was apparent that "The rush of the working classes from Detroit continues, and there is now scarcely a good house to rent. High, very high rents in Detroit are causing the stampede."[283] Not only were Detroit labourers finding cheap lodgings in Windsor, Windsor men were finding good employment in Detroit. The *Essex Review* thought that the prime purpose of the ferries was to bring "Windsor mechanics, laborers, artisans and clerks, going to and returning from work in a foreign country." Windsorites regularly attended Detroit shows and circuses, and on the Fourth of July American visitors flooded Windsor's streets and went on excursions to Sandwich's Sulphur Springs. In so many ways the area already seemed to form one economic and social unit, though a tragic incident in 1883 highlighted the distinctions that still divided the two communities.

The ferry *Hope* was making one of its routine runs from Detroit to Windsor on the evening of August 19, 1883. Several knots of couples were around the promenade deck when shots suddenly rang out. A man appeared pursuing a woman, and as he cornered her near a smokestack he fired twice into her body. She died as the *Hope* arrived at the Windsor shore. The killer was Luke Phipps, a Detroit bartender, and the victim was his wife, a woman who had left him repeatedly for other men. At Phipps' trial in Sandwich, the fact of the murder seemed beyond dispute; scores of people had witnessed it. The question was, on which side of the river had the act been committed? Michigan did not have the death penalty, so if the crime was committed in U.S. waters, Canada had no jurisdiction, and the most Phipps could suffer was life in prison. Canada still mandated capital punishment for murder. The opening of Phipps' trial in April 1884, was disrupted when his Canadian defence counsel, Solomon White, failed to appear. The judge insisted on proceeding, and the prisoner's Detroit lawyer did his best. The Detroit press was fascinated by the case, and a reporter commented on the quaintness of the proceedings:

> There is in Canada a certain dignity of procedure, a sort of old world air, about the stately movement of justice that rather impresses the American on-looker. The flowing black silk robes of judge and counsel; those white, well laundried arrangements, whatever their name is [tabs] that the Judge wears at his neck... all tend to make the scene seem unreal to American eyes and gives it the resemblance to an old-fashioned George III court act in a play.[284]

Detroiters clung to every report of the Phipps case, with its lurid details of sex and betrayal, all conducted in this nearby but surprisingly strange locale. Solomon White eventually appeared (after several prosecution witnesses had already testified) and led defence evidence to the effect that Mrs. Phipps had been unfaithful. When he asked the judge if he should present evidence as to the site of the crime, the judge did not think it necessary. "Very well your lordship," White responded, "Then our case is finished." And so was his client, as without any dispute raised as to the location of the crime, Phipps was doomed. The jury was compelled to conclude that the crime was committed on the Canadian side.

A public hanging at the Sandwich jail was a significant public event. It was a carefully choreographed ritual in which every detail of the condemned man's last day was meticulously recorded and later broadcast in the press. At his execution in June (barely two months after his trial), a ticket-only crowd watched in awe as Phipps played his part bravely, taking religious instruction, thanking the jail staff, and, once the noose was tightened, indicating that he was ready to die. In addition to the crowd at the jail yard, thousands of Detroiters lined roofs on the far side of the river and with telescopes tried to follow the dramatic events occurring in Sandwich.

Despite the peculiar British traditions that still appeared on the Canadian side, it was apparent that there was a great deal in common between the peoples at the strait. Some were left wondering why the border restrictions existed at all, and perhaps Canada (and particularly Windsor) might be better off if the land at the strait were part of one country.

Political Unionists

Advocates for the annexation of Canada to the United States had come to the forefront by the late 1880s, and the movement was nowhere as strong as it was in Windsor. If the National Policy had brought some investment across the border, it also meant that high tariffs effectively precluded Windsor and Essex County producers from selling their goods in the lucrative Detroit market. The Windsor *Clarion* attributed the growth of annexationist sentiment to the fact that:

> The people here have every opportunity of seeing how injuriously the tariff between the United States and Canada affects them… They know that in many lines the prices in Detroit are lower by just the amount of the tariff. They see a city of one quarter of a million on one bank of a river while on the other bank… the population is less than ten thousand.[285]

One local politician who was unafraid of advocating for annexation, or as it was more diplomatically termed, "political union," was Luke Phipp's inept counsel, Solomon White. A prominent, if unsuccessful, criminal lawyer whose clients were sentenced to hang with alarming frequency, White had more success in his business pursuits, which included a 500-acre stockyard and profitable farms and vineyards. [286] From his mother, Angelique Fortier, White inherited his Catholic faith and fluency in French, both desirable political assets in North

120

Essex. He had barely been called to the bar in 1878 when he was elected to the provincial assembly. After his defeat by Pacaud in 1886, White returned to his farms and businesses but remained involved in public life. Even though he was descended from one of the oldest families in the county, and his grandfather, John White, had fought for the British cause in both the Revolutionary War and the War of 1812, White became an avid campaigner for union with the United States. In January of 1889, he pronounced himself an annexationist, and in a speech at Laing's Hall in Windsor he "explained the benefits that would be derived from political union... He predicted a rapid and healthy growth of political union between the two countries."[287]

As a border-area farmer, it was apparent to White that the tariff system was barring producers from selling to a large, receptive market right next door. Annexationism had reached such a stage of public acceptance that when White ran for Mayor of Windsor in 1889, both he and his opponent, Michael Twomey, supported political union. The Toronto *Globe*, a newspaper that rarely paid any attention to events south of London, was aghast. Here was a Canadian town supporting avowed annexationists, and "from this it appears that two-thirds of the people of Windsor entertain political opinions for which they should, according to The Empire, be shot in their tracks." But perhaps they should not be too harshly condemned, for Windsor people understood "how vastly they and the country are injured by the abominable taxes placed on international trade." Other editorialists across the province began to question Windsor's loyalty, but were consoled by the fact that "Windsor people had but little choice in the matter, and the trade restrictions but cold comfort out of the result."[288]

Yet there was no excuse for White's victory by acclamation at the municipal election of 1890. While it may have been an embarrassment in other parts of the province, support for political union was obviously an asset to a political career in the border lands. Still, White as an annexationist and prominent member of the Conservative Party had become something of an embarrassment. This discomfort was compounded when White took advantage of a split in the Liberal vote to return to the provincial assembly in June 1890. When White was informed that his party chief Macdonald was surprised by his election, he responded, "Sir John is perfectly aware of the growing sentiment in favour of annexation in this section of Ontario."[289] Ironically, the movement had generated no great interest in the U.S. Few Americans were interested in or willing to commit any resources to adding Canadian territory to the republic. One of the exceptions was a Detroit newspaper, the *Evening News*, which regularly published editorials advocating American expansion to the north. Annexationism retained strong support among farmers, and inevitably became an issue when a general election was called in 1891. Liberals favoured greater free trade with the U.S., a policy some feared was merely slow political union. Macdonald, with his cry of "A British subject I was born—a British subject I will die," wrapped himself in the flag and defied his opponents. The 1891 election would be, in one historian's estimation, "the closest approach to a plebiscite on annexation in Canada's history."[290]

In North Essex, a familiar figure re-emerged to advance the Liberal cause. William McGregor had abandoned Windsor after his business failure in 1877 and political defeat in 1878. Moving to Winnipeg in about 1882, he worked for his brother's livestock business and recouped some of his losses. He returned to Windsor in 1887 and revived his livery and real estate businesses. If Macdonald was playing the patriotism card, Laurier had staked Liberal prospects on "unrestricted reciprocity"—that is, free trade, but not annexation, with the United States. As the Liberal candidate, McGregor chaired a mass rally at the Opera House where banners proclaiming "Away With Customs Between Detroit and Windsor" and "Free Trade with 70,000,000 People" expressed public displeasure with the tariff barriers. In the March vote, McGregor soundly defeated Patterson. In the eyes of the Toronto *Globe*, he had overturned the "Tory hive" at the strait and slightly redeemed the area from its traitorous past.[291] Beyond politics, it was McGregor's most recent business schemes which had begun to reshape the community.

Expansion

In March 1890, William McGregor shared with the town council his plans to expand the streetcar system. McGregor had recently become a stockholder and the driving force behind the street railway, the "Sandwich, Windsor and Amherstburg Railway Company." This corporation, the successor to the original streetcar line between Windsor and Sandwich, had been incorporated in 1887 and was intent on extending its limited services. As the operator of the railway, McGregor outlined their plans to lay tracks along Wyandotte Street to Walkerville, and in due course to extend the line along Ouellette Avenue to Tecumseh Road. An extension to Amherstburg remained a wistful hope. For the most part, McGregor was compelled to rely on horsepower. However, for a brief period he obtained a locomotive, and Windsor residents could take a local commute on a real steam railway.

It took a Detroit entrepreneur, Colonel Joseph Clarke, to make a dramatic shift in how Windsor moved. In February 1891, Clarke bought out McGregor and the other stockholders and took over the S.W. & A. He

An S.W. & A. Streetcar.

had new bonds issued for the company and used the capital to electrify the routes. By the late summer of 1891 the horses were gone, and on August 15th the electric cars of the S.W. & A. made their first trip from Windsor to Sandwich. The S.W. & A. also bought out Tringham's old line along the river and built a new track east from Ouellette along Wyandotte Street. When these tracks were joined, a "belt-line" service connected commuters between Windsor and Walkerville.

These new lines uniting the three communities were powered by electric dynamos far larger than those available to Tringham. By 1894, a coal-fired powerhouse with two generators supplied 250 horsepower for the streetcars with excess capacity available for the lighting system. While it was a private service, the street railway had shown itself to be an indispensable part of urban life. In 1893, it was proposed that "council should carefully guard the interests of our working population by providing cheap fares" since the street railways were the principal mode of transport from Windsor to "Sandwich or Walkerville which are practically part of Windsor." Goods and people were now rapidly moving between the neighbourhoods at the strait as if they were one community.[292]

The growth of the 1880s also meant that this population could not be contained within the town limits as set in the 1850s. In March 1887, the town council expressed its desire to annex all that portion of Sandwich West Township up to the town of Sandwich. A year later, they tempered this ambition and only sought to add the developed lands as far as Campbell Avenue. By that time, assessors put the town's population at 8,600, and with the addition of these new lands the community could even consider application for city status. In March 1889, one bold member of Council, Robert Timms, put forward the notion that Windsor should absorb Walkerville, as the two communities were almost one. For that matter, he argued, "the taking in of Sandwich on the west and Walkerville on the east would make Windsor the prettiest city in Canada."[293] While such grand notions would have to wait, provincial approval was granted to annex that portion of Sandwich West up to Campbell Avenue. On January 1, 1889, Windsor gained an additional 292 acres and expanded by almost fifteen percent. It would be almost thirty years before it would expand again.

Sandwich residents showed no particular interest in joining the growing town to their north. They appeared to be satisfied with what they had, even though without any railway connections they had painfully little. Few new businesses were coming to the town, although the Sulphur Springs still drew crowds from Detroit during the summer. Perhaps due to the lack of a regular supply of customers, the Brighton Beach Hotel had closed in about 1887. The town's streets were unpaved, and after the spring it was reported that they were covered with "vast amounts of dust."[294]

By contrast, Walkerville had a great deal to lose by any annexation to Windsor. Hiram Walker's personal fief (still only an unincorporated post office village in Sandwich East Township) had benefited by the construction of rail and ferry connections and was regularly adding new factories. Up until 1888, the village had been mostly made up of various Walker enterprises, including the distillery, the Walker malt house, cooperage and lumber yard. After that year a number of new industries took advantage of the rail and ferry connections to relocate along Fifth Street (Walker Road). One of them, the metal works of the Kerr Brothers, had already been in Walkerville for a few years and were at least partially independent of the Walkers. However, when they incorporated as the Kerr Engine Company in 1890, E.C. Walker became president of the firm. The newcomers, including the Walkerville Malleable Iron Company, Parke Davis pharmaceuticals and the Globe Furniture Company (the majority of the shares held by the Walker family), made this community a dynamo and something of a rival to Windsor. Hiram Walker was not above poaching from Windsor, and in 1888 he offered inducements to the Barnum Wire and Iron Works to relocate from Windsor to a larger, free site in his town.[295] The first true industrial conglomeration in the area was coming together along Walker Road.

With his community growing at such a pace, "Annexation could only have been repugnant to the eldest Walker. Powerful as he was in Walkerville, as part of the larger Windsor setting his influence would have diminished considerably."[296] Walker backed the petition to incorporate Walkerville as a town, since this step would relieve him of the personal obligation to maintain the police and fire department and still enable him to negotiate deals to provide lighting and water to 'his' town. On April 7, 1890, Walkerville was incorporated, and its first mayor would be the founder's nephew, H.A. Walker. A Detroit newspaper, the *Journal*, published an exposé on the new town which it called "the queerest, quaintest place in all Christendom." According to the writer, the residents of Walkerville lived in a "condition of dependency" under the despotic control of Hiram Walker.[297] Local pride had been grievously wounded, and at a public meeting (held in Walker's bottling plant) the Detroit journalist was condemned for disseminating untruths and mindless insults. Walker could depend upon his subjects to rise to his defence while he quietly soldiered on with business as usual.

Compelled to look to the future without its neighbours, Windsor was doing just fine in the 1880s. It was undergoing what one newspaper described as a "quiet boom," and by 1888 the town's assessors noted that the population had grown to 8,602. Even the Detroit newspapers were beginning to take note of events across the river: the Detroit *Free Press* commented in 1889 that:

> Very few towns in Canada can boast of so solid and healthful a growth as Detroit's Canadian suburb. The rise of the place has been most gratifying and of such a nature that it has now secured a hold that will ere many years place it in the front rank of Canadian cities.[298]

In the mind of its new mayor, Solomon White, there was no doubt that Windsor should march in the front rank. At his swearing-in in January, 1890, White lauded Windsor as "the most progressive and prosperous town in the dominion—now, in fact a city." Six months later, the Toronto *Globe* reported that White had been working on the city incorporation project for quite some time, and that he envisioned annexing both Sandwich and all the intervening lands into Windsor.[299] The first tangible step was taken just before the end of White's tenure as mayor when, in December of 1890, the town council resolved to make an application for incorporation. Growth over the past seven years had not been rapid, and if anything had been somewhat sporadic (see Appendix C). Still, the Dominion census of 1891 showed that the town had a population of just over 10,000, and while Windsor remained a modest place, only one third the size of London and a fifth that of Hamilton, it was still large enough to become a city.

Solomon White would not see through the incorporation project. His enthusiasm for political union with the United States was becoming an embarrassment, and at a meeting in Paris, Ontario, he was hissed off the stage while the crowd roared out "God Save the Queen." He would be defeated in 1892 and his successor as mayor, Oscar Fleming, would take a decidedly more cautious approach. A handsome, strong-jawed young lawyer, Fleming came from that long tradition of Scottish leaders who approached problems with due deliberation.[300] The incorporation of Windsor was not even listed among the first three objectives of his administration. Unlike White, he

Oscar Fleming.

saw no reason to seek further annexations since the town already held "ample territory." A far more pressing concern was searching for ways to finance roads and sewers and improve the town's drinking water. While Cameron and Curry had made a fortune laying out lots and building houses, they had not had to shoulder the cost of the roads and services these new residences needed. By January 1892, Fleming observed that "the debt of the town has assumed tremendous proportions" and that further improvements had to be put on hold.[301]

A meeting to discuss incorporation was called for January 27, 1891, at the militia drill shed. It was sparsely attended, and a Detroit *Free Press* reporter observed that it adjourned "without accomplishing any great good or harm." But the process was well underway, and clerk Lusted wrote to Stratford and St. Thomas, two towns that had recently experienced advancement to city status, to inquire how it had affected their finances.[302] Convinced that there were no financial drawbacks, and after a local plebiscite favoured the move, Fleming and the town council formally authorized Lusted to petition the Ontario legislature in February 1892, for a special act incorporating Windsor as a city. Ironically, Solomon White, the man who had initiated the incorporation but who had been ousted from the mayor's chair by Fleming, was called on to introduce the bill in the provincial assembly.[303]

After the bill was given a third reading on April 5, 1892, Windsor's incorporation would come into effect on May 24th—the same day as Queen Victoria's birthday. This was no coincidence: the date had been selected deliberately to add patriotic weight to the occasion. At All Saints' Church, Canon Hincks gave a sermon on the Queen's birthday in which he extolled

126

the British connection, and in a shot at Solomon White, the Canon made it clear that he "did not take much stock in annexation."[304] Enthusiasm for the Empire and the Queen had taken a firm hold in Windsor, and a huge "Welcome Tower" was erected at the foot of Ouellette Avenue. As the focal point of the celebration, it was:

> A monster tower, the design having been taken from one of the tower peaks of Windsor Castle… A large portrait of Her Majesty hangs from the spire encircled in a wreath of evergreens. The four sides of the tower bear inscriptions such as "God Save The Queen, 1819–1892.[305]

That weekend's events were probably the greatest display of public exuberance until the Freedom Festival several decades later. Toronto's "Royal Grenadier" militia regiment had been invited to take part as had the local 21st Fusiliers and a squadron of cavalry from Kingsville. The militia boys were resplendent in their red coats and infectious in their youthful enthusiasm. The night before the official ceremony, gangs of "Grens" paraded up and down the main street, dragging carts carrying local girls, as fireworks were set off on street corners. On the morning of May 24, 1892, Windsor officially and soberly celebrated its elevation to the status of a city. Services giving thanks were held at All Saints' Church and St. Andrew's. The city was jammed with more than 40,000 visitors as tourists from Michigan and Ohio sailed over to see the show. At the parade and trooping of the colours, the massed militia regiments were the centre of attention and were then followed by the fraternal organizations, the Sons of England, the St. George's Society and the Orange Lodge. As the day wore on, there were races and football games. More prominent members of society adjourned to the British American Hotel where a formal dinner was served that evening.

Ironically, the great celebration of May 24th, no matter how wholesome, was an indication of the social unease that was to mark the coming decades. The tenor of the proceedings had been wholly British and Protestant. The emphasis had been placed on the royal connection and the enduring ties of loyalty to the Crown. There was little place made at the incorporation parade for blacks, or for that matter, Irish, French or American residents. Significant elements of the community existed at its periphery, and the coming years would reveal the difficulty in reconciling their allegiance to each other and to their new city.

Baseball, about 1900, at what would become the intersection of Wyandotte Street and Drouillard Road.

128

Chapter Eight
Victorian Windsor: 1893–1900

ELEVATION TO THE STATUS of a city did nothing to alleviate the rifts that lurked beneath the surface of Windsor society. Even if French-Catholics were a strong presence in the northern part of Essex County, the municipal directories of the early 1890s record a city that was largely Anglo-Saxon and over two-thirds Protestant. Windsor was therefore susceptible to the strong forces of anti-Catholicism that were sweeping across North America. In the American Midwest, the American Protective Association was virulently anti-Catholic, and one of its journals, the *Patriotic American*, was widely circulated in Michigan and Ontario. It is not surprising that the movement spread across the Detroit River and that the first Ontario branch of the "Protestant Protective Association" was formed in Windsor late in 1891. The secretive P.P.A. required its members to swear that they would never hire, buy from, or vote for, a Catholic; each member took a solemn oath that they "denounce the Pope... his priests and emissaries and the diabolical work of the Roman Catholic Church."[306] Oscar E. Fleming, the first mayor of the City of Windsor and a prominent member of the legal establishment, was an early and avid member of the P.P.A.

This organization was well-represented in commercial and political circles and sought to isolate Catholic businesses and remove Catholics from public offices. The raw nerves of religious bigotry were first exposed by the most visible Catholic institution in the city, Hôtel-Dieu Hospital. In 1890, the hospital had requested and received a remission of its water rates as a charitable organization. The following year a further petition, signed by some of the area's most prominent Protestants, including H.B. Walker, Dr. Coventry and Canon Hincks of All Saints', again sought remission. No sooner had this motion been passed by Council than rumours spread that this exemption was part of a Catholic cabal to swindle honest Protestants. Even though the remission motion had been presented by a Presbyterian, Robert Sutherland, he was dismissed as a pliant tool of the priests and a "poor Protestant." The grant would be raised in the municipal election of 1892 and used as a tool by Fleming to rally Protestant support and defeat Sutherland in the mayor's contest. Hôtel-Dieu again became the focus of religious controversy when Essex County's venerable lion, Colonel Arthur Rankin, died there in March 1893. Shortly before his death, the Colonel converted to Catholicism, a conversion the ardently anti-Catholic newspaper the *Quill* attributed to coercion from Father Wagner and the nuns. The Colonel's son, George Rankin, published a rebuttal and pointed out that Rankin had been raised at a Catholic school, that he had always associated with Catholics, and that he had been partial to that faith. George Rankin considered these ugly rumours to be a manifestation of the "abnormal spirit of religious prosecution"[307] which had recently come to blemish Windsor's public life.

Blemish or not, Mayor Oscar Fleming presented himself to the public as the champion of a threatened Protestantism. One of his first acts as mayor in January 1892, was to propose Major Guillot of the militia as Chief of Police. The *Weekly Record* thought that the appointment of Guillot, a man who was known to look down on Catholics, had revealed "Mayor Fleming and the aldermen who owe their election to the anti-Catholic organization called the Patriotic Sons of America, are only carrying out the pre-election programs arranged for them."[308] Another patron of the P.P.A. was the former mayor of Sandwich, G.W. Mason. He publicly condemned the Catholic Men's Benevolent Association (a mutual insurance society) as a malevolent force who "meet at night with guns and swords and ... go to church with guns." One individual thought that this torrent of bigotry had gone far enough. Archibald McNee, an elder in the Baptist Church and the editor of the local newspaper the *Evening Record*, abhorred the P.P.A. and advocated religious toleration. He pointed out that Windsor employed 43 persons in 1893 and only four of them (three being policemen) were Catholics. For a community in which a third of the residents were Catholic, that religious group was already vastly underrepresented in the public service.

The *Evening Record* recounted a confrontation in Sandwich between Mason and the current mayor, François Girardot, in which the latter tore into the P.P.A. as a bigoted group of malcontents. The C.M.B.A. provided insurance to its members: it had no guns or swords and it did not conduct drills. Girardot confronted Mason with the fact that for decades he had lived peacefully among Catholics and done business with them and asked, "Could you state a single instance where the Catholics have used their religion to damage their Protestant fellow-citizens?"[309] The general public responded and in the civic elections in January 1894, all P.P.A. candidates, save one, were defeated. The Stratford *Beacon* saluted this result and noted that while Windsor may have been the first Ontario outpost of this intolerant group, it now deserved "much credit for the uprooting of this pernicious organization."[310]

Prejudice of a different sort affected Windsor's black citizens. McDougall Street, the focus of black life, had become a compact, self-reliant community, with the Walker House Hotel at the corner of Robinson Street and the nearby Frontier Club and the B.M.E. Church practically next to each other. "McDougall Street [is] a street unique in Canada," one impressive observed, "It is a thoroughfare closely settled on each side for more than a mile by negroes." While McDougall Street was a haven to its residents, it was also a measure of the prevailing racial intolerance, for blacks were limited to this neighbourhood and their prospects of moving to other parts of the city were non-existent. Moreover, for any black youngster it was apparent that advancement to a position beyond that of labourer was largely out of reach. The guarded welcome extended to blacks during the Civil War years had ended, and "Earlier postures of acceptance shown by whites could now turn to gestures of rejection." The pseudo-science of racial superiority in the 1890s resulted in blacks in Canada "sliding down an inclined plane from mere neglect to active dislike."[311] The school system remained the principal source of friction between the black and white communities.

Barely five years after Windsor's schools had been integrated, a dispute arose out of the realignment of boundaries. In 1896, several predominantly white neighbourhoods were ordered to send their children to the mostly black Mercer Street School. A number of parents objected, and a girl was quoted as refusing to "go to school with those horrid colored people." The Detroit *Free Press* reported this racial unrest, and that even H.T. Ellis, the Chairman of the Board of Education, refused to send his child to the Mercer School. Ellis denied the accusation. Still, the schools remained the focal point of white attempts to isolate their black neighbours. In 1898, the principal of the Mercer School reported that several parents were transferring their children and she asked the Board to "help her overcome the prejudice against her school." The transfers were denied and "the vagrant sheep must be brought home to the Mercer-st. fold."[312] Essex County experienced even more in the way of racial tensions in the schools. In Harrow, the small student population did not warrant separate schools for blacks and whites. Miss Patterson, the school teacher, was ordered in 1894 to keep the races separate in her classroom. She refused, and was promptly fired.[313]

131

Mercer St. School.

Tainted Water

In addition to this racial discord, in the winter of 1891 diphtheria ripped through the town. In the first week there were four deaths, and green placards were posted on infected houses along Aylmer Street to warn of the presence of the disease. "Imperfect sewerage is claimed to be the cause of it all," a newspaper claimed. The following year was even worse, and the Medical Health Officer reported that in 1892 there were 90 cases of diphtheria and 19 deaths, while four persons died of scarlet fever.[314] For the past several years, Dr. John Coventry had taken the lead in warning that the quality of Windsor's water had become literally a life and death issue. He argued that the location of Windsor's water inlet downstream of Walkerville's sewage discharge meant that the water was bound to be tainted. Finally, in 1893, a by-law was put forward to finance the building of a new intake some distance away from Walkerville. The proposal met the determined opposition of the *Evening Record*, which considered the expenditure completely unnecessary and that all this nonsense about "bacteria" was wildly overblown.[315] The by-law was defeated. The following year eight citizens died of water-borne cholera.[316]

In lieu of real action, the city brought a lawsuit against Walkerville, alleging that it was the source of tainted water. When the case was called in September of 1893, the judge strongly suggested that the parties compromise, and an agreement was struck and embodied in a court order that a joint water intake to cost not less than $55,000 be constructed near Askin's Point upstream of Walkerville's sewers. Walkerville would bear a tenth of the cost and Windsor the rest. In light of Windsor ratepayers' unwillingness to bear any further increases, the order was never complied with.

The failure to deal with the water problem came to a dramatic head in February 1896. Hiram Walker's massive stockyards at Walker and Tecumseh Roads needed a large reservoir to contain the waste of the thousands of animals that passed through the yards. In February of that year, the reservoir was breached and a huge river of raw sewage surged down Walker Road and inexorably flowed into the Detroit River. The smell must have been terrific as Walkerville was all but inundated by this flood of liquid manure. Even worse, the foul mess surged into Windsor's intake close to the shore and, for a period before the valves could be closed, pure sewage flowed through Windsor's water system. Sickness inevitably followed, and over 200 cases of typhoid fever were reported. Miraculously, there were no deaths. But news of this horrific event reached Toronto and the Provincial Board of Health intervened. The Mayor and Medical Officer were summoned to Toronto by the Board's Dr. Bryce, who reminded them of the 1893 court order. Yet even after Bryce's letter ordering the city to take action was read to the Council, the members refused to comply. They felt that the problem was solved, as they had built another intake a bit farther into the river.[317] In 1897, Coventry convinced the water board to buy an advanced filtration system. It had already been demonstrated that filtration could reduce death rates from typhoid by as much as 80%. But Windsor's leadership would have none of it, and the following year they repudiated the contract.[318] It would not be until the next century that Coventry's warnings were finally given weight.

PANIC OF 1893

The threat of disease and discrimination were far from the only problems confronting the citizens of the new city. The "Panic of 1893" triggered an economic downturn in American business that left 25,000 Detroit workers, a third of the total force, unemployed. Mayor Hazen Pingree opened up public land for home gardens and "Pingree's Potato Patches" provided food for many families who would have otherwise gone hungry. Inevitably, the acute economic stress rippled through Canada. As money tightened and businesses went bankrupt, one reaction to the crisis was a rise in protectionist sentiment. The McKinley tariff of 1890 raised the duty on imports to the U.S., and America's trading partners bore the brunt. The Dingley Act of 1897 would raise tariffs to 52%, the highest in American history. One 1894 congressional proposal to prohibit persons from crossing the border to work in the U.S. was noted by the Detroit *News-Tribune* as "obviously aimed at Windsor. Nominally, it affects the entire border, but Windsor is really the point of attack." In 1896, Detroit congressman John Corliss proposed a bill to prohibit Canadians from working in the U.S. In a heated response, the *Evening Record* listed the many businesses in Essex County which were owned by Americans, and whose staff travelled back and forth across the border. The newspaper described the complicated interaction along the border, where an American might have a family in Canada but work in the U.S. Tradesmen worked in a Detroit factory one week and in a Windsor one the next, and "so it goes, through an endless maze of employment and relationship." [319]

The Panic of 1893 had shown Windsor's dependence on Detroit's economy. As the *Evening Record* reported late in 1893, "The monetary panic among our neighbours early in the year had more effect on Windsor's progress than any place in Canada owing to the close business relations between Windsor and Detroit." [320] When business fell off, so did the number of trains running through Windsor. The Grand Trunk Railway, one of the city's major employers, cut workers' hours as well as their pay. The downturn would also have an impact on the real estate trade. Working men could not afford huge down payments and could often only afford to buy a house in installments. By 1894, when work was scarce, even this was getting difficult, and the *Evening Record* felt that "until the industrial classes recuperate from the past dull times, not so much property will change hands." In order to provide some employment, Hiram Walker hired men during the winter of 1894 to clear brush. Over one hundred men, all of them Detroiters, crossed the river to work at Paquette's Bush in what was essentially a make-work project. As the *Evening Record* described it, "No howl went up from any Canadian journal" over Americans coming over to Canada in hard times in search of work. [321]

BICYCLE MANIA

One way out of the depression was to encourage innovative new industries that would attract capital and encourage employment. The answer came from an industry that had been around for decades, but in the 1890s emerged as popular leisure activity that for many became a daily necessity. The invention of the chain drive for bicycles in the late 1870s transferred power from the pedals to the rear wheel and made them safer and easier to ride. As Toronto *Evening News* observed, "The ranks of the cyclists increase daily; the enthusiasts grow more enthusiastic... and the Bicyclist Owns the Town." Starting in 1892, Windsor streets featured an annual bicycle race where young men would try to outdo each other to find the fastest machine and the cleverest tactics to speed about the city's streets. The "Windsor Wheelmen" represented the city at meets, including the Belle Isle Road race of 1893, where the finest athletes in the U.S. were on display. Beyond the road races, bicycles offered ordinary people a mobility they had never possessed before. Now they were able to move beyond the limitations of the streetcar or train and venture modest distances on their own. Some bicyclists abused this new freedom and became "scorchers" who raced along the roads and sidewalks, heedlessly endangering pedestrians. However, for most riders, the bicycle represented a "new freedom, a great multiplication of power for men, and especially for women..."[322]

This was a particularly shocking development for Victorian sensibilities, and many were alarmed by the number of young ladies who had become avid bicyclists. Women of the late 19th century were usually encouraged to refrain from engaging in physical activity and were encouraged to keep themselves sheathed inside the confines of corsets which accentuated the female bosom and buttocks. Such clothing discouraged even modest exercise and constricted the activity of most women. In the bicycle, the "New Woman" found a way to exert and exercise herself, and as more and more women took to the streets, the *Evening Record* asked the question that was on the minds of all right-thinking men: "Is cycling for women immodest?" It concluded that only certain kinds of female sportswear, such as "bloomers which reach to the ankle," were acceptable. However, they strongly disapproved of any woman who:

> Consents to ride through the streets with the contour of a portion of her limbs on exhibition to the passing throng, which very often contains vile and lecherous men whose glance is an insult to a pure-minded, modest woman.[323]

The writer was not opposed to physical exercise, for Canada's women had to develop their bodies in order to become good wives and mothers, but any display of "the female nether limbs" should be suppressed.

In Windsor, the craze expanded from racing to include the manufacture of bicycles. Due to its location adjacent to Detroit, Windsor had access to a growing array of industrial enterprises and machinists who were turning out the most advanced products. Fred S. Evans of Windsor took advantage of this, and as secretary-treasurer of the Dominion (after 1894, the Canadian) Typograph Company produced not only equipment for setting type, but in time, bicycles. An apprentice at the plant recalled how an ad in the Detroit *News* for "an assembly man, a floor man" had resulted in the appearance of two red-haired applicants. The superintendent had explained that only one man was needed. The two men, Horace and John Dodge, explained "We're brothers and we always work together; if you haven't got room for two of us, neither of us will start. That's that!"[324] Both were hired. Fred Evans was an inveterate tinkerer who was always attempting to develop a better product. He provided a factory in the Medbury Block on Sandwich west of Ouellette where the Dodges had access to the latest precision instruments. This enabled them to develop and patent an improved bicycle bearing in 1895. By that time, they had entered into a partnership with Evans, and the "Evans & Dodge Bicycle" became a Canadian classic.[325]

Even though they continued to live in Detroit and commute to Windsor, the Dodge brothers became local fixtures. They liked to drink in taverns on both sides of the river, and Horace became a star rider for the Windsor Wheelmen, earning a respectable finish at the great Belle Isle race of 1893. It is a measure of the fluidity of the border that in July 1896, Horace married Anna Thompson during his lunch break at the Windsor plant and set up a

THE E. & D. BICYCLE

Is the Only 80 Gear **ROADSTER** Absolutely Dust Proof.

Cornell University test shows the E. & D. Bicycle chain to have only one-half of the per cent friction running without oil. It is guaranteed to be interchangeable at every point. Runs as easy geared to 80 as others geared at 66. EXAMINE THIS WHEEL BEFORE BUYING ANY OTHER.

Canadian Typograph Co. (Ltd.) **Windsor, Ont.**

An ad for an Evans & Dodge Bicycle in the *Evening Record,* April 16, 1896.

home with her in Detroit. The Dodge brothers would leave Windsor in 1900, but "their nine-year stint in Canada gave them much-needed experience as machinists and as managers"[326] and proved that Windsor plants had facilities which offered precision machining as good as any in the Midwest.

MASTERPIECE ON THE WATERFRONT

While many Windsor businesses were affected by the protectionist storms of the 1890s, one continued to prosper and expand. The public's appetite for whisky remained as strong as ever, and Hiram Walker's distillery continued to record huge profits. A federal regulation requiring whisky to be matured for at least two years led to the erection of new warehouses, and by 1890 the distillery had storage capacity for five million gallons.[327] Walker's product was especially popular in gentlemen's clubs and was labelled "Club Whisky." When American competitors required the word "Canada" to be inserted on the label to distinguish it from their products, Walker obliged, and in 1889 "Canada" was added to the top of the label. The following year "Canadian" was dropped to the bottom to precede "Club." The new name gave the brand an exotic flair and "Canadian Club" gained even further popularity among American drinkers.

In 1890, the operations were restructured and Hiram Walker & Sons continued as a separate distillery manufacturer distinct from the founder's other ventures. One of these included Walker's substantial real estate holdings that spread south from the river and were controlled by him through the Walkerville Land and Building Company. There was a hierarchical order in the way in which the town was being laid out. The founder himself was not present and resided in his Detroit mansion. His supervisors lived in a series of fine brick duplexes designed by Mason & Rice of Detroit and laid out on Second Street (Devonshire Road) between 1884 and 1890. Distillery employees lived in one-storey clapboard houses that lined both sides of Third Street (Argyle Road).[328] Land speculators took advantage of the existence of the street railway that connected the community to Windsor and Detroit to expand the residential section. Yet, the Walkerville *Mercury* warned on April 19, 1890, that "There are so many real estate rumours about that this, that, and the other property has been purchased by Detroit and other syndicates at fabulous prices, that it would be well perhaps if 'our boys' would wait a little before purchasing their lots."[329] Heedless of these warnings, nine days after the editorial Windsor real estate men Cameron and Curry, and a syndicate of Detroit capitalists, registered Walkerville's first subdivision.

Thanks to the contribution of the Walker firm, the town was able to operate without incurring a yearly debt. At a year-end meeting, Walkerville's aldermen noted how prosperous and well-kept was their town, and one concluded that other places "always looked shabby when compared with their trim and neat little town." It was an attitude that struck a Windsor reporter as cloying "mutual admiration."[330]

As for the company itself, the time had come to build the landmark headquarters for the Walker distillery. Mason & Rice was again hired to design an elegant waterfront building based on the Florentine renaissance structure, the Palazzo Pandolfini. The exterior was a display of terra cotta ornaments and design. The interior, designed by twenty-three year old Albert Kahn, was an eclectic array of Mexican onyx, Egyptian marbles, fine mahogany and Circassian walnut panelling. Born in Germany, Kahn had grown up in modest circumstances in Detroit, and while a teenager became an office boy for Mason & Rice. In 1891, he won a scholarship to study in Europe, and many of the Italian and German motifs he absorbed during his studies would be reflected in the interior of the Hiram Walker office.[331] When the building was dedicated in September 1894, the Walkers put on an elaborate fete with the Chicago Mandolin Orchestra playing in the lobby. Outside, the massed militia regiments and bands gave the ceremony an almost state occasion. A local reporter thought the exterior had no equal, but that the interior "is unlike anything ever seen." The Windsor area had never seen any structure so sophisticated or luxurious, a testament to the Walker family's taste and wealth. It would also be the first of many displays of virtuosity by Albert Kahn.

Hiram Walker main office.

Recovery

Canadian Typograph, initially the producer of intricate printing machines and then a mass producer of bicycles, had emerged as a major employer in the city. In 1896, a reporter from the *Evening Record* toured the plant where he observed eighty skilled hands at work producing some of the most sophisticated machinery of the times. The reporter was escorted by the mechanical superintendent, John Dodge, who explained the assembly process and noted that the leading journal of bicycle manufacturers, "The Referee," had complimented their ball bearing design as being superior to anything else on the market. The reporter gave a vivid description of the back rooms of the plant where the "E & D" bicycles were produced and assembled:

> Here are the four gas brazing furnaces, also a row of iron assembling tables with radial drills… Here is also the plating room, with its array of dinamos, tubs and chemicals necessary for the plating work that is now observed on all bicycles… bicycle frames are subjected to several coats of enamel varnish, after each of which they are placed in large ovens, where a high rate of temperature is kept up.[332]

It was a glimpse of the highly organized production factory which in a few decades would characterize the city. Demand was high for their products, especially the "E & D" bicycles. The City of London police had put in a huge order so that they could "run down the festive scorcher." By 1898, Canadian Typograph employees were working all holidays on sixteen-hour shifts. This relentless pace illustrated the gruelling nature of factory work in the 1890s, as men on these extended shifts had little time or energy left for family or recreation. While the Typograph men worked exhausting hours, the press also noted that the Grand Trunk Railway intended to dismiss scores of older workers and replace them with younger, cheaper staff.[333] Mere existence remained a precarious proposition for those at the bottom of the labouring class.

In response, the 1890s saw the first glimmerings of a union movement. In 1891, the Tailor's Union of Windsor ordered a strike when merchants refused to increase their wages. The withdrawal of services was quietly resolved, but in the coming weeks all those workers who had had the gall to go on strike were fired and replaced.[334] Unions appreciated that they were in a vulnerable position, but they did have the power of numbers. By the late 1890s, the Labor Day parades had become a display of the cohesion among the skilled trade workers, as groups of bricklayers, masons, plumbers and longshoremen exercised their right to parade down Windsor's streets.

It was a measure of Windsor's renewed prosperity that by the late 1890s, there were calls to extend the street lighting system. In order to do this, the city's power plant would have to be expanded. The *Evening Record* proposed that the community place electric power under the direction of commissioners similar to the system that operated the police department and the water system. Windsor already had a unique system of government that delegated to separate boards the responsibility for municipal utilities. Since 1888, Windsor had a Waterworks Commission that was an efficient (but not legally authorized) system of supervising the construction of water mains. It was not regularized until an 1898 provincial statute ratified the previous acts of the waterworks commissioners. When a Woodstock reporter asked city clerk Stephen Lusted to describe the status of Windsor's utilities, he replied that "as to the Municipal ownership of waterworks, lighting plants, etc. I am now as always strongly in favour of that plan, as affording the best and cheapest services, always providing that such works be arranged and controlled by a commission in each instance, and not by the Municipal Council."[335] Windsor was unique in having both its electric power and water provided by municipally run commissions. In much of Ontario, private companies supplied public demands, and while this freed the taxpayer from obligations it could result in unreliable monopolies. The Ontario Natural Gas Company (backed by the Walkers) had discovered a gas field in Gosfield Township, and in 1894 they were granted a ten-year franchise to pipe natural gas into the city. Other utilities such as telephones and street railways remained in private hands, and one of these monopolies, the Detroit-Windsor ferry, had continually been the focus of public dissatisfaction.

By the later 1890s, the economy was recovering and employment was again rising. Commercial sales were better than ever, and while merchants were never completely satisfied, they reported healthy revenues.[336] Some of the recovery was tinged with luck, such as the discovery of an "immense salt block" adjacent to the C.P.R. lands by the riverfront. A mine was immediately sunk and salt exported by the rail line that existed next door. Windsor had not abandoned giving bonuses as a method of encouraging business. However, it was now barred from making grants, so in 1896 a by-law was passed exempting the Windsor Salt Works from taxes for ten years. As the economic recovery gained momentum, more American companies moved at least some of their operations to the border cities. In a comment on an American proposal to halt cross-border trade, the *Evening Record* warned that "more than three-quarters of the business in Essex County is carried on under the auspices of American citizens." Thanks in part to the National Policy (and the easy availability of land), American capitalists held a huge array of branch plants in the border cities. The newspaper listed several of them, from the major firms such as Parke-

Davis pharmaceuticals and Hiram Walker distillery to the Globe Furniture Factory, Penberthy Injector and the Walkerville Malleable Iron Works.[337] There was a substantial American investment in the border area that provided much of the community's employment, and in return fed profits back to Detroit capitalists.

By the 1890s, it was apparent that the Detroit/Windsor area had emerged as a distinct region with its own identity. One of the unintended consequences of the National Policy was the creation of a vast array of American branch plants just across the border from Detroit. The workers at these plants would go back and forth in (as the *Evening Record* called it) an "endless maze of employment and relationships." The Dodge brothers were a good, but far from unique, example of industrial workers and innovators who worked on whichever side of this growing metropolis suited them at the moment. Moreover, the relationship had become cultural as well as economic. Windsor residents were regular attendees of the Detroit theatre scene and on Sundays the Detroit *Free Press* was the newspaper of choice in Windsor. Sports teams from either side of the river regularly challenged each other. The technical existence of an international border was only a slight inconvenience in what was now a region that was neither entirely American nor Canadian.

A Modern World

In March of 1895, the old St. Andrew's Church had been gutted by fire. Barely a year later, a fine new Romanesque structure was dedicated at the corner of Park and Victoria. Not only was the exterior impressive, the interior had the latest "American hot blast system" furnace and both gas and electric lighting. This beautiful and functional structure was a sign of the times. In so many ways, the 1890s was the first modern decade. Electric streetcars brought workers back and forth from residential areas to their factories. This clean, dependable method transported the public without the dirt and smell of horse-drawn carriages. Streets were lighted with electric lamps powered by central stations. The gentlemen who walked those streets read newspapers that carried the latest international events and fashions from Europe. They returned to homes heated and lighted by natural gas. The residents of urban Ontario were becoming accustomed to a system of utilities and services that no one would have dreamed possible only thirty years previously.

Victorians valued progress, and in 1894 John Curry, the successful real estate developer, headed the project to erect a municipal library. He saw to the acquisition of the Lambie Hall, a former (and somewhat dilapidated) Methodist chapel, and supervised its renovation for library purposes. The library opened in December 1894, and in his dedicatory speech Curry noted that a free public library had been added to the collection of "modern conveniences" available to the people of Windsor.[338] Six years later Windsor would be among the first Ontario cities to seek a Carnegie grant to build a permanent facility to replace its first and "very primitive" structure.

It was another measure of modernity that a vibrant sporting scene had become a regular part of city life. For the first time sports scores began to edge out church notices as news items. Lacrosse and football matches were regularly staged in Windsor between neighbouring communities. Windsor footballers had an entry in the "Peninsular Association Football League" and regularly took on Michigan teams. In November 1895, a Windsor football team played the Detroit MAA club in the Thanksgiving Day game and defeated them. A new addition to organized sport was hockey. In 1898, Windsor, a new entry in the Ontario Hockey Association, played Sarnia for the championship. The game was played in Windsor and, despite its enthusiastic fans, Windsor lost 6-5. The *Evening Record* took a gamble and predicted that hockey "will prove a great drawing card in the future."[339]

Far more than baseball or football, the most noteworthy sporting event was the seasonal racing meet at the Windsor Driving Park. In 1884, W.G. Curry of the Essex County bank became the principal promoter of the Windsor Fair Ground and Driving Park Association. Together with his brother John Curry and Alexander Cameron, the investors bought a tract of land and intended to build on it "a first-class driving park and fair ground." The directors shrewdly estimated that they could draw huge numbers of Michiganders, as well as Americans from Ohio and even New York. "Horsemen will visit us from all over this continent," they predicted, "and will do much to make Windsor known." Their plans succeeded to the extent that the Windsor track, located in a bucolic setting on Ouellette Avenue a mile south of the ferry, was an instant success with punters from across the Midwest. At the first meet, held in 1894, the Lieutenant Governor presided over the initial races and complimented the organizers for their interest in horse breeding. He apparently ignored the crowd, which had no interest at all in the breeds but was instead clustered around the betting wickets. The grandstand was filled to overflowing with more than 4,000 persons, most of them Detroiters. Despite the popularity of the races, the practical use for horses had declined to the extent that almost all the crowd arrived at the park by electric streetcar.[340]

On a more elevated level, an evening at the Opera House remained one of the city's finer entertainment options. Construction of an Opera House on Sandwich Street had been started early in 1880, but due to a lack of funding

Belle Archer. Appearing in "A Contented Woman" at the Detroit Lyceum "the most beautiful woman now before the public." Evening Record December 21, 1899.

was delayed by two years before John Davis saw to its completion around 1882. A practical man, Davis used the ground floor for commercial purposes such as Hiram's Grocery, while the upper floor held the gallery theatre, which had a capacity for about 800 patrons. In 1894, the famous Mohawk poet Pauline Johnson performed "The Cry of an Indian Wife" in native costume before a Windsor Opera House audience. Unfortunately, it was difficult for the Opera House to compete with the variety of entertainment available in Detroit. Theatre-goers had a vibrant selection available across the river, and the Whitney and the White Horse Tavern featured shows direct from the New York stage. In 1899, Detroit's Lyceum staged Belle Archer, one of the most beautiful actresses of the day, in the comedy "A Contented Woman." Even more sensational was the 1900 appearance of the international celebrity Lilly Langtry in the play "The Degenerates." Detroit's moral arbiters protested, so the promoters were forced to move the show's venue to the more accommodating Windsor Opera House.[341]

Not everyone was pleased with these modern displays, and some thought that urban life was inherently immoral and that "urban growth posed a serious menace to the future of the [Canadian] nation."[342] Social conservatives felt that life on the land was the only way to live and they had misgivings about the rise of cities such as Windsor. Still, they could rest easy that Essex County as a whole remained overwhelmingly rural. For that matter, the border communities were separated by township lands that in places stretched to the Detroit River. Even though the street railway ran through the townships and connected Windsor to Sandwich, the local farmers had no interest in maintaining the right of way, and urban dwellers were infuriated that they left the tracks to be overcome by weeds and blocked by cattle.[343]

The passions and causes of the 1890s were felt by most residents in varying degrees of intensity. Windsor residents were not immune when gold-fever struck in 1897 and thousands of young men, and a few women, headed to the Yukon. Windsor churches held "Klondike socials," where guests were given picks and shovels and (symbolically) climbed the Chilkoot Pass. More serious individuals joined the "Windsor Yukon Mining Company," a small group of adventurers under G.W. Gauthier who headed out for the gold fields in 1898. Gauthier sent back regular reports to the editor of the *Evening Record* describing the expedition's progress; however, his company made no fabulous discoveries and Gauthier concluded many of his reports with comments on who had abandoned the project and returned to the border towns.[344]

Church Life—"I am a Catholic"

Victorians celebrated their leisure time in ways that were usually restrained and distinctly churchy. The *Evening Record* described a typical winter evening in 1897:

> Last night was a busy one in the city. The rinks were all running at full blast, the ladies of St. Andrews were holding a monthly social, the public library was giving one of its literary evenings, the Knights of Pythias were celebrating their 34th anniversary of the order and special services were going on at the Windsor-ave Methodist church. There was something to suit all tastes.[345]

Among young people, religious meetings remained popular and the "Detroit Union of Christian Endeavor" comprised Protestant youths from both sides of the river. Revival services were often held outside churches during the warmer months, and celebrated religious leaders would be brought into the city to preach for the occasion. Religious feast days, such as the Ascension, were treated as quasi-state occasions and at All Saints' Anglican, the fraternal order of Knights Templar paraded to the church in full uniform. Despite having over 500 members and numbering mayors and magistrates among its flock, St. Andrew's Presbyterian was deeply divided by quarrels in the early 1890s. But thanks to the leadership of Rev. J.C. Tolmie, the congregation regained its direction and unity. Tolmie was also a formidable preacher, and when he preached on the evils of gambling (everything from poker games, horse racing and even the stock exchange were condemned as sinful pleasures) the church was "crowded with people of all denominations, even the aisles being seated with chairs." As one newspaper observed, "Mr. Tolmie has a way of talking right out in meeting," and he once used a sermon to castigate those supposed Christians who set themselves up as the defenders of Protestantism in order to strike at another faith. Despite the presence of a number of his congregation in the P.P.A., Tolmie's sermon was an unabashed attack on the bigotry of that organization. Not everyone was pleased with his plain speaking, and during one "Week of Prayer," Canon Hincks of All Saints' refused to take part in the service as Tolmie "had used slang phrases in the pulpit."[346]

In addition to the mainstream churches, offbeat sects occasionally caught the disapproving eye of the authorities. The "Flying Rollers," an offshoot of an English cult, had a following in Windsor. This sect encouraged its male members to let their hair and beards grow long and follow the "cleansing of the blood" ritual, whereby the church's Messenger was responsible for deflowering the congregation's virgins. "Prince Michael" (a.k.a. Michael Mills) was the Messenger in the Midwest, and he fulfilled his duties with gusto. In 1894, he went a step further and announced that wives were henceforth to be considered common property and rotated among the church's men. When the Windsor leader of the Flying Rollers, Rev. D.L. Mackay, published a tract to this effect, Magistrate Bartlet termed it a "lewd and wicked publication." It was a sad commentary, Bartlet thought, for Mackay to have left such an august body as the Presbyterians in favour of such a questionable sect. He sent Mackay to the Central Prison for four months, where his first punishment would be the sheering off of his luxuriant locks.[347]

Yet, it was among the Roman Catholics that the most bitter dispute was about to emerge. The visit of the Bishop of London, Fergus Patrick McEvay, to administer the sacrament of Confirmation to the children of St. Alphonsus Parish on Sunday, September 17, 1899, was not supposed to be a controversial affair. The youngsters, all in their best, would be addressed by the Bishop while their beaming parents looked on. The lay leaders of the Church, Francis Cleary in English and Senator Charles Casgrain in French, welcomed the Bishop and explained how Windsor's two Catholic schools were run on Church principles, but under the control of the Board of Education. Both men conceded that this was an unusual arrangement, but for years Protestants and Catholics had co-operated and the system worked to their mutual satisfaction. The Bishop would have none of it. He bluntly told them that this was not within the law, and that this "conglomeration of compromises" had to stop. He further reminded them that "in some localities these [Catholic school] rights have been unjustly invaded, as in Manitoba." McEvay, a product of his time, had watched helplessly as the constitutional guarantees that had been given to Manitoba Catholics to have their own schools had been quashed during the 1890s by an aggressive Protestant majority. The previous year he had given a speech about this unjust treatment, and now he warned Windsor's Catholics: "We have enemies enough all around us."[348] He directed them to establish a separate school board, and to give weight to his words he made it clear that any

Catholic who opposed this order would be denied the sacraments; that is, they would be excommunicated.

According to the Amherstburg *Echo,* the Bishop's edict "caused a sensation in the city." The Toronto *Globe* was quick to jump on this as another example of the medieval autocracy of the Catholic leadership, or what it labelled the "arbitrary power" of the Bishop in ordering his people to obey "backed by the terrors of excommunication." There was a good deal of grassroots opposition to McEvay. The townships around Windsor had similar school systems, and Father Semande, the parish priest of Sandwich, called a meeting and tried to explain to his flock why they had to create a separate school board. One parishioner, Remi Janisse, stood up and defied the priest.[349] The existing public school was entirely Catholic except for two children. Catholic prayers were read four times a day and an image of the Blessed Virgin presided over the classroom. To convert this into a separate school made no sense, for it would mean the loss of most of the property tax revenues that supported the school. All Semande could do was to remind Janisse that the bishop had given his order, and that anyone who did not comply would be refused the sacraments.

Those who wished to hold out against the Bishop looked to one man, Dr. Charles Casgrain. Originally from Quebec, the doctor had made his life at the strait and had become the acknowledged head of the French-Canadian community. He had founded Essex County's St. Jean Baptiste Society and had served eighteen years on the school board. In this capacity he had personally supervised the construction of St. Alphonsus school. An active Conservative, he had attended the 1883 convention in which a French-Canadian faction proposed creating a "Catholic League" within the Conservative Party. Casgrain spoke strongly against the idea, arguing that such a league would only foster a religious divide within the party. The proposal was defeated. Sir John A. Macdonald took note, and in gratitude Casgrain was appointed to the Senate in 1886. While he undoubtedly disagreed with McEvay, whose edict challenged much of what he had built up over the years, Casgrain was left in a quandary. When a delegation of leading Catholics attended at his house to discuss the dilemma, he received them cordially, but turned away their request for his leadership. "I am a Catholic" was his simple response. To have opposed McEvay would have meant expulsion from his church and his community; Casgrain knew that his only option was submission. In November 1901, the Windsor Separate School Board was created, and the following month it petitioned the Minister of Education for ownership of St. Alphonsus and St. Francis schools. But the public board was not about to part with its property, and the stage was set for years of acrimonious dispute.

COMMUNITY AT WAR

While the Catholic community may have suffered fissures, a strong sense of imperial identity united the Protestant Anglo-Celtic majority at the strait. Walkerville celebrated Queen Victoria's 60th year on the throne in 1897 with the dedication of a splendid fountain. The town was also large enough and brimming with enough patriotism to sponsor one of the companies of the 21st Fusiliers. Membership in the militia was a mark of distinction, and young men who excelled in sports frequently spent the summer in military training. At parades such as the city incorporation or the Queen's birthday, the 21st Fusiliers were the centre of attention. Yet, unlike their American counterparts who were off seeking glory in the Spanish-American war, it seemed that the young men of Windsor would have to content themselves with the local parade ground. Their only excitement came in July of 1899, when some of the Fusiliers were dispatched to London to help quell a street railway strike. Few would have believed that international events were about to have an impact on this small Victorian city.

When war broke out between Britain and the Boer republics in southern Africa in 1899, a wave of patriotism overcame Windsor. Editorials proclaimed the justice of the British cause and denounced a pro-Boer rally in Detroit as "bloodthirsty fulminations." Sixteen local volunteers from the militia were accepted for service. One of them was Walter White. Nineteen years old and a fine athlete, White loved militia life and invariably turned out on parade

The 21st Battalion receiving colours.

in an impeccable uniform. So impressed were his officers that he became the battalion's colour sergeant. As the "Transvaal Volunteers" pulled out of the Grand Trunk station on October 20th, 1899, to go to war, they were cheered by a huge crowd who waved the Union Jack and sang "God Save the Queen." A few months later, letters from some volunteers gave a picture of a not-so-glorious conflict in which the soldier's lot was mostly unrelenting drudgery. Still, there was time for some relaxation, and Private John Robinson wrote home that "The Windsor boys have got a football and it does not get very much rest." Other Windsor soldiers were at the spearhead of battle. During the initial assault on Paardeberg in February 1900, the Canadian attack was repulsed with heavy losses. One of those killed was Walter White.[350] "What will become of the poor boy's body?" his grieving father asked a reporter.

His loss, and the death of another Windsor soldier, Hospital Sergeant Harry Barr, of enteric fever in April 1900, did not diminish the imperial enthusiasm that existed at least among the British segment (all of the volunteers had Anglo-Celtic names with the exception of Victor Marentette) in the border area. Barely a week after Walter White's death came the news of a great British victory: the relief of Ladysmith. A massive public celebration was held to mark the triumph and an effigy of the Boer leader Paul Kruger was paraded through Windsor's streets and then torn apart. A year after the original contingent had left Windsor, returning troops were met at the G.T.R. station by a welcoming crowd that formed a line of torches to honour the veterans. In 1906, a memorial designed by the great monumental sculptor Walter Allward to those who had been lost in South Africa was dedicated outside the post office on Pitt Street.

CENTURY'S END

In March 1899, John Coventry, who had headed a decade-long crusade to improve Windsor's drinking water and who had often incurred the ridicule of the local press, was again appointed Medical Health Officer. City Clerk Stephen Lusted in an uncharacteristically effusive letter welcomed his re-appointment as evidence that "public interests of the most important character have been removed from serious jeopardy and peace restored to a much-disturbed and too long suffering community."[351] In October 1897, at Coventry's insistence and also due to a threat by underwriters to downgrade the city's borrowing and insurance rating, Windsor's water intake had been moved farther out into the river beyond shore contamination. Costing $40,000, this work had been undertaken grudgingly by the administration of Mayor John Davis to preserve the city's credit. Davis had been acclaimed as mayor a remarkable three times and elected twice. He was known as a pragmatic businessman (the largest single taxpayer in the community) who dedicated himself and Council to reduce expenditures and ensure the city's solvency. While he resisted Coventry's earlier plans for a water filtration system, he was compelled to approve the intake extension. It would take until the 20th century for effective water treatment facilities such as filtration and chlorination to be installed.

At the turn of the century, Windsor remained a modest city of 11,000. Even with the aid of the National Policy, its growth had not been spectacular. Shops opened, employed a few men for a time, and then either folded or moved elsewhere. The first decade after incorporation as a city was something of a disappointment for the "over-expansion of the railways and rampant land speculation of the 1880s had fuelled a boom whose expectations could not be maintained."[352] Windsor would inevitably share the fate of its larger neighbour Detroit. Between the Civil War and 1900, Detroit's growth had also been unspectacular. In the railway age, location along the water route became less consequential, and as "The initial main rail lines ran well south of Detroit and brought profits to cities such as Chicago and Cleveland located on the East-West axis," Detroit and Windsor were being by-passed.[353] There were other factors working against expansion.

In late 1899, a chill went through the business community when it was learned that Fred Evans and his bicycle plant were going to leave Windsor. The E & D Bicycle Company had been amalgamated with several others to form the National Cycle and Automobile Company in 1899. This American-based firm was shortly thereafter bought out by Canadian Cycle & Motor (CCM) and all future production would be centred in Toronto. "Already Toronto is claiming the consolidated concern," the *Evening Record* reported, and Windsor would lose up to 100 jobs.[354] Windsor simply could not compete with the larger centres which were attracting new capital and jobs. The newspaper lamented the loss of the bicycle and typograph industries, and that their departure "leaves an aching void that would be hard to fill." It seemed at the time an irreplaceable loss, and that Windsor would be condemned to be a city featuring a series of low-paying, transient concerns. At Mayor John Davis's annual dinner in 1900, one alderman shrugged in resignation that Windsor "will never be more than a residence city." It was becoming apparent that factories were choosing to locate in central cities such as Hamilton and Brantford, and the *Evening Record* commented that "Windsor for some time has been almost at a standstill, and there has even been some talk of the city losing some of the industries she already possesses."[355]

Windsor ended the century on a note of economic uncertainty. Yet, while the city and its fellow border communities were hard to distinguish from similar

Ontario municipalities, they nurtured the potential for a unique urban centre. The border towns still had a viable industrial presence along Walker Road. Even the factories that had departed, such as Canadian Typograph, had left behind them scores of highly trained mechanics. Supplementing them were hundreds more skilled tradesmen in Detroit who could easily cross the border to man new industries. Windsor had emerged as a transnational region with a keen international workforce and significant potential for industrial growth. Part American, part Canadian, and having an ethnic and racial mixture different from the rest of the province, it carried the seeds of a dynamic new technology that would fan an unprecedented industrial flame. No one could have imagined that this small, struggling community, hardly more than a town, would within half a century emerge as one of Canada's major cities and the fourth-largest centre of industrial production in the nation.

Appendix A

**POPULATION GROWTH IN WINDSOR
AND COMPARABLE MUNICIPALITIES**

Year	Windsor	Sandwich	London	Toronto	Hamilton
1851	c. 300	c.450	7,035	30,775	14,112
1861	2,501	988	11,555	44,821	19,096
1871	4,253	1,160	18,000	59,000	26,880
1881	6,561	1,143	27,876	96,196	36,661

SOURCE: Robert Cancian, Karol F. Dycha, Larry L. Kulisek, and Trevor Price, <u>Windsor: A Statistical Package</u> (Windsor: Essex County Historical Society, 1983)

Appendix B

RACIAL AND RELIGIOUS COMPOSITION OF WINDSOR, 1864

Ward	Population	Black	Catholic	U.S. Born	Windsor/ Sandwich Born
1	884	132	234	353	92
2	1,452	430	278	517	211
3	243	8	139	24	111
Total	2,579	570	651	894	414
Percentage		22%	25%	35%	16%

SOURCE: Windsor Public Library, Windsor census of 1864

Appendix C

POPULATION AND ASSESSMENT OF WINDSOR: 1886-1892

Year	Population	Assessed value of land
1886	9,331	$2,356,720
1887	9,608	$2,462,575
1888	8,602	$2,684,450
1889	10,038	$4,221,970
1890	10,528	$4,878,493
1891	10,416	$5,023,766
1892	10,929	$5,187,821

SOURCE: Windsor Municipal Archives, RG 2 B II/4 City Clerk Letterbook

Appendix D: Maps

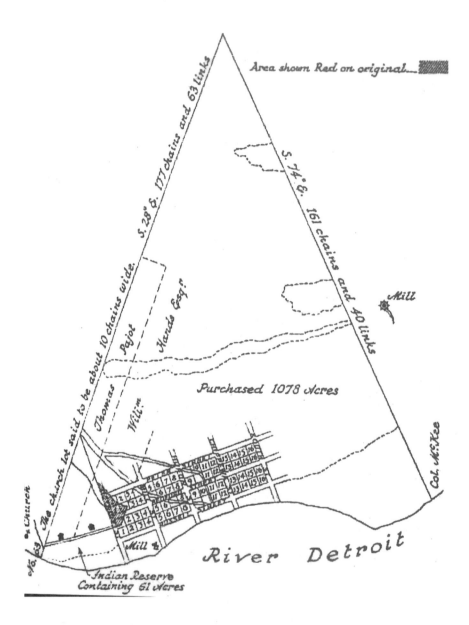

Plan for the Town of Sandwich, prepared by A. Iredell, July 12, 1797, with the base of the triangle along the Detroit River constituting the front of the town. Map courtesy of the Windsor Community Museum.

154

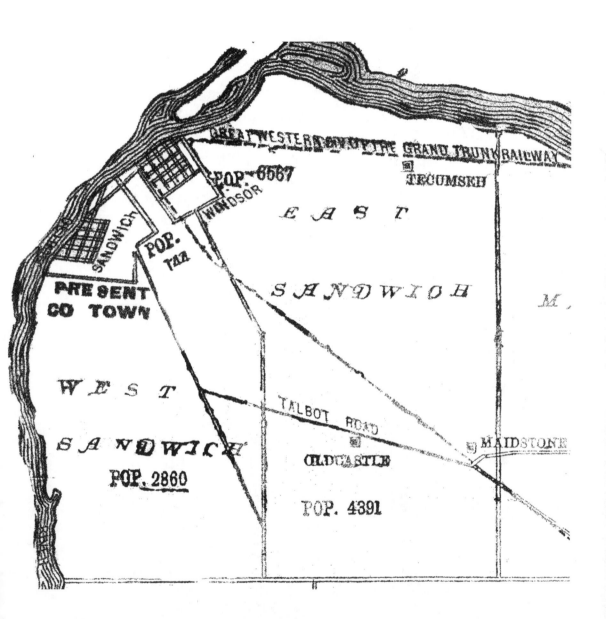

The towns of Sandwich and Windsor, divided by county lands. Map originally appeared in the *Amherstburg Echo*, December 12, 1884.

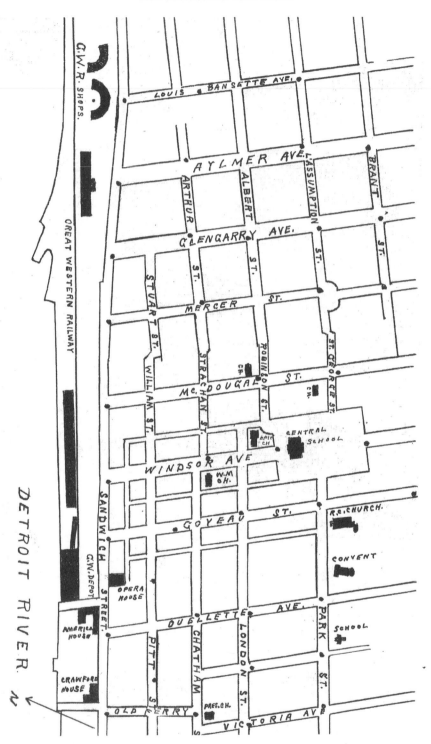

Town of Windsor, Charles E. Goad, July 1876. Map courtesy of the Windsor Community Museum.

Selected Bibliography

Manuscript Sources

Windsor Municipal Archives:

Record Group 2, AIV—By-laws and Minutes of the town council of Windsor

Record Group 2, B—Letter book of the Windsor town clerk

University of Windsor Archives: Alexander Bartlet diaries

Canadian Transportation Commission Archives: Decisions of the Railway Transportation Committee

Ontario Archives: Buell papers; Alvin D. McCurdy fonds

National Archives of Canada: Sir John A. Macdonald papers

Published Sources

Cancian, Robert, Karol Dycha, Larry Kulisek, Trevor Price, Windsor: A Statistical Package (Windsor, 1983)

Chauvin, Francis X., Hiram Walker, His Life and His Work and the Development of the Walker Institutions in Walkerville, Ontario (1927)

Douglas, R. Alan, Uppermost Canada: The Western District and the Detroit Frontier 1800-1850 (Detroit: Wayne State University Press, 2001)

_____, John Prince 1796-1870: A Collection of Documents (Toronto: The Champlain Society, 1980)

Hoskins, Ronald G., "Hiram Walker and the Origins and Development of Walkerville, Ontario" Ontario History 64 (September 1972) 122-31

_____, A Historical Survey of the Town of Walkerville... (University of Windsor, Master of Arts thesis, 1964)

Lajeunesse, Ernest J., The Windsor Border Region (Toronto: The Champlain Society, 1960)

Philip Mason, The Ambassador Bridge: A Monument to Progress (Detroit: Wayne State University Press, 1987)

Morrison, Neil F., Garden Gateway to Canada (Toronto: Ryerson Press, 1954)

Power, Michael and Daniel J. Brock et. al., Gather Up the Fragments: A History of the Diocese of London (London: Diocese of London, 2008)

Pryke, K.G. and L.L. Kulisek eds. The Western District: Papers from the Western District Conference (Windsor: 1983)

Endnotes

ENDNOTE TO INTRODUCTION

1 Louis Hennepin, <u>A New Discovery of a Vast Country in America...</u> (London: M. Bentley, 1698) as quoted in Philip P. Mason, <u>The Ambassador Bridge: A Monument to Progress</u> (Detroit: Wayne State University Press, 1987) 23

ENDNOTES TO CHAPTER ONE

2 The account of the naming of Windsor is taken from reports from local historian George F. Macdonald, in Windsor <u>Daily Star</u>, Thomas Brophey, "One Hundred Years of Progress Is observed..." September 5, 1936; and Sandwich <u>Canadian Emigrant</u> September 13, 1836

3 R. Alan Douglas, <u>Uppermost Canada: The Western District and the Detroit Frontier, 1800-1850</u> (Detroit: Wayne State University Press, 2001) 267, fn. 54: the Douglas book is the pre-eminent account of the early British settlement at the strait.

4 E.A. Theller, <u>Canada in 1837-38</u>, (Philadelphia, 1841) vol. 1, 114, as quoted in Frederick H. Armstrong, "James Dougall and the Founding of Windsor, Ontario" <u>Ontario History</u>, 76, No. 1 (March, 1984) 52; the Armstrong article is the source for the preceding information concerning the Dougall family; on the Scots see T.M. Devine, <u>To the Ends of the Earth: Scotland's Global Diaspora, 1750-2010</u>, (Washington: Smithsonian Books, 2011)

5 Richard Weyhing, "Gascon Exaggerations" The Rise of Antoine Laumet dit de Lamothe, Sieur de Cadillac, the Foundation of Colonial Detroit, and the origins of the Fox Wars" in Robert Engelbert and Guillaume Teasdale, <u>French and Indians: In the Heart of North America, 1630-1815</u> (East Lansing: Michigan State University, 2013) 77-112

6 The finest work on the origins of the French settlement remains Ernest J. Lajeunesse's <u>The Windsor Border Region: Canada's Southernmost Frontier</u> (Toronto: Champlain Society and University of Toronto Press, 1960) – on the settlement of the south shore, see lii to lxv

7 Ibid., xcvi-ii

8 Ronald G. Hoskins, "Angus Mackintosh, the Baron of Moy Hall" in K.G. Pryke and L.L. Kulisek, The Western District: Papers From the Western District Conference (Windsor: Essex County Historical Society, Occasional Papers No. 2, 1983) 149

9 See Guillaume Teasdale, The French of Orchard Country: Territory, Landscape and Ethnicity in the Detroit River Region, 1680s-1810 (Toronto: Phd. Thesis, York University, 2010) quote from page 221; a thorough account of the origins of the orchards in the French settlements is given in Chapter 5—"The French of Orchard Country"

10 Hoskins, "Angus Mackintosh" 150; Unfortunately, Moy Hall was demolished in November, 1912

11 Peter Russell to J.G. Simcoe, December 9, 1797, in E.A. Cruikshank and A.F. Hunter eds. The Correspondence of the Honourable Peter Russell vol. II—1797-1798 (Toronto: Ontario Historical Society, 1935) 38; and see Donald Lafrenière and Douglas Rivet, The Forgotten Capital: A Historical Atlas of Sandwich, Ontario (April, 2009)

12 Douglas, Uppermost Canada 9

13 Christopher Headon, "Richard Pollard" vol. VI, Dictionary of Canadian Biography (Toronto: University of Toronto Press, 1987) 599-601

14 John Clarke, "The Role of Political Position and Family and Economic Linkage in Land Speculation in the Western District of Upper Canada, 1788-1815" Canadian Geographer 19, No. 1, (1975) 18-34

15 The early description of Sandwich comes from Douglas, Uppermost Canada Chapter 1 "Connections"; the quote describing Assumption Church from Michael Power and Daniel J. Brock, et al., Gather up the Fragments: A History of the Diocese of London (London: Diocese of London, 2008) 157

16 Douglas, Uppermost Canada 40

17 J. Mackay Hitsman, The Incredible War of 1812: A Military History (Toronto: revised edition by Robin Brass Studio, 1999) updated by Donald E. Graves, 66-7

18 Douglas, Uppermost Canada 87

19 Robert Gourlay, Statistical Account of Upper Canada, vol. 1, (London: Simpkin and Marshall, 1822) 280

20 "Sketches of the Upper Lakes" in Pittsburgh Post-Gazette, May 1, 1819; as quoted in Scott Martelle, Detroit: A Biography (Chicago: Chicago Review Press, 2012) 29

21 John Clarke, "James Baby" vol. VI, Dictionary of Canadian Biography (Toronto: University of Toronto Press, 1987) 21-2

22 John Clarke, "François Baby" in vol. VIII, Dictionary of Canadian Biography (Toronto: University of Toronto Press, 1985) 33-5

23 Dufaux to Hubert, October 9, 1795 in Lajeunesse, The Windsor Border Region 146

24 Frederick H. Armstrong, "The Oligarchy of the Western District of Upper Canada, 1788-1841" Historical Papers/Communications Historiques, 12, No. 1 (1977) 86-102

25 Aileen Dunham, Political Unrest in Upper Canada, 1815—1836 (Toronto: McClelland & Stewart, 1963) "Industrial depression and a redundant population in the British Isles gave force to the movement and Canada acquired value as an asylum for the surplus poor of Great Britain." at 22; on the Family Compact, see Robert E. Saunders, "What Was the Family Compact?" Ontario History 49 (1957) 165

26 Alan Douglas, ed., John Prince, 1796-1870: A Collection of Documents (Toronto: Champlain Society, 1980) lxii

27 Patrick Shirreff, A Tour Through North America (Edinburgh: Oliver & Boyd, 1835) 216 (as quoted in Douglas, Uppermost Canada 137)

28 Sandwich Canadian Emigrant July 20, 1833

29 Ibid., February 21, 1835

30 Willis F. Dunbar, revised by George S. May, Michigan: A History of the Wolverine State (Grand Rapids: William B. Eerdmans, revised ed. 1980) 261-2

31 Douglas, Uppermost Canada 138

32 Ibid., 142

33 Essex County Registry Office, lot 85, First Concession, Plan 106, surveyed September 23, 1835; on the layout of the early streets, see the description in Douglas, Uppermost Canada 140-5

34 Sandwich Canadian Emigrant October 13, 1832

35 Ibid., August 15, 1835

36 Anna Murphy Jameson, Winter Studies and Summer Rambles in Canada, (London: Saunders & Otley, 1838) (Coles reprint, 1972) 315-6

37 Sandwich Canadian Emigrant, August 25, 1836

38 Sandwich Western Herald, November 6, 1838; Detroit comment in Detroit Free Press, December 20, 1838

39 Gerald M. Craig, Upper Canada: The Formative Years, 1784-1841 (Toronto: McClelland & Stewart, 1963) 237

40 Sandwich Canadian Emigrant September 20, 1836

Endnotes To Chapter Two

41 Andrew Bonthius, "The Patriot War of 1837-1838: Locofocoism With a Gun?" Labour/Le Travail 52 (Fall, 2003) 12; the quote is taken from the Huron Commercial Advertiser December 15, 1837; see also, Oscar A. Kinchen, The Rise and Fall of the Patriot Hunters (N.Y., Bookman Associates, 1956) and Edwin C. Guillet, The Lives and Times of the Patriots (Toronto: University of Toronto Press, 1968 reprint)

42 Prince to Hamilton, December 28, 1837, in Douglas, John Prince, 16-7

43 Sandwich Western Herald May 29, 1838

44 Ibid., January 23, 1838

45 Ronald J. Eady, "Anti-American Sentiment in Essex County in the Wake of the Rebellion of 1837" Ontario History 56 (March, 1969) No. 1, 2; attack on the British officers described in the Western Herald May 22, 1838

46 Francis Cleary, "The Battle of Windsor," Essex Historical Society Papers and Addresses, II (1915) account of Friend Palmer, 30

47 This account of the Battle of Windsor is drawn largely from Alan Douglas, "The Battle of Windsor" Ontario History 61 (September, 1969) No. 3, 137-152

48 Cleary, "The Battle of Windsor" account of John D. Sullivan, 15

49 Prince to Colonel Chichester, December 19, 1838, as quoted in Alan Douglas, "Battle of Windsor" 143

50 Douglas, "The Battle of Windsor" 146

51 Arthur to Colborne, December 8, 1838 in Charles R. Sanderson, ed., The Arthur Papers: Being the Papers Mainly Confidential, Private, and Demi-Official of Sir George Arthur (Toronto: University of Toronto Press, 1947) Part II, 429

52 Halifax Times, as quoted in the Sandwich Western Herald February 28, 1839

53 Excerpt from the House of Lords debate, May 27, 1839; as quoted in Alan Douglas, John Prince, 38; and see Normanby to Arthur, June 12, 1839 in Sanderson, The Arthur Papers, Part III, 167

54 Detroit Free Press editorial "Canadian Affairs" December 6, 1838; and see Detroit Morning Post December 4, 1838 as quoted in the Western Herald December 20, 1838

55 Sandwich <u>Western Herald</u> "Agriculture" June 13, 1839

56 Cleary, "The Battle for Windsor" account of Victor Ouellette, 33; the phrase "Scottish reflection" is attributable to Alan Douglas

57 Armstrong, "James Dougall..." at 54; comments of a Sandwich resident, see Sandwich <u>Western Herald</u>, May 16, 1839 "The 'Town' of Sandwich"

58 Douglas, <u>Uppermost Canada</u>, 144

59 Pierre Hector Morin to LaFontaine, November 15, 1844; in Douglas, <u>John Prince</u>, 67

60 Douglas, <u>Uppermost Canada</u>, 190

61 Robin Winks, <u>The Blacks in Canada: A History</u>, (Montreal & Kingston: McGill-Queen's University Press, 1997, 2nd ed.) 145; on Elliott's "lashing ring" see above, 51; on the "refuse of the States" comment, see the grand jury address of Charles Eliot in 1832, in Sandwich <u>Canadian Emigrant</u> January 19, 1832

62 Sandwich <u>Western Herald</u> "Temperance Meeting" January 16, 1840; on the growth of temperance in Upper Canada see Craig, <u>Upper Canada</u>, 208

63 Armstrong, "James Dougall" 55; on the 1849 fire, see Windsor Public Library, Local History Collection, book 3c

64 Clarke, "François Baby" 35

Endnotes To Chapter Three

65 Sandwich <u>Canadian Emigrant</u> August 16, 1836

66 See the discussion of the impact of the end of the Corn Laws on the development of the Great Western Railway in Russell D. Smith, "The Early Years of the Great Western Railway" <u>Ontario History</u>, 60 (Dec., 1968) 207

67 John McCallum, "Urban and Commercial Development until 1850"—"By the middle of the nineteenth century Western Ontario had become one vast granary and London one of its principal market towns." As reprinted in R. Douglas Francis and Donald B. Smith, <u>Readings in Canadian History: Pre-Confederation</u> (5th ed.) (Toronto: Harcourt Brace, 1998) 349

68 as quoted in Neil Morrison, <u>Garden Gateway</u> 31

69 Donald R. Beer, <u>Sir Allan Napier MacNab</u> (Hamilton: Dictionary of Hamilton Biography, 1984) 210

70 As quoted in Smith, "The Early Years..." 211

71 Armstrong, "James Dougall and the Founding..." 56

72 Ronald G. Hoskins, <u>CN Riverfront Lands A Historical Survey, 1749-1955</u> (Windsor: September, 1989) 28; on Daniel Goyeau's sale, see Essex County Registry Office, lot 83, Concession 1, instrument No. 226 registered August 20, 1851

73 Accounts of the arrival of the Great Western in Windsor: see Alan Douglas, <u>John Prince</u>... 129

74 See comments in Morrison, <u>Garden Gateway</u> on the rush to use the Great Western in 1855, at 33

75 See the provincial inquiry into the disaster; Province of Canada, <u>Journal of the Legislative Assembly</u>, XIII Session, 1854-55. Appendix YY; on the Norwegians, see Joan Magee, <u>A Scandinavian Heritage</u> (Toronto: Dundurn Local History Series 3, 1985) 17—25; the Windsor Community Museum currently has on loan a watch given by the railway to Margret McEwan for her efforts to assist the dying. It is engraved, "...for her Christian Charity to the German Emigrants..." July, 1854

76 Amherstburg <u>Echo</u> December 11, 1891

77 <u>Detroit Daily Advertiser</u> June 10, 1854; as quoted in Morrison, <u>Garden Gateway</u>, 40-1

78 Essex County Registry Office, Plan 91, being part of lot 82, First Concession, registered on December 20, 1853

79 Windsor <u>Herald</u> October 24, 1856 "Talbot and Windsor Gravel Road"; on S.S. Macdonell see, Windsor Library, local scrapbooks, vol. 4 "Col. S.S. Macdonnell Windsor's First Mayor" 4; <u>The Canadian Biographical Dictionary and Portrait Gallery of Eminent and Self-Made Men</u>, Ontario Volume, 1880; on the by-law, see Windsor Municipal Archives, R.G. 2A, Council Records and By-laws, Village of Windsor, By-law 26 IV, "A By Law to Permit the Talbot and Windsor Road Company to Build a Road" passed July 9, 1855

80 Robert Cancian, Karol Dycha, Larry Kulisek, Trevor Price, <u>Windsor: A Statistical Package</u> (Windsor: 1983) "Population Growth in Windsor and Suburbs: 1851-1981" 8

81 Martin J. Havran, "Windsor—Its First Hundred Years" <u>Ontario History</u>, 45 (1954) No 3, 184

82 Windsor <u>Herald</u> May 26, 1855, "Laying the Corner Stone of the Court House and Gaol"; and see, Keith Wagland and Harold Kalman, "Mackenzie Hall: A New use for the Essex County Courthouse" (June, 1981)

83 Power and Brock, <u>Gather up the Fragments</u> 172

84 Windsor <u>Herald</u> July 14, 1855; see also, Windsor Community Museum, PM 75 "Through Ninety Years, 1855-1945" All Saints' Church; on the Congregationalists, see Windsor <u>Herald</u> February 10, 1855

85 Windsor Municipal Archives, R.G. 2A, Council Records, By-laws, By-law No. 10 of the Village of Windsor, passed May 1, 1854

86 Havran, "Windsor—Its First Hundred Years" – "It (town hall) was not merely a building, it was a Council Chamber, police headquarters, opera house and market all in one;" 185

87 Windsor Public Library, local history scrapbook 3(b) 8 "Call for Windsor-Sandwich Amalgamation 82 Years Early"

88 Windsor <u>Herald</u> July 14, 1855; the article refers to the Sandwich <u>Oak</u>, copies of the newspaper are no longer extant

89 Letter E.H. Dewar to the Windsor <u>Herald</u> July 11, 1855; the Windsor Cricket Club "made a very impressive appearance being all dressed alike." These splendid outfits were no match for dexterity and Windsor lost to Chatham, see Windsor <u>Herald</u> August 25, 1855

90 F.P. Gavin, "First Grammar School Established in 1854: Wonderful Advancement Since That Time" <u>Essex County Historical Society Papers and Addresses</u>, vol. 3, 1916, 98; on the private toll roads, see Windsor Municipal Archives, R.G. 2A, Council Records of By-laws, By-law No. 26 IV "By-law to permit the Talbot and Windsor Road Company to build a road"; on the water pump, see Windsor <u>Herald</u> December 26, 1856; on the "Grand Coulee" see the surface map on Registered Plan No. 91 (Essex County Registry Office); and comments on the drain by Dr. R. Carney in "Through Ninety Years" All Saints' Church, 6

91 Much of the early work on the career of Hiram Walker can be found in the biography commissioned by his sons being Francis X. Chauvin, <u>Hiram Walker, His Life and His Work and the Development of the Walker Institutions in Walkerville, Ontario</u> (1927); this was widely used in both of Ronald G. Hoskin's outstanding articles being, "Hiram Walker and the Origins and Development of Walkerville, Ontario" <u>Ontario History</u> 64 (Sept. 1972) 122-31; and "Hiram Walker A Man of Two Countries" <u>Detroit in Perspective: A Journal of Regional History</u> 2 (Winter, 1975) No. 2, 97—110

92 <u>County of Essex Gazeteer and General and Business Directory for 1866-67</u> (Woodstock: Sutherland and Company, 1867) 128; as quoted in Hoskins, "Hiram Walker and the Origins…" 124

93 Douglas, <u>John Prince</u>, diary August 1, 1859, 169

94 John O'Farrell, "Henry Walton Bibb" vol. VIII <u>Dictionary of Canadian Biography</u> (Toronto: University of Toronto Press, 1985) 89-90

95 Sandwich <u>Voice of the Fugitive</u>, January 1, 1851; on the black press and Henry Bibb, see Silverman, <u>Unwelcome Guests</u>, 144-7; Black refugees frequently stayed in Windsor and found work on the Great Western Railway, see Patrick Brode, <u>The Odyssey of John Anderson</u> (Toronto: University of Toronto Press/Osgoode Society, 1989) 13

96 Afua Cooper, "The Search for Mary Bibb, Black Woman Teacher in Nineteenth-Century Canada West" <u>Ontario History</u> 83 (March, 1991) No. 1, 47; on the separate coloured schools, see Jason H. Silverman and Donna J. Gillie, "The Pursuit of Knowledge Under Difficulties": Education and the Fugitive Slave in Canada" <u>Ontario History</u> 74 (June, 1982) No. 2, 95-112

97 Kristin McLaren, "'We had No Desire to Be Set Apart' Forced Segregation of Black Students in Canada West Public Schools and Myths of British Egalitarianism" in Barrington Walker, ed., <u>The History of Immigration and Racism in Canada</u> (Toronto: Canadian Scholars' Press, 2008) 73

98 Silverman, "The Pursuit of Knowledge" 103

99 On Prince's comment, see Douglas, <u>John Prince</u>, 156; on the Sandwich Baptist Church, see Windsor Community Museum, PM 1208, <u>Religious Structures of Architectural and Cultural Diversity</u>

100 John Prince diaries, July 31, 1854; in Douglas, <u>John Prince</u>, 132; Two years later Prince had the satisfaction of defeating Rankin in the election for the legislative council

101 Windsor <u>Herald</u> January 13, 1855

102 Smith, "The Early Years of the Great Western," 222

103 Windsor <u>Herald</u> May 5, 1855

104 <u>Detroit Daily Advertiser</u> September 12, 1854; as quoted in Morrison, <u>Garden Gateway</u> 35-6

ENDNOTES TO CHAPTER FOUR

105 Detroit <u>Free Press</u> September 21, 1860

106 Ian Radforth, <u>Royal Spectacle: The 1860 Visit of the Prince of Wales to Canada and the United States</u> (Toronto: University of Toronto Press, 2004) 314

107 Radforth, <u>Royal Spectacle</u>, 74-5

108 R. Alan Douglas, "John Prince" vol. IX, <u>Dictionary of Canadian Biography</u> (Toronto: University of Toronto Press, 1976) 646

109 As reported in the Detroit <u>Free Press</u> January 8 and 9, 1858, and Toronto <u>Globe</u> "McLeod Elected After all!" January 8, 1858 and "The Essex Election" January 11, 1858

110 Toronto <u>Globe</u> July 11, 1861, "Mr. Rankin Elected!"; and see Donald Swainson, "John O'Connor" vol. XI, <u>Dictionary of Canadian Biography</u> (Toronto: University of Toronto Press, 1982) 649; on Rankin as "a doubtful member" who supported no party—see Hamilton <u>Spectator</u> "The Doubtful Members" July 17, 1861

111 Patrick Brode, "Colonel Rankin's Canadian Lancers in the American Civil War" <u>Detroit in Perspective: A Journal of Regional History</u> 4 (Spring, 1980) 170–7

112 Detroit <u>Free Press</u> reported (and later retracted) that "fortifications were being erected immediately opposite this city (Detroit), and other warlike preparations were being made" see "The Fortifications At Windsor" January 3, 1862; on the Mayor's letter asking for military aid, see—James Dougall to Sir W.F. Williams, December 27, 1861; as quoted in Morrison, <u>Garden Gateway</u>, 52; no copy of that letter appears to currently exist in the collection of the Windsor Community Museum

113 Detroit <u>Advertiser and Tribune</u> editorial, August 17, 1863; on the Skedaddle Guard and real estate in Windsor, see <u>Advertiser and Tribune</u> April 18, 1863

114 <u>Ibid.</u>, July 16, 1864

115 Chauvin, <u>Hiram Walker</u>..., Chapter 10, p. 6; on horses for the federal cavalry see Detroit <u>Advertiser & Tribune</u>, -"quite a considerable traffic is being carried on between the farmers across the river and the army horse contractors" May 21, 1863

116 Detroit <u>Advertiser and Tribune</u>, "Over the River" July 16, 1864

117 J.M.S. Careless, <u>Toronto to 1918: An Illustrated History</u> (Toronto: James Lorimer & Co., 1984) 73

118 Dougall was mayor from 1859 to 1861. Macdonell served from 1864 till 1867 and was followed by Dougall who was mayor again until 1869. A brief interruption to the Scottish hegemony was the two term mayoralty from 1862–1863 of the popular baker and volunteer fireman, Mark Richards.

119 On Kingston, see Alan G. Green, "Immigrants in the City: Kingston as Revealed in the Census Manuscripts of 1871" in Gerald Tulchinsky, <u>To Preserve & Defend: Essays on Kingston in the Nineteenth Century</u> (Montreal and London: McGill-Queen's University Press, 1976) at 318-9

120 Hull News, April 27, 1861; as reported in the Chatham Tri-Weekly Planet May 21, 1861

121 On François Caron, see Windsor Evening Record, D.B. Shepherd, "Magistrates Past and Present" May 23, 1917

122 John P. Comiskey, My Heart's Best Wishes for You: A Biography of Archbishop John Walsh (Kingston: McGill-Queen's University Press, 2012) 17-8; and see, J.E. Robert Choquette, "Pierre-Adolphe Pinsoneault" vol. XI Dictionary of Canadian Biography (Toronto: University of Toronto Press, 1982) 692-5; and see Power and Brock, Gather up the Fragments 17-23: "Bishop Pinsoneault did not know how to govern and could not leave well enough alone." At 17

123 University of Windsor Archives, Alexander Bartlet diaries, July 7, 1864; and see Detroit Advertiser and Tribune "Secesh Pic-Nic At Windsor" July 7, 1864

124 Jennifer L. Weber, Copperheads: The Rise and fall of Lincoln's Opponents in the North (N.Y: Oxford University Press, 2006) 10

125 Detroit Free Press "Mr. Vallandigham at Windsor" August 26, 1863; and see Frank L. Klement, The Limits of Dissent: Clement L. Vallandigham & The Civil War (Lexington: The University Press of Kentucky, 1970)

126 Klement, The Limits of Dissent, 165

127 On John Yates Beall, see Beall and Lucas, Memoir of John Yates Beall, (1865); on Bennet Burleigh, see Roger T. Stearn, "Bennet Gordon Burleigh" Oxford Dictionary of National Biography (Oxford: Oxford University Press, 2006)

128 The *Philo Parsons* Incident was described in the newspapers of the day, but the most complete report can be found in the legal case concerning Burleigh's extradition hearing in Toronto, In The Matter of Bennet G. Burley (January, 1865) vol. 1, N.S., Law Journal 20-2

129 Detroit Free Press September 22, 1864; and Detroit Advertiser & Tribune "The Rebel Pirates" September 22, 1864

130 Alexander Bartlet diaries, September 21, 1864; on S.S. Macdonell's actions, see Windsor Record, as reported in the Toronto Globe September 23, 1864; ultimately, Beall was seized and executed by federal authorities. Burleigh was also apprehended but escaped. After the war he became one of the most famous Victorian journalists and covered the British Empire's wars for the Daily Telegraph.

131 Robin Winks, Canada and the United States, 293-4

132 Detroit Free Press editorial "Public Meeting in Windsor" December 22, 1864

133 Carl Betke, "Gilbert McMicken" vol. XII Dictionary of Canadian Biography (Toronto: University of Toronto Press, 1990) 675-9

134 Detroit <u>Advertiser & Tribune</u> editorial "The Passport Order" January 2, 1865

135 Detroit <u>Advertiser and Tribune</u> "The Canadian Volunteers and the Funeral Pageant" April 21, 1865

136 Detroit <u>Free Press</u> "Coming Back" May 9, 1865

137 Robin Winks, <u>Canada and the United States</u>, 323-6; on the Fenians generally, see David A. Wilson, <u>Thomas D'Arcy McGee: The Extreme Moderate, 1857-1868</u> vol. 2 (Montreal & Kingston: McGill-Queen's University Press, 2011) 221-4

138 <u>Alexander Bartlet diaries</u>, February 1, 1866 and March 10, 1866; on the Chatham Volunteers, see Chatham <u>Weekly Planet</u> "Our Brave Volunteers At the Front" March 15, 1866

139 <u>Alexander Bartlet diaries</u>, March 16 and 17, 1866; on St. Patrick's Day in Toronto see, Wilson, <u>Thomas D'Arcy McGee</u>, 265; on the mass meeting in Detroit, see Chatham <u>Weekly Planet</u> "Fenianism in Detroit" March 15, 1866; on Detroit's reaction to the Fenians, see Detroit <u>Advertiser & Tribune</u> "The Fenian Scare" March 12, 1866

140 On the Fenian assault, see Peter Vronsky, <u>Ridgeway: The American Fenian Invasion and the 1866 Battle that Made Canada</u>, (Toronto: Penguin Books, 2011); on Windsor's reaction, see Detroit <u>Advertiser & Tribune</u> June 2-3, 1866

141 <u>Alexander Bartlet diaries</u>, October 30, 1866

142 Brode, "Arthur Rankin" 885; and see, <u>Confederation Debates</u>, March 10, 1865 (Ottawa: King's printer, 1951) 916

143 The Confederation Day race riot is covered in the Detroit <u>Advertiser and Tribune</u> "Confederation Day At Windsor" July 2, 1867 and <u>Alexander Bartlet diaries</u>, July 1 and 2, 1867

Endnotes To Chapter Five

144 On the 1849 fire, see Detroit <u>Advertiser and Tribune</u> April 16, 1849; on the 1859 fire at the Great Western depot, see Detroit <u>Free Press</u> "Three Destructive Fires" April 26, 1859

145 Detroit <u>Advertiser and Tribune</u> "Fire Department in Windsor" May 6, 1867; on the by-laws enacted to recognize Windsor's vulnerability, see Municipal Archives, R.G. 2 AV-2/3, By-law 105 passed December 3, 1867 "to prevent the erection of wooden buildings;" on the 1867 fire, see <u>Advertiser and Tribune</u> "Disastrous Fire in Windsor" December 2, 1867

146 Detroit <u>Free Press</u> "Where Next? Incendiaries at Work in Windsor" October 13, 1871

147 Donald Cameron to Alexander Bartlet, November 15, 1872, in Windsor <u>Essex Record</u> November 21, 1872

148 Windsor <u>Essex Record</u> "Water Works By-Law Carried" February 8, 1872

149 *An Act Respecting the Water Works in the Town of Windsor* <u>Statutes of Ontario</u> 1874, Chapter 79; on Walkerville and the pipes, see Hiram walker to Water Committee, August 11, 1875, as reported in the <u>Evening Record</u> August 20, 1875

150 Windsor <u>Essex Record</u> "Big Land Purchase" August 21, 1874

151 Windsor <u>Essex Record</u> "The River Ferries" February 20, 1874; on William McGregor's views, see <u>Essex Record</u> "Meeting on Saturday Night" December 19, 1873

152 Ontario Archives, F62-MV307, Buell Papers, Alexander Cameron to A.N. Buell, January 12, 1869

153 Windsor <u>Essex Record</u> December 1, 1871

154 On the Sandwich Mineral Springs, see Frederick Neal, <u>The Town of Sandwich</u> (Sandwich: 1909; reprinted Essex County Historical Association, 1979) 58-61; and see, London <u>Free Press</u> "Sandwich Sulphur" November 3, 1866; Detroit <u>Advertiser & Tribune</u> "The Sandwich Sulphur Springs" July 28, 1868 and "Sulphur Spring" August 4, 1868

155 Windsor <u>Essex Record</u> "Windsor Gas Works" August 30, 1877 and "The Gas Works" May 4, 1877

156 Windsor <u>Essex Record</u> June 6, 1873; Windsor Municipal Archives, R.G. 2 AV-2/6, By-law 202 "Respecting the Sandwich and Windsor Passenger Railway Company…" passed July 1, 1873—opening up London Street as a public highway; and see <u>Essex Record</u> editorial "The Street Railway" February 22, 1872—which blasted the owners of the Sandwich Gravel Road Company who had been actively trying to stop the street railway project; "blocking improvement by the old cant about (so-called) vested rights." On the initial run, see <u>Essex Record</u> "Street Railway" July 24, 1874

157 "A By-law to Establish Fire Companies in the town of Windsor…" as reported in Windsor <u>Essex Record</u> February 18, 1876; on the high regard for firemen, see comments of town alderman Foster, "The boys (volunteer firemen) were very faithful in the discharge of their duties; they were not backward in putting their lives in danger, and they deserved all the encouragement the Council could give them." Windsor <u>Essex Record</u> "Town Council" June 22, 1877

158 Windsor <u>Essex Record</u> "Meeting of Town Council" November 23, 1871

159 David Roussel, The Windsor Justice Facility (Windsor: 1999) 6; on the police reorganization, see Municipal Archives, R.G. 2 AV-2/6 By-law 254 passed February 14, 1876 "To establish organize and regulate a Police Force…"

160 There was a controversy in the Anglican Church when the Rev. Hurst suddenly resigned in November, 1873. As he explained, he had been put in charge by Bishop Cronyn for the purpose of "rescuing the church from the overwhelming financial difficulties that had overtaken it and closed its doors." Windsor Essex Record November 14, 1873

161 Windsor Community Museum, PM 411, Central Methodist Church Golden Jubilee, 1873-1923

162 Lincoln Road United Church Archives, Letter from John Semmens, first pastor to Rev. H.A. Graham, November 15, 1915; as quoted in Ronald G. Hoskins, A Historical Survey of the Town of Walkerville… (University of Windsor, M.A. thesis, 1964) 27; on the Walkerville Fire Brigade, see Hoskins, at 31-3

163 Michael Power, "James Theodore Wagner" vol. XII, Dictionary of Canadian Biography, (Toronto: University of Toronto Press, 1990) 1077-8; and see Power and Brock, Gather up the Fragments… "St. Alphonsus" 172; on Macdonell's grant of land for St. Alphonsus, see Evening Record "St. Alphonsus Parish: A Bit of Interesting Local Ecclesiastical History" March 11, 1901—"S.S. Macdonnell had recently bought for speculative purposes a section of the Goyeau farm and he generously came to the aid of Father Point and for the nominal consideration of $1, deeded 1 ½ acres of ground at the corner of Goyeau and Park sts."

164 Windsor Community Museum, Memoirs of St. Mary's Academy, 1866-1977 (no author, no publication information); Betty Wamsley, "Blessing of Graduates…" Windsor Daily Star November 15, 1951; and see Evening Record "St. Alphonsus Parish…" March 11, 1901—on the arrival of the Holy Names Sisters—"It was somewhat irregular for a religious community to precede a regular priest in an unorganized parish…"

165 The original conveyance of the four acre site to the Province for the Ordinance department was effected by instrument no. 260 executed December 4, 1839 and registered February 4, 1840—Essex County Registry Office, Abstract of title for lot 84 in Concession One;

Macdonell's plan for the park was registered January 6, 1855 as Registered Plan 96;

Registered Plan 95, registered on August 6, 1861 carried a copy of the by-law passed by the Windsor Town Council on May 9, 1859 which by-law laid out the roads around the "proposed park in Windsor heretofore known as the Barrack Square which has been lately purchased by this Corporation from the Ordinance Department of the Government."

However, there is no record of such a conveyance to the town in the Essex County Registry office, nor do the Clerk's records contain a copy a by-law enabling the purchase. Nevertheless, all parties assumed that the town owned the site. Likewise, while there is no record of a conveyance to the School Board, such a transfer also appeared to be unchallenged. The decision to use the site for school purposes was not universally popular and during a Town Council meeting in 1875, J.C. Patterson held that:

"In his opinion it was a mistake to place the central school where it is,

because that square was designated for a park, and would have been

better retained exclusively for that purpose."

Mayor Cameron responded: "Sixteen years ago the Council appropriated the school lot for a park, and nothing has been done to carry out the purposes then formed." See Windsor Essex Record March 19, 1875

It would not be until 1892 that provincial officials discovered that despite the intention of the Province to convey the land to the municipality in 1859 for $1,600 that the purchase price had never been paid. Apparently, this was because the Province had declared the town's by-law to be invalid. By 1892, provincial authorities were no longer concerned about such niceties but more interested in getting their money. They demanded payment plus interest.

At a Council meeting in January 1892, one member protested the town's innocence—"The town officials well knew that the land had never been paid for, but as the government officials never asked for the price, they did not think it was their business to call their attention to it." see Amherstburg Echo January 8, 1892

The matter was finally put to rest when the Province executed a deed to Windsor over what eventually became the City Hall site on May 17, 1897.

166 The dedication of the Central School is described in Windsor Essex Record December 1, 1871

167 Windsor Essex Record January 11, 1872

168 Address by James Dougall at the laying of the cornerstone of the Windsor Central School, in Windsor Essex Record November 30, 1871; On occasion, one denomination or other thought they were being short-changed. In 1877, a "Protestant Taxpayer" wrote an enraged letter to the Essex Record complaining that the picket fence around the "Catholic School" (St. Alphonsus) was far nicer than the one around the "Central Protestant School." "Is the Catholic position of this community wealthier than the Protestant, or have they a majority on the Board?" he fumed. Essex Record May 18, 1877

169 Windsor <u>Evening Record</u> F.P. Gavin, "First Grammar School established in 1854" May 23, 1917; and Windsor <u>Daily Star</u>, Neil Morrison, "Windsor Secondary Schools Had Humble Start" November 17, 1945

170 See the memoir by Alexander Black, "Windsor Public Schools" in the Windsor <u>Evening Record</u> May 23, 1917: "These quarters became so foul that the late Dr. Coventry, as medical health officer, condemned the building as unsanitary."

171 Michael Power and Mark G. McGowan, "Denis O'Connor" vol. XIV, <u>Dictionary of Canadian Biography</u>, (Toronto: University of Toronto Press, 1998) 789-92

172 Windsor <u>Essex Record</u> "Assumption College, Sandwich" June 23, 1881

173 on cricket, see Detroit <u>Advertiser and Tribune</u> "The Windsor Cricket Club" May 9, 1867; and "Cricket Match" July 2, 1868; while cricket was still frequently played, and the "Detroit Peninsulars" were a prestigious cricket club, baseball had become the more dominant sport by the 1870s—see the contest between the Sandwich "Avalanche" and Windsor "Auroras" at Ouellette Square (formerly the site for cricket matches) <u>Essex Record</u> "Base Ball" July 4, 1873; on football, see <u>Essex Record</u>, "Foot Ball" November 13 and 20 1879; on "Tableaux Vivants" see <u>Essex Record</u> February 1, 1872

174 On nude bathing see editorial in the <u>Essex Record</u> against the morality by-law that forbade bathing in the river and suggesting that certain areas be set aside and, " if set apart for that purpose, we have no doubt the boys would confine themselves"; two boys arrested see <u>Essex Record</u> "Caught Swimming" September 9, 1880; and see Windsor Municipal Archives, R.G. 2 AV-2/4, By-law 112 passed March 30 1868 "For the regulation of Public Morals..." on the Williams brothel, see <u>Essex Record</u> "A Disreputable House Broken Up" August 9, 1877

175 Walter Griffith, "A Little Bit of old France Set Down in Sandwich West" <u>Radio Sketches...Essex County-Detroit Area</u> (Essex County Historical Association, 1963) April 29, 1950, 73-4

176 Hector Charlesworth, <u>Candid Chronicles</u> (Toronto: MacMillan Company, 1925) 31

177 Detroit <u>Advertiser and Tribune</u> "Reciprocity Across the River" February 27, 1866

178 Detroit <u>Advertiser and Tribune</u> "Grand Railway Excursion" January 10, 1867; on the gauge problem, see Robert F. Legget, <u>Railroads of Canada</u> (Vancouver: Douglas, David & Charles, 1973) 46-8

179 Detroit <u>Advertiser and Tribune</u> "Grand Railway Excursion" January 10, 1867

180 Robert D. Tennant, Jr. <u>Canada Southern Country</u> (Erin, ON, Boston Mills Press, 1991) 11-23; quote on the engineering of the Canada Southern in Douglas N.W.

Smith, <u>The New York Central in Canada: Southern Ontario Lines—Volume 1</u> (Trackside Canada, 1998) 11

181 Walter Griffith, "Along the Detroit River in the 1880's" <u>Radio Sketches...</u> May 19, 1948, 41

182 Philip Mason, <u>The Ambassador Bridge</u> 42: there is a thorough examination of the tunnel and bridge proposals of the 19th century in Chapter 1

183 F.J. Holton, D.H. Bedford, Francis Cleary, <u>History of the Windsor and Detroit Ferries</u> (reprinted from the papers and records, vol. XVI, Ontario Historical Society) 6-9; and Windsor Public Library, Local History Collection, William Oxford, <u>The Steamers: The Story of the Detroit-Windsor Ferry Boats</u> Chapter 5; on whether the *Great Western* would float, see Hoskins, <u>Walkerville</u> 36; and see "Jenking's Ship Yard in <u>Evening Record</u> March 28, 1872, which describes a typical day at that yard—"three steamers are upon the stocks; and the rattle and noise which arrests the car on approaching the place, shows plainly enough that business in that quarter is being directed by a vigorous and pushing mind."

184 Letter from "An Old Grumbler" in <u>Essex Record</u> March 28, 1873

185 Holton, Bedford & Cleary, <u>Windsor and Detroit Ferries</u> 10; and see editorial in Windsor <u>Essex Record</u> "The River Ferries" February 20, 1874

186 On the ferry wharves, see Hoskins, <u>CN Riverfront Lands...</u> 43; and Windsor <u>Essex Record</u>, "Town Council" March 28, 1873; on the ferries ramming each other, see Amherstburg <u>Echo</u>, "The Ferry War at Windsor" December 26, 1879; and <u>Echo</u>, January 9, 1880: "Since the opposition ferry boat started on the route between Windsor and Detroit an incessant rivalry has been kept up, and one way it shows itself is in the racing of the boats at fullest speed back and forward across the river. By such a course, the lives of the passengers are placed in constant danger."

187 National Archives of Canada, M.G. 27, Sir John A. Macdonald Papers, vol, 1-2, Macdonald to O'Connor, December 26, 1870: "According to your suggestion I had a long and satisfactory conversation with the Archbishop..."

188 Windsor <u>Essex Record</u> "The Essex Election" August 8, 1872; on O'Connor as a representative of Catholic interests, see Buja, <u>Arthur Rankin...</u> 136

189 The best account of William McGregor's early career can be found in David Roberts, <u>In the Shadow of Detroit: Gordon M. McGregor, Ford of Canada, and Motoropolis</u> (Detroit: Wayne State University Press, 2006) 11-3

190 See Edward Chancellor, <u>Devil Take the Hindmost: A History of Financial Speculation</u> (N.Y: Farrar Straus Giroux, 1999) "By 1877, it was estimated that only a fifth of the labour force was in regular employment." At 186; and see Charles R.

Kindleberger, Manias, Panics, and Crashes: A History of Financial Crises (Revised ed.) (N.Y. Basic books, 1989) 144-5

191 JoEllen Vinyard, The Irish on the Urban Frontier: Nineteenth Century Detroit, 1850-1880 (New York: Arno Press, 1976) 127

192 Windsor Essex Record "A Great Want Supplied" May 15, 1874

193 Francis Chauvin, Hiram Walker... Chapter 16, page 3; on the depression, see "Town Council" December 24, 1875; and "Soup Kitchen" February 9, 1877

194 Windsor Essex Record "Street Opening" August 18, 1876

195 On the sewer project as a "make work" project, see Windsor Essex Record "Town Council" August 9, 1877; there were continual problems associated with the quality of the bricks used and the presence of lime in the bricks, see Essex Record "Meeting of the Board of Works" August 23, 1877; on the failure to provide sewers in 1872, see Evening Record "A Flea..." June 19, 1874

196 The assessment records for 1874 indicated that Windsor had 6,000 residents. The Dominion Census of 1881 showed a population of 6,561; see Cancian et al... Windsor a Statistical Package, 8; on Bradstreet's Commercial Register, see Amherstburg Echo March 1, 1878

Endnotes To Chapter Six

197 R.T. Naylor, The History of Canadian Business, 1867-1914, vol. 2 (Toronto: James Lorimer, 1975) 107; while Naylor categorically condemns bonusing, other historians have viewed it as part of the business process of that time—see Paul Maroney, "Municipal Bonusing in Kingston, Ontario, 1873-1914" Ontario History 85 (June, 1993) 119: "Certainly Kingston's bonused companies performed comparatively well" at 136; and see Elizabeth Bloomfield, "Municipal Bonusing of Industry: The Legislative Framework in Ontario to 1930" Urban History Review 9.3 (February, 1981) 59

198 Windsor Essex Record January 8, 1875

199 Robert D. Tennant, Canada Southern Country 33, 62 and 117; Douglas N.W. Smith, The New York Central 17-8

200 On protests against the bonus, see Windsor Essex Record "That $30,000 Bonus Question" November 20, 1879; on meetings in favour of it see, Essex Record "The Proposed Bonus" November 13, 1879

201 Detroit <u>Post and Tribune</u> December 1, 1879; Detroit <u>Free Press</u>, December 5, 1879; and see Patrick Brode, "Alexander Cameron and the Flowering of the County of Essex, 1853-1893" Occasional Paper No. 4, Essex County Historical Society, 1987, 14-5

202 *An Act to Consolidate the Debt of the Town of Windsor* (1881) <u>Statutes of Ontario</u>, Chapter 48

203 On the National Policy see Peter B. Waite, <u>Canada 1874-1896: Arduous Destiny</u> (Toronto: McClelland and Stewart, 1971) "Clearly, in the National Policy— Mackenzie protested against that title—the Conservatives were on to a good thing." 81; and see, Randall White, <u>Fur Trade to Free Trade…</u> (Toronto: Dundurn Press, 1988) 62-5

204 Windsor <u>Essex Record</u> "Town Council" February 19, 1875: Patterson—"The sentiment of the entire country was strongly in favor of curtailing the use of liquor…"

205 Windsor <u>Essex Record</u> "A Political Revolution" September 19, 1878

206 R.T. Naylor, <u>The History of Canadian Business..</u> 73

207 On Parke Davis see, Hoskins, <u>Town of Walkerville…</u> 71-2; the hardware branch plants see Windsor Municipal Archives, Minutes of the Town Council, R.G. 2 AIV 1/2., April 3, 1882

208 Windsor <u>Evening Record</u> "The Corliss Bill' May 29, 1896

209 Windsor <u>Evening Record</u> "A Big Brewery" June 27, 1893 and obituary for Louis Griesinger, October 7, 1902; and see William Marentette, "Brewed in Windsor: The British American Brewery: 1882-1969" <u>Walkerville Times</u> No. 11 (November, 2000); Carlings eventually bought the British American Brewery and the Windsor plant was closed in 1969. In 1985, the O'Keefe Brewery in British Columbia re-launched "Cincinnati Cream" and on the label noted—"original since 1882."

And see, Allen Winn Sneath, <u>Brewed in Canada…</u> (Toronto: Dundurn Group, 2001) 47-8; Peter H. Blum, <u>Brewed in Detroit: Breweries and Beers Since 1830</u> (Detroit: Wayne State University Press, 1999) 288-9

210 on the special rate on taxpayers, see Windsor Community Museum, R.G. 2 AV 2/10, By-law 368 "for the consolidation of the Debt…" passed August 26, 1881

211 Barbara Lazenby Craig, "State Medicine in Transition: Battling Smallpox in Ontario, 1882-1885" <u>Ontario History</u> 75 (December, 1983) 319 at 330; and see Windsor Community Museum, P.M. 13, <u>Biography of John Coventry, M.D. 1836-1902</u>

212 Windsor <u>Essex Record</u> "The Mayoralty" December 24, 1879; on the outcry that Coventry remain as mayor, see <u>Essex Record</u> December 22, 1881—"the financial concerns of the town are still in a condition to require his (Coventry's) skill and experiences for yet a little longer."

213 <u>Commemorative Biographical Record of Essex, Ontario</u> (Toronto: J.H. Beers, 1905) 139

214 Holton, Bedford and Cleary, <u>Windsor and Detroit Ferries...</u> 11

215 Windsor Municipal Archives R.G. 2 AIV 1/3, Minutes of Town Council, January 21, 1884

216 Stephen Lusted, "Development of Public Works" Windsor <u>Evening Record</u> May 23, 1917; on the Sandwich Street controversy, see Amherstburg <u>Echo</u> August 22, 1884 and October 10, 1884

217 Windsor Municipal Archives, R.G. 2 AIV 1/3, Minutes of Windsor Town Council, January 21, 1884; on Coventry's introduction of the sewer by-laws, same source, January 15, 1883; on the need to drain the Coulie, see Amherstburg <u>Echo</u> April 6, 1883, and February 1, 1884—"During the year a large sewer is to be made along Ouellette avenue, which will extend from a small creek about two miles back of Windsor, to the Detroit River. This will be the most important sewer in the town, and will entirely drain the swamp back of Windsor."

218 Windsor <u>Border Cities Star</u> "Oldest Ex-Mayor Still Living ..." April 29, 1922

219 Amherstburg <u>Echo</u> June 30, 1882

220 Windsor <u>Essex Record</u> "Sandwich" September 1, 1881

221 Hoskins, <u>The Town of Walkerville...</u> 40-1

222 Michael Bliss, <u>Plague: A Story of Smallpox in Montreal</u> (Toronto: Harper Collins, 1991) 40

223 One of these councillors was Dr. Peter Aikman, a colourful if questionable practitioner who "after years of experimental study developed ORANGEINE... a remedy for the relief of all forms of pain." Windsor <u>Evening Record</u> December 17, 1904; early in his practice, Aikman had become sexually involved with a patient and was charged with "alleged undue familiarity" with a Mrs. Eddington; Amherstburg <u>Echo</u> July 12, 1878

On the construction of the pest house, see Windsor municipal Archives, R.G. 2 AV-2/6, By-law 217 passed December 29, 1873, "To acquire a parcel of land whereon to build an Hospital and for other purposes..."

224 Windsor Essex Record "An Hospital Case" January 8, 1880; on the 1877 smallpox outbreak, see Essex Record "Town Council" June 22, 1877

225 Windsor Municipal Archives, R.G. 2, AIV 1/3. Minutes of the Town Council of Windsor, May 10, 1882; on the outbreak, see Windsor Essex Record "Small Pox In Town" April 20, 1882

226 Windsor Essex Record "Town Council" May 11, 1882; on the persistence of the epidemic, see Amherstburg Echo June 9, 1882

227 Windsor Municipal Archives, R.G. 2 AV 2/11 By-law 409, passed November 19, 1883

228 Craig, "State Medicine in Transition…" 331; on Montreal, see Bliss, Plague

229 Amherstburg Echo April 26, 1889—"Six years ago the Buchanan Bros. The wealthiest distillers in Louisville Ky. got into some revenue trouble.. the Buchanans fled to Canada, locating in Windsor."

230 Amherstburg Echo "St. Jean Baptiste" June 29, 1883; on Church excursions see Windsor Essex Record "Dominion Day in Windsor" July 8, 1880

231 Windsor Essex Record "Criminal Statistics" January 8, 1880

232 Amherstburg Echo March 26, 1880; on wife beaters, see Echo July 19 and August 2, 1878

233 Windsor Essex Record "Board of Education" March 8, 1876; on J.C. Patterson's inspection of the black school,, see Essex Record December 8, 1876

234 Ontario Archives, Alvin D. McCurdy fonds F-2076-14-0-3, unidentified newspaper comment "Windsor's School Privileges" September 6, 1883; and Detroit Evening News September 6, 1883

235 Dunn v Board of Education for the Town of Windsor (1883) 6 Ontario Reports 125-8

236 On the origins of the Windsor Telephone Exchange, see Windsor Daily Star "22 Phone Subscribers On City List in 1880" July 10, 1954; and see Windsor Essex Record "New Enterprise" December 18, 1879; on Tringham's Sandwich pottery, see Windsor Essex Record November 14, 1872; on Tringham's life, see obituary in Amherstburg Echo August, 1886

237 New York, *Electrical World,* "The Telephone" December 15, 1883; on the underwater cable, (which followed a circuitous course from Windsor to Walkerville, under the Detroit River to the tip of Belle Isle and from there to Detroit) see Windsor Essex Record January 23, 1880; telephones to Leamington, Essex Record May 4, 1882; Tringham sells his exchange, Essex Record July 29, 1880

238 Neil Morrison, "The Telephone Comes to Essex County" in Radio Sketches.. 35-7; on 290 telephones in use in 1894, see Windsor Evening Record September 7, 1894

239 On street lights, see Amherstburg Echo November 14, 1884, and February 6, 1885

240 Windsor Municipal Archives, R.G. 2 AV-2/14, By-law 491passed March 15, 1886; on Bangham's inspiration of the electric street railway, see Windsor Evening Record, "Windsor had First Electric Car to Operate in America" May 23, 1917

241 The first test run is described in Border Cities Star, G.M. Brown, "Story of Initial Trip is Recalled" July 21, 1928

242 New York, Electrical World, June 26, 1886, as quoted in Fred Angus, "Electric Traction 1886-1986" Canadian Rail 395 (November-December, 1986) 185-6; and see M. Peter Murphy, "Commemorating the Fiftieth Anniversary of the Abandonment of Electric Street Car and Interurban Service in Many of Canada's Cities" Canadian Rail 532 (September-October, 2009) – "Canada's first electric railway was the Windsor Electric Street railway, engineered by Charles Van Depoele..." at 175

243 As quoted in Border Cities Star July 21, 1928

244 J.M.S. Careless, Toronto to 1918: An Illustrated History (Toronto: James Lorimer, 1984) 138; on the difference between the impact of streetcars in Toronto and Windsor see, Gilbert A. Stelter and Alan F.J. Artibise, The Canadian City: Essays in Urban and Social History (Ottawa: Carleton University Press, 1984)—"Thus, Toronto is thoroughly typical in that the desire to gain access to the centre of the city on the part of a few well-to-do suburbanites preceded the desire to escape the city by its residents." At 87

245 Windsor Municipal Archives, R.G. 2 AIV 1/3, Minutes of the Windsor Town Council, June 14, 1886

246 Windsor Clarion January 9, 1886

247 Amherstburg Echo March 21, 1884

248 Essex County Registry Office, lands to the west of Windsor being registered Plans 260 and 261 registered on September 28, 1883 and 282 registered on October 6, 1885; and see Patrick Brode, "Alexander Cameron and the Flowering of the County of Essex, 1853-1893" Occasional Paper no. 4, Essex County Historical Society, 1987 , 16; on John Curry, see Windsor Daily Star Sybil Watts, "Old Curry Home..." July 29, 1948

249 Amherstburg Echo September 28, 1883

250 Essex County Registry Office, Registered Plan 360, registered April 28, 1890

251 On the "core-ring configuration" see Gilbert A. Stelter and Alan F.J. Artibise, Power and Place: Canadian Urban Development in the North American Context (Vancouver: University of British Columbia Press, 1986) 9

252 Amherstburg Echo April 9, 1886

253 On the by-laws to separate from the County, see Windsor Municipal Archives, R.G. 2 AV-2/10, By-law 334 passed June 30, 1879, "...to authorize withdrawal from the jurisdiction of the County of Essex" and By-law 347 passed February 9, 1880, ratifying and confirming the above; on reaction to the separation, see Amherstburg Echo June 20, 1879—"Scarcely any interest seems to be taken in the matter."; on criminal costs, see Echo December 5, 1885

254 Ibid., "Essex Electric Railway Company" July 19, 1886

ENDNOTES TO CHAPTER SEVEN

255 Ronald G. Hoskins, A Historical Survey of the Town of Walkerville... (University of Windsor Master's Thesis, 1964) 49-63

256 Windsor Municipal Archives, R.G. 2 AIV 1-4, Minutes of the town council, July 30, 1888; on the C.P.R.'s expansion in Ontario see, W. Kaye Lamb, History of the Canadian Pacific Railway (New York: Macmillan, 1977) 94-7

257 Archives of the Canadian Transport Commission, Decision of the Railway Committee of the Privy Council, November 19, 1889; on the debate of the Canadian Pacific proposals, see Windsor Municipal Archives, R.G. 2, AIV 1-4 Minutes of the town council, October 24, 1888; and Amherstburg Echo October 19 and 26, 1888

258 Windsor Evening Record "Windsor in It" February 14, 1895

259 Amherstburg Echo March 27, 1888; on the ferry license issue, see Holton et al., History of the Windsor and Detroit Ferries 12

260 On the confrontation between Morton and Drake, see Amherstburg Echo November 16, 1888; and Minutes of the town council, the offending ink blot is found on the entry for October 15, 1888; on Patterson's role in advocating for the town, see Amherstburg Echo October 19, 1888

261 See Amherstburg Echo November 19, 1886—"Over a year ago the government inspector condemned the high school building and notified the school board of the liability of the school grant being forfeited unless a new building was erected." And

Windsor Daily Star Neil Morrison, "Windsor Secondary Schools Had Humble Start" November 17, 1945

262 Windsor Essex Record "Base Ball—A Noble Play" August 18, 1881

263 Amherstburg Echo October 26, 1888

264 Windsor Weekly Record "Do We Get The Children?" October 21, 1892

265 On the dissention at All Saints' Anglican, see Amherstburg Echo January 12, 1883 and April 13, 1883; on the Methodists, see Windsor Essex Record "Addresses and Presentations" July 8, 1880

266 London Free Press June 5, 1888; on Mercer Street Baptist Church, see Amherstburg Echo April 20, 1888

267 Amherstburg Echo August 30, 1889

268 Amhersburg Echo August 17 and 21, 1888; Jonathan V. Plaut in The Jews of Windsor, 1790-1990: A Historical Chronicle (Toronto: Dundurn Press, 2007) erroneously indicates that, "Windsor's founding Jewish community established their first synagogue in the 1890s." 54

269 Amherstburg Echo August 24, 1888; on attitudes towards the Salvation Army, see Echo—"Some person or perhaps numbers of persons pelted the Salvation Army (American Branch) with rotten apples & mud, while parading the streets on Sunday evening the 19th September." October 1, 1886; on American and English Salvationists, see Echo February 1, 1889

270 Walter Griffith, "More Recollections of Old Time Windsor" in Radio Sketches... Essex County-Detroit Area 143

271 Amherstburg Echo "Sam Jones in Windsor" July 6, 1888; on "Red Hot" Methodism, see Echo March 11, 1881; on temperance, Echo May 18, 1889; The temperance movement in Windsor was only a fragment of a larger campaign to improve the human condition. Protestant reformers hoped to instill values which would make society more sober, decorous and religious. In this, they drew heavily from their parent Churches in the U.S; see, F.L. Barron, "The American Origins of the Temperance movement in Ontario, 1828-1850" The Canadian Review of American Studies, 11, No. 2 (Fall, 1980) 132

272 Amherstburg Echo March 5, 1886; even the area's Member of Parliament reflected a relaxed attitude towards tippling. In response to a proposal to prohibit the manufacture and sale of liquor, J.C. Patterson responded that such acts "are an interference with individual liberty; they are an interference with our civil rights." Patterson concluded that prohibition destroyed the moral fibre of the community

by depriving it of choice and that, "It is impossible to legislate men into a state of virtue." House of Commons debates (Canada) June 8, 1887, 853

273 Windsor Evening Record editorial "Prohibition Plebiscite" January 4, 1894; on the plebiscite, see Windsor Municipal Archives, City Clerk Letterbook, R.G. 2 B II /4, report on the Prohibition Plebiscite, male voters yes—598, male voters no—726: female voters yes-76, female voters no—54, page 23

274 Amherstburg Echo June 5, 1885

275 Windsor Le Progrès July 14, 1881

276 Amherstburg Echo January 21, 1887; on Laurier's tour of Windsor, see Echo December 17, 1886; the animosity created over the "Ross Bible" issue had encouraged a strong Catholic vote for the Liberals. The impact of this was especially apparent in ridings such as North Essex – "The government won North Essex for the first time, converting the Conservative majority of 326 in 1883 into a Liberal (Pacaud) margin of 79" see A. Margaret Evans, Sir Oliver Mowat (Toronto: University of Toronto Press, 1992) 245

277 David and Rosemary Gagan, For Patients of Moderate Means: A Social History of the Voluntary Public General Hospital in Canada, 1890-1950 (Kingston: McGill-Queen's university Press, 2002) 1-5

278 Windsor Weekly Record "The Hotel Dieu" December 16, 1892

279 Catholic Record January 15, 1887; as reprinted in Comiskey, My Heart's Best Wishes for You fn. 22, p. 223

280 Diocese of London Archives, P 15400, letter from Sisters of St. Joseph to Bishop McEvay, October 11, 1905; On the Cardinal's approval of the Colored Mission, see Amherstburg Echo May 18, 1888—"the Cardinal Prefect of the Congregation of the Propaganda expresses profound satisfaction at the reverend gentleman's efforts to establish a colored mission in Windsor."

on the community effort to build Hotel Dieu, see Windsor Daily Star Neil Morrison, "Hotel Dieu 60 Years Old" September 11, 1948; on the hospital's opening, see Detroit Free Press "Windsor" October 14, 1889

on the few Catholic converts, see Windsor Evening record "Windsor Statistics' January 6, 1990: of 886 black citizens only 24 identified as Catholics.

281 Richard Oestreicher, "Changing Patterns of Class Relations in Detroit, 1880-1900" Detroit in Perspective: A Journal of Regional History 3 No. 3 (Spring, 1979) 146-7; and see Arthur M. Woodford, This Is Detroit, 1701-2001 (Detroit: Wayne State University Press, 2001) 79-81; on Alexander Cameron as "Croesus" see Amherstburg Echo April 11, 1890

282 Brode, <u>Alexander Cameron</u>, 19

283 Amherstburg <u>Echo</u> May 6, 1881

284 Detroit <u>Free Press</u> "To Be Hanged" April 26, 1884

285 Windsor <u>Clarion</u>, undated as quoted in the Toronto <u>Daily Mail</u> January 3, 1889; as reproduced in Donald F. Warner, <u>The Idea of Continental Union: Agitation for the Annexation of Canada to the United States 1849-1893</u> (Lexington: University of Kentucky Press, 1960)

286 In addition to his lacklustre defence of Luke Phipps, White had had two other clients, Hardinge and Greenwood condemned to death in 1883. They escaped the noose by breaking out of the Sandwich Gaol.

287 Amherstburg <u>Echo</u> February 1, 1889

288 Welland <u>Tribune</u> January 18, 1889; comments in the Toronto <u>Globe</u>, editorial "Windsor Election" January 8, 1889

289 Warner, <u>The Idea of Continental Union</u>… 202; on White as a liability to the Conservatives, see the Toronto <u>Globe</u> January 8, 1890 which carried the attack by James Cleary the Catholic Archbishop of Kingston on the provincial Conservative leader W.R. Meredith in which Cleary alleged that it was Meredith's advisor, "Sol. White (who) struck out straight for Annexation and delivered to the world his manifesto against British connection"

290 Warner, <u>Continental Union</u>, 225

291 Toronto <u>Globe</u> February 20 and March 6, 1891

292 Windsor <u>Evening Record</u> editorial, "The Electric Railway" April 22, 1893; on Colonel Clarke, see his obituary in Windsor <u>Evening Record</u> "Col. Clarke Dead" October 1, 1894; on McGregor's expansion of the street railway to Walkerville, see Amherstburg <u>Echo</u> March 21 & 28, 1890, and Windsor Municipal Archives, R.G. 2 AIV 1-4, Minutes of the town council, March 17, 1890; on the powerhouse, see <u>Evening Record</u> "At The Power House" May 12, 1894

293 Amherstburg <u>Echo</u> March 22, 1889; on the 1887 motion for annexation, see Windsor Municipal Archives, R.G. 2 AIV 1-4, Minutes of the town council, March 21, 1887

294 Amherstburg <u>Echo</u> May 24, 1889

295 Hoskins, <u>A Historical Survey of the Town of Walkerville</u>, which gives a thorough account of the various industrial developments in the town after 1888, see 70-8

296 Ronald G. Hoskins, "Hiram Walker and the Origins and Development of Walkerville, Ontario" <u>Ontario History</u> 64 (September, 1972) 130; and see *An Act to Incorporate the Town of Walkerville* <u>Statutes of Ontario</u> 1890, chapter 108

297 Detroit <u>Journal</u> "Neither Town Or City" May 10, 1890

298 As quoted in the Amherstburg <u>Echo</u> August 16, 1890

299 Toronto <u>Globe</u> August 21, 1890 "Windsor to become a City"

300 See "Oscar Fleming" in <u>Commemorative Biographical Record of the County of Essex</u> (Toronto: J.H. Beers, 1905) 42-3; on White as an embarrassment, see Windsor <u>Weekly Record</u> March 18, 1892

301 Windsor Municipal Archives, R.G. 2 AIV 1-4, Minutes of the town council, January 19, 1891 and January 18, 1892

302 Windsor Municipal Archives, R.G. 2 B II /2, Letterbook of the Town Clerk, Lusted to Mayors of Stratford and St. Thomas, January 22, 1891, p. 448-9; on the meeting in the drill shed, see Detroit <u>Free Press</u> January 28, 1891

303 Patrick Brode, "Solomon White and the Incorporation of the City of Windsor" (Windsor: Essex County Historical Society, Occasional Paper No. 6, 1994) 8

304 See Amherstburg <u>Echo</u> May 29, 1891

305 Toronto <u>Globe</u> May 24, 1892

ENDNOTES TO CHAPTER EIGHT

306 James Watt, "Anti-Catholic Nativism in Canada: The Protestant Protective Association," <u>Canadian Historical Review</u> 48 (1967) 45—"For six years the P.P.A. worked secretly to protect the institutions of Canada against what it alleged to be a Roman Catholic conspiracy to take control of the state... the P.P.A. discriminated against Catholics personally by boycotting their businesses, and also attempted to drive Catholics out of political life." 45; and see James Watt, "Anti-Catholicism in Ontario Politics: The Role of the Protestant Protective Association in the 1894 Election" <u>Ontario History</u> 59 (June, 1967) No. 2—"Sometime late in 1891 the P.P.A. jumped from Detroit to Windsor and from this beachhead it quickly spread throughout southwestern Ontario." 57

307 Windsor <u>Evening Record</u> "A Memorandum from Geo. C. Rankin" March 20, 1893

308 Windsor <u>Weekly Record</u> editorial "The Chief of Police" January 29, 1892; on the controversy over the water rate remission for Hotel Dieu, see speech of Robert Sutherland at the nomination meeting—"certain parties would seek for their own ends to make out that I was the nominee of the Catholics... I learned from all directions that my unscrupulous opponents were circulating contemptible and untrue reports that I

had been willing to grant a remission of water rates to the Hotel Dieu and refuse the like to the Home of the Friendless" Windsor Weekly Record January 1, 1892

309 Windsor Evening Record "Meeting In Sandwich" December 30, 1893; Fleming and his council colleagues did not appreciate McNee's attacks and they sued the *Evening Record* for libel. The case was settled out of court in March 1894, Evening Record "Libel Case Settled" March 14, 1894

310 Ibid., editorial "As Others See Us" January 5, 1894

311 Winks, The Blacks in Canada, 292; on McDougall Street—see Margaret Claire Kilroy, "Local Historic Places in Essex County" vol. I Essex Historical Society Papers and Addresses (1913) 25

312 Windsor Evening Record "Color Prejudice" May 5, 1898; on the school boundary dispute of 1893, see Evening Record "The Children Strike" October 26, 1893 and letter from H.T. Ellis, Chairman of the Board of Education, October 28, 1893; on racist comments in the press, see Evening Record comments on the Emancipation Day celebration meeting of "de culled breddern" August 1, 1893

313 Windsor Evening Record "The Color Line" May 1, 1894

314 On the 1891 diphtheria epidemic, see Amherstburg Echo January 16, 1891; on the report of the Medical Health Officer, Echo December 16, 1892

315 Windsor Evening Record editorial "Shades of Esculapius" October 7, 1897 – recounting a professorial lecture that held that—"bacteria was a blessing rather than a source of danger" and that, "The city had a narrow escape recently from incurring an expenditure of about a hundred thousand dollars to run our water intake pipe above Walkerville just to avoid those blessings.." on the newspaper's crusade against a new intake, see Evening Record editorial "Stop It" July 5, 1893

316 Windsor Evening Record "The Quarantine Hospital" January 9, 1895; on the records of deaths for 1894, see Evening Record January 8, 1895

317 Windsor Municipal Archives, City Council Minutebook, R.G. 2, Special Meeting of July 20, 1896; on the sewage flood in Walkerville, see Amherstburg Echo February 28, 1896—"The utmost alarm was caused in Windsor, on Wednesday, when word was received that the Walker's reservoir of liquid manure had burst and let the contents flow into the river, just above the spot where the city gets its water supply."; on the City Council's reaction to the problem see Windsor Evening Record "Filter Scheme" July 23, 1896, and editorial "The Water Board's Dilemma" July 24, 1896—that it was impossible to "extract any logic from the attitude of the inflexible Dr. Bryce."

318 The history of Coventry's attempt to purchase a filter is given in the Amherstburg Echo of May 17, 1901

319 As reported in Windsor <u>Evening Record</u>, editorial, "Folly of Griffin's Bill" April 16, 1894; on U.S. tariff policy, see, Ernest R. May, <u>Imperial Democracy: The Emergence of America as a Great Power</u> (N.Y. Harcourt, Brace, 1961) at 112; and Lewis L. Gould, <u>The Presidency of William McKinley</u> (Lawrence: Regents Press of Kansas, 1980)—William McKinley's comments at 26; on the Corliss bill, see <u>Evening Record</u> "The Corliss Bill" May 29, 1896; on the hard times resulting from the Panic of 1893 in the Detroit area, see H. Roger Grant, "Pingree's Potato Patches: A Study of Self-help during the Depression of the 1890's" <u>Detroit in Perspective: A Journal of Regional History</u> 4 No. 2 (Winter, 1980) 61-73

320 Windsor <u>Evening Record</u> "Building Operations" November 4, 1893; on reduced hours for G.T.R. trainmen, see Amherstburg <u>Echo</u> January 19, 1894

321 Windsor <u>Evening Record</u> editorial "A Striking Contrast" April 25, 1896

322 Windsor <u>Evening Record</u> "People on Wheels" July 13, 1896; on "The ranks of the cyclists…" see Toronto <u>Globe</u> "On the Wheel" May 4, 1895; generally, see Glen Norcliffe, <u>The Ride to Modernity: The Bicycle in Canada, 1869-1900</u> (Toronto: University of Toronto Press, 2001)

323 Windsor <u>Evening Record</u> "The Real Question" October 27, 1894

324 Walter G. Griffiths, Reminiscences, October 1951, 2-5, Ford Motor Company oral history project, as quoted in Charles K. Hyde, <u>The Dodge Brothers: The Men, the Motor Cars, and the Legacy</u> (Detroit: Wayne State University Press, 2005) 15

325 <u>Ibid.</u>, Hyde, 16-17; on Fred Evans, see Windsor <u>Evening Record</u>, "A New Manufactory" August 4, 1898—" F.S. Evans is nothing if not enterprising. In fact, if it wasn't for Mr. Evans Windsor wouldn't be on the map as far as manufacturing is concerned."

326 Hyde, 18

327 Ronald G. Hoskins, "Hiram Walker" in vol. XII <u>Dictionary of Canadian Biography</u> (Toronto: University of Toronto Press, 1990) 1079-81

328 Windsor Community Museum, the Goad Survey of 1884 does not show any of the managerial duplexes in existence. By the Goad survey of 1890, all three duplexes being 516-518, 546-548 and 580-582 Devonshire are apparent. As for the worker's cottages, see reports from Windsor Architectural Conservation Advisory Committee, 1980—on 646 Argyle Street which notes that according to the Goad Survey of 1884, cottages lined this street from Wyandotte to Tuscarora.

329 Walkerville <u>Mercury</u> April 19, 1890; on the incorporation of Walkerville see *An Act to Incorporate the Town of Walkerville,* <u>Statutes of Ontario</u>, c. 108, assented to April 7, 1890; on Cameron and Curry's speculation in Walkerville, see Detroit <u>Free</u>

Press March 25, 1890—credited John Curry as the "engineer of the scheme."; on Parke Davis, see the comment in Windsor Evening Record—"Parke Davis & Co. have begun manufacturing antitoxin, the new diphtheria and consumption cure." March 6, 1895

330 Windsor Evening Record "Walkerville's Record" December 23, 1898

331 W. Hawkins Ferry, The Legacy of Albert Kahn, (Detroit: Wayne State University Press, 1970) – "Sketches Kahn had done in Venice and Orleans provided inspiration for the fireplaces and panelling in the lavish individual executive offices and sketches he had done in Nuremberg gave him ideas for the details in the dark, cozy Sample Room, that inner sanctum of the establishment." 9

332 Windsor Evening Record "A Winner" February 29, 1896

333 On the Grand Trunk Railway shedding older staff see, Windsor Evening Record, "City Siftings" April 5, 1898; On the Typograph Company selling to the London Police and working overtime, see, Evening Record "City Siftings" April 5, 1898—"Starting today the Typograph Co's staff will work sixteen hours a day in order to keep up with the rush for the popular E & D."

334 Amherstburg Echo March 13, 1891 and July 10, 1891—"A number of new hands have been engaged and the merchant tailors declare that under no circumstances will they take back those who were instrumental in the strike a few months ago."; on the Labor Day parade see Windsor Evening Record "Labor Day" September 1, 1897

335 Windsor Municipal Archives, City Clerk's letterbook, R.G. 2 B II/5, Lusted to Andrew Patullo, December 7, 1898; on the regularization of the waterworks commissioners, see—An Act Respecting the Waterworks in the City of Windsor, Statutes of Ontario 1898, chapter 58; on expanding the street lights, see Windsor Evening Record "The City Lighting" July 12, 1895; on the creation of corporate utility monopolies, see Christopher Armstrong and H.V. Nelles, Monopoly's Moment: The Organization and Regulation of Canadian Utilities, 1830-1930, (Philadelphia: Temple University Press, 1986);

On natural gas in Windsor, see Evening Record "Windsor Will Get It" July 25, 1893; and "It's coming Here" February 9, 1894

336 Windsor Evening Record "Happy Merchants" December 29, 1896; on new American branch plants, see "Building Boom" April 11, 1900

337 Windsor Evening Record "The Corliss Bill" May 29, 1896; on the salt mine, see Evening Record "The C.P.R. Salt Block" November 4, 1893; Windsor Municipal Archives, By-law 908 passed November 27, 1896 to exempt Windsor Salt Works from taxation for ten years

338 Windsor <u>Evening Record</u> ""The Library Opened" December 5, 1894; and see, Lorne Bruce, <u>Free Books for All: The Public Library Movement in Ontario, 1850-1930</u> (Toronto: Dundurn Press, 1994) 62

339 Windsor <u>Evening Record</u> "Great Hockey" January 25, 1898; on Windsor beating Detroit in the Thanksgiving Day game, see <u>Evening Record</u> November 22, 1895

340 Windsor <u>Evening Record</u> "Away They Go!" June 7, 1894—"But the popular mode of reaching the track was by electric car."; The official name of the organization, the "Windsor Fair Ground and Driving Park Association" had been planned as early as 1884 with W.G. Curry (brother of the banker John) as the principal promoter, see Amherstburg <u>Echo</u> March 21, 1884; It was not until 1893 that the promoters began to erect the structures and arrange for a racing meet. Windsor <u>Evening Record</u> May 6, 1893

341 Windsor <u>Evening Record</u> "Windsor Gets It" April 5, 1900; on the Windsor Opera House, see Windsor <u>Star</u> Carl Morgan, "Windsor's own Opera House once part of Smith's store" August 20, 1976: in which he recounts research by Frederick Hall of the University of Windsor entitled—"Musical Life in Windsor 1875-1901"

342 Paul Rutherford, "Tomorrow's Metropolis: The Urban Reform Movement in Canada, 1880-1920" in Gilbert A. Stetler and Alan F.J. Artibise, <u>The Canadian City: Essays in Urban and Social History</u> (Ottawa: Carleton University Press, 1984) 436; on the criticism of cities see Carl Berger, <u>The Sense of Power: Studies in the Ideas of Canadian Imperialism: 1867-1914</u> (Toronto: University of Toronto Press, 1970) 177-9

343 Windsor Municipal Archives, City Clerk letterbook, R.G. 2 B II-4 Stephen Lusted to Jacques Pajot, Reeve of Sandwich West—"I am directed by the City Council to ask you to co-operate with the Public Works Committee of the city in cleaning out the ditch on the southerly side of London Street (Street Railway Line) from the westerly to easterly line of your township.. said portion of the ditch having been largely obstructed by cattle and by unchecked growth of grass and weeds." There is no record of any compliance.

344 On the Gauthier expedition, see Windsor <u>Evening Record</u> "Reached Skaguay" May 6, 1898; and "From White Pass" May 9, 1898

345 Windsor <u>Evening Record</u> February 20, 1897

346 On Tolmie as unifying the Presbyterians, see <u>Evening Record</u> "Presbyterians Meet" January 9, 1895; condemning intolerance, Amherstburg <u>Echo</u> January 26, 1894; on offending Canon Hincks, <u>Echo</u> January 19, 1894

347 The "Flying Rollers" were the off-shoot of an English sect created by John Wroe in the mid-1800s that outlawed shaving and hair-cutting and encouraged the ritual

of "cleansing of the blood" whereby virgins were deflowered by the Church's leader. Members emigrated to Australia, Canada and the U.S. There was a particularly active group in the Windsor-Detroit area; see Windsor Evening Record, "A Curious Story" November 5, 1897; and "Heavily Fined' May 15, 1899

348 On McEvay's edict to the Windsor Catholics, see Windsor Evening Record "Bishop McEvay" September 18, 1899; on McEvay, see Power and Brock, Gather up the Fragments at 41-8; I would like to thank Michael Power for his comments on this incident

349 Windsor Evening Record "Bishop's Mandate' October 6, 1899; on Toronto editorials, see Globe "Windsor School Controversy" September 29, 1899, and October 4, 1899

350 On the volunteers' send-off, see Windsor Evening Record "Transvaal Volunteers" October 20, 1899; on the death of Walter White, see, "Late Sergeant White" February 21, 1900; on Essex county men in the Anglo-Boer war, see Sandy Antal and Kevin R. Shackleton, Duty Nobly Done: The Official History of the Essex and Kent Scottish Regiment (Windsor: Walkerville Publishing, 2006) 151-3

351 Windsor Municipal Archives, R.G. 2 B II/5, Lusted to Coventry, March 25, 1899; In a speech to the YMCA in 1893, Coventry warned against the "impure character of Windsor's water supply…A supply of pure water would be an important factor in the promotion of temperance." Windsor Evening Record January 20, 1893; his warnings were not well received, and in 1895, Alderman Shepherd welcomed Coventry's removal as Health Officer.. "the doctor gave us too much 'water' for the good of the town. He was scaring people away with his water lectures." Evening Record July 4, 1895

352 See Price and Kulisek, 30

353 Melvin G. Holli, "The Impact of Automobile Manufacturing upon Detroit" Detroit in Perspective: A Journal of Regional History 2 No. 3 (Spring, 1976) 177

354 Windsor Evening Record "Amalgamated" October 30, 1899; and "The Bicycle Factory" editorial October 31, 1899; on Fred Evans selling out to the American firm of National Cycle & Automobile, see "To Make Bicycles" November 20, 1899; On Windsor as a "residence city" see comments of Alderman Gagnier at Mayor Davis's dinner, in Evening Record "Festive Aldermen" January 27, 1900

355 Ibid., "Want More Public Spirit" May 6, 1904

Index